MW00653501

Rabindranath Tagore, Amartya Sen, and the Early Indian Classical Period

Rabindranath Tagore, Amartya Sen, and the Early Indian Classical Period

The Obligations of Power

Neal Leavitt

LEXINGTON BOOKS
Lanham • Boulder • New York • London

Published by Lexington Books
An imprint of The Rowman & Littlefield Publishing Group, Inc.
4501 Forbes Boulevard, Suite 200, Lanham, Maryland 20706
www.rowman.com

86-90 Paul Street, London EC2A 4NE

Copyright © 2022 by The Rowman & Littlefield Publishing Group, Inc.

All rights reserved. No part of this book may be reproduced in any form or by any elec-
tronic or mechanical means, including information storage and retrieval systems, without
written permission from the publisher, except by a reviewer who may quote passages
in a review.

British Library Cataloguing in Publication Information Available

Library of Congress Cataloging-in-Publication Data

Names: Leavitt, Neal, 1974– author.
Title: Rabindranath Tagore, Amartya Sen, and the early Indian classical period : the
    obligations of power / Neal Leavitt.
Description: Lanham, Maryland : Lexington Books, [2022] | Includes bibliographical
    references and index.
Identifiers: LCCN 2022034660 (print) | LCCN 2022034661 (ebook) |
    ISBN 9781666915679 (cloth) | ISBN 9781666915686 (ebook)
Subjects: LCSH: Power (Social sciences) | Political violence—Prevention. | Tagore,
    Rabindranath, 1861–1941—Political and social views. | Sen, Amartya, 1933—Political
    and social views.
Classification: LCC JC330 .L356 2022 (print) | LCC JC330 (ebook) | DDC
    303.3/3—dc23/eng/20220816
LC record available at https://lccn.loc.gov/2022034660
LC ebook record available at https://lccn.loc.gov/2022034661

∞™ The paper used in this publication meets the minimum requirements of American
National Standard for Information Sciences—Permanence of Paper for Printed Library
Materials, ANSI/NISO Z39.48-1992.

Contents

Preface

In this book, I develop the idea of the obligations of power in the thought of Rabindranath Tagore and Amartya Sen. Whereas thinkers in the social contract tradition derive the primary obligations in the international system from the notion of a contract or an agreement, Tagore and Sen focus on the ethical obligations that flow from asymmetries of power. Persons in positions of greater power have greater responsibilities in the view of both thinkers.

To Tagore and Sen, individuals and societies do not need to enter into contracts with each other to understood why the intentional bombing of civilian populations is unjust or morally wrong. Instead, the removal of abuses of power is a foundational moral norm in the view of both thinkers. Persons can understand why abuses of power are unjust independent of the decisions of the head of state. But a second key feature of Tagore and Sen's ethical thinking is their tendency to locate the idea of the obligations of power in the reflections of Buddha. In *The Idea of Justice*, for instance, Sen notes that "The perspective of obligations of power was presented powerfully by Gautama Buddha in Sutta Nipata."[1] The ethical standard Sen invokes to criticize the social contract tradition is also articulated in this collection of early Buddhist discourses. Likewise, when Tagore states that "things that are living are so easily hurt: therefore they require protection" he is drawing attention to the Sutta Nipata and especially the Metta Sutta.[2] The notion that adult human beings should use their powers or their capabilities to protect— and not oppress—the fragile life around them is the central image in this Buddhist discourse.

From this point of view, the twin pillars of Tagore and Sen's ethical and political philosophy—their concern with promoting the growth and development of all persons while diminishing abuses of power—can be traced back to the early Indian classical period. The Sutta Nipata and the Ashokan inscriptions are source texts for many of their ethical and political ideas. Clarifying this line of influence is an important goal in this study. But a second reason for focusing on the idea of the obligations of power in the writings of Tagore and Sen involves the concrete recommendations Tagore and especially Sen develop based on this idea. Sen in *Peace and Democratic Society* indicates that the idea of the obligations of power is essential for understanding why Calcutta had a lower homicide rate than any other large urban area in the world in 2005. The twin focus on diminishing abuses of power and protecting persons from extreme deprivation has shown itself to enhance human security in this city.[3] Sen makes a similar point in foreign policy. When Sen notes that "Bangladesh is probably the safest place to live in, in the subcontinent" he is drawing attention to the dangers persons in India and Pakistan have been exposed to because of the commitment of Indian and Pakistani heads of state to a nuclear arsenal.[4] The human security of persons is enhanced when heads of state jointly forgo the production of nuclear weapons and place limits on their conventional arsenals, in Sen's view.

Interpreted in this way, Tagore and Sen do more than offer an interpretation of Buddha and Ashoka's ideas. They also use these ideas in their own analyses of contemporary events. Norms of nonviolence, rooted in the idea of the obligations of power, are needed in both the democratic and the nondemocratic societies of the world in the view of both thinkers. The idea of the obligations of power provides a better foundation for thinking about human security than the social contract tradition.

NOTES

1. See introduction, note 23.
2. Tagore, *Nationalism* (New York: Macmillan, 1917), 95.
3. See introduction, pages 14–16 and 154–59.
4. Sen, *The Argumentative Indian*, 258.

Acknowledgments

I would like to thank Natalie McKnight, dean of the College of General Studies at Boston University, for her moral and intellectual support during this project, as well as the awarding of a sabbatical semester in the early stages of research. I would also like to thank Kevin Stoehr, humanities department chair at Boston University, for his wise counsel and patience during the Covid era which we still find ourselves in. Anastaysa Chandra, Gabriella Walsh, Daniel M., and Andrea Ventura each read through different versions of the manuscript and offered comments and feedback. Anil Mundra also very graciously read through the manuscript and offered extensive comments during a very busy time. Eric Kuntzman, Rachel Kirkland, and Jasper Mislak at Rowman & Littlefield's Lexington Books provided excellent editorial advice throughout. The final typed copy of the text was checked for accuracy by Mary Wheelehan. I am most grateful to her for bringing to light errors which had escaped my own eyes and for assistance with the large number of editorial decisions that needed to be made regarding spellings and capitalizations in the manuscript. Irene and Kyle, and my mother, father, and brother helped me at every step of the way.

Introduction

In Amartya Sen's essay "The Contemporary Relevance of Buddha," Sen makes a comment about Rabindranath Tagore. Sen states:

> The great poet and novelist Rabindranath Tagore once remarked that he was extremely sad that he was not alive when Gautama Buddha was still around. Tagore very much wished he could have had conversations with Buddha.[1]

On the surface, this comment might seem innocuous. Sen indicates that Tagore was drawn to the ideas of Buddha but in such a way that he wanted to converse with Buddha more. Tagore believed he had much to learn from an encounter with Buddha. But as one reads on in Sen's essay this comment gains in significance. In particular, Sen indicates that Tagore was especially drawn to Buddha's "reasoned approach" to "ethics, society and political life."[2] It was the reasoning, interpersonal aspects of Buddha's thinking that most interested Tagore.

Sen's recollection of Tagore is noteworthy in its own right. It is based on first-hand experience and opens a window into Tagore's mental and emotional life.[3] It is not mediated by what various commentators have said. Sen's description of this event also shifts the emphasis of his account of Tagore. While many scholars tend to locate Tagore's thought within the framework of Upanishadic doctrine and ascribe a religious basis to Tagore's ethical ideas, Sen focuses on Tagore's abiding interest in Buddha, who, in Sen's view, expressed a very strong "theoretical skepticism of God" and who completely disaggregated his ethical arguments from religious disputations.[4] There is an engagement with radical doubts in Tagore's writings that is often glossed over in accounts of Tagore's life.

Sen's focus on the importance of Buddha to Tagore, coupled with Sen's very strong characterization of the ethical strategy of the Sutta Nipata, which untangles ethical questions from debates about God, is revealing. To Sen, Buddha and Tagore are better understood in terms of the figure of "the

argumentative Indian" in Indian history.[5] It is the peaceful exchange of reasons between persons—and not the commitment to what is ineffable—that
best characterizes the lives of these two Indian persons, in Sen's view. But
how, exactly, does Tagore describe Buddha in his own writings? And what
significance does Tagore ascribe to the history of Buddhism in his works?

Consider, in this context, Tagore's comment about Buddha in *The Religion
of Man*. Tagore states:

> We must never forget to-day that a mere movement is not valuable in itself, that
> it may be a sign of a dangerous form of inertia. We must be reminded that a
> great upheaval of spirit, a universal realization of the true dignity of man once
> caused by Buddha's teachings in India, started a movement for centuries which
> produced illuminations of literature, art, science, and numerous efforts of public
> beneficence. This was a movement whose motive force was not some additional
> accession of knowledge or power or urging of some overwhelming passion. It
> was an inspiration for freedom, the freedom which enables us to realize dharma,
> the Truth of eternal Man.[6]

In this passage, Tagore frames Buddha's life and teachings in terms of his
ethical message. Buddha did not encourage persons to gain power over their
neighbors or to seek out a life of desire without bounds. Instead, Buddha's
goal was to promote the freedom and equality of all persons through acts
of public reasoning. Public reasoning—and especially the public critique of
radically hierarchical and non-egalitarian ideas—is central to both Buddha's
ethical teaching and the social movement of Buddhism, in Tagore's view.

Tagore understands Buddha and the early history of Buddhism through
the idea of an "upheaval of spirit." A social movement that seeks to promote
the growth and development of all individuals—through "illuminations of
literature, art, science, and numerous efforts of public beneficence"—was
the fruit of Buddha's ideas. But a second feature of Tagore's interpretation of
Buddha is connected to Tagore's understanding of the international system.
Protecting persons from abuses of power while promoting the growth and
development of all persons is central to the foreign policy internationalism
that Tagore espoused.

Tagore's account of the foreign policy implications of Buddha's ideas is
found in Tagore's text *Nationalism*—which was first delivered in lectures
Tagore gave during World War I. In a key passage, Tagore states:

> I cannot help but bring to your mind those days when the whole of eastern
> Asia from Burma to Japan was united with India in closest friendship, the only
> natural tie which can exist between nations. There was a living communication
> of hearts, a nervous system evolved through which messages ran about the
> deepest needs of humanity. We did not stand in fear of each other; we did not

need to arm ourselves to keep each other in check; our relation was not that of self-interest, of exploration or spoliation of each other's pocket; ideals and ideas were exchanged, gifts of the highest love were offered and taken; no difference in language and customs hindered us in approaching each other heart to heart; no pride of race consciousness or superiority, physical or mental, marred our relation; our arts and literatures put forth new leaves and flowers under the influence of this sunlight of united hearts, and races belonging to different lands and languages and histories acknowledged the highest unity of man and the deepest bound of love.[7]

The descriptions Tagore presents in this passage cover precisely the same ground he went on to discuss fifteen years later in *The Religion of Man*. It is the spread of Buddhism throughout Asia that Tagore is referring to here. More precisely, Tagore believed that Buddha's focus on the freedom and equality of all persons blended with other streams of language, art and material culture in Asia. The peaceful exchange of reasons led to "new leaves and flowers" of literature wherever the persons who followed Buddha went.

Tagore sees the initial expansion of Buddhism in Asia as a period of growth and development in the mental and emotional lives of numerous different peoples. The theme of "enlightenment"—which is commonly associated with a period of European history starting in the eighteenth century—is also rooted in the early Indian classical period in Tagore's writings. But while the positive description of the relation between different peoples is the main theme in the quotation from *Nationalism* it is also the case that Tagore uses the initial peaceful expansion of Buddhism in Asia as a vantage point from which to view contemporary events. Tagore is speaking against the backdrop of the colonial period and World War I when he made this remark. And this context shades the meaning of his words. The clause "We did not stand in fear of each other; we did not need to arm ourselves to keep each other in check"—as well as the clause "our relation was not that of self-interest, of exploration or spoliation of each other's pocket"—is both a description of the spread of Buddhism throughout Asia and an indirect reference to the relation between states in the period leading up to the First World War. Tagore is contrasting the social movement Buddha set in motion with the international system established by the European nation states in their quest for power and territory.

Interpreted in this way, Tagore uses the initial spread of Buddha's ideas in Asia to critique the contemporary competition for power in the international system. There are ways of thinking about the relations between peoples and societies that do not lead with the ideas of violence and territorial gain. An authoritarian politics is not the only possibility a society can pursue. But even this point understates the influence of Buddha's ideas on this passage in

Nationalism. In the first verse of the Attadanda Sutta, Buddha notes that "fear is born from arming oneself: just look at how people fight!"[8] In Buddha's view, the decision to take up arms and threaten other groups of people inevitably leads to more conflict and struggle. Persons and groups will respond violently to the threat of violence emanating from other people. And when seen through this lens the passage in *Nationalism* takes on a third meaning. Tagore's comment that "We did not stand in fear of each other; we did not need to arm ourselves to keep each other in check" is also a new expression of the theme of the Attadanda Sutta. Tagore thinks about fear and the human decision to arm a group of people in a similar way to Buddha.

THE DISCOURSE ON THE ARROW

Tagore's analysis of the international system is grounded in the history of Buddhism and Buddha's ethical ideas. The texts *Nationalism* and *The Religion of Man* cannot be understood in abstraction from these concerns. But Tagore's interest in Buddha is not limited to Buddha's comments about the dignity of the person or the inevitable effects of armed hostility. Tagore also makes several epistemological observations when interpreting Buddha's ideas. The theme of "how do we know?" is central to Tagore's discussion.

The epistemological aspect of Tagore's interpretation is highlighted in another passage from *The Religion of Man*. Tagore states:

> When somebody asked Buddha about the original cause of existence he sternly said that such questioning was futile and irrelevant. Did he not mean that it went beyond the human sphere as our goal—that though such a question might be legitimately asked in the region of cosmic philosophy or science, it had nothing to do with man's dharma, man's inner nature, in which love finds its utter fulfillment.[9]

Here Tagore makes a comment on Buddha's method. To Buddha, some questions are interesting from a scientific or a speculative point of view but that does not mean that these questions have ethical significance or that a person must have a well-developed cosmic philosophy or religious doctrine to act in an ethical manner. A person does not need to answer all questions in order to act in an altruistic way or to love other people.

Tagore understands Buddha's ethical teaching as confined to "the human sphere." The idea that god created the world—or the idea that the world is eternal—are consciously and intentionally avoided in Buddha's public statements. Moreover, the story from the early Buddhist discourses Tagore refers to in the passage from *The Religion of Man* seems to confirm this idea. In particular, "The Shorter Discourse to Malunkyaputta"—the Cula-Malunkyaputta Sutta—communicates this point. Buddha states:

> So, Malunkyaputta, remember what is undisclosed by me as undisclosed, and what is disclosed by me as disclosed. And what is undisclosed by me? "The cosmos is eternal," is undisclosed by me. "The cosmos is not eternal" is undisclosed by me. "The cosmos is finite" . . . "The cosmos is infinite" . . . "The soul and the body are the same" . . . "The soul is one thing and the body is another" . . . "After death a Tathagata exists" . . . "After death a Tathagata does not exist" . . . "After death a Tathagata both exists and does not exist" . . . "After death a Tathagata neither exists nor does not exist," is undisclosed by me.[10]

Here Buddha indicates that there are many ideas that he will not comment on—one way or the other. Questions about the origin of the cosmos or the immortality of the soul are not central to the justifications of Buddha's dharma in this discourse. Instead, Buddha indicates in this discourse that he is concerned with (1) the causes of suffering, and (2) the way to remove the causes of suffering.[11] These themes are at the center of Buddha's teachings, not speculative doctrines of various sorts. And the specific example Buddha gives in the discourse is the example of a man who has been shot with an arrow. What is important to this man is removing the arrow. Reflecting on the creation of the world or the idea that the world is eternal will not help this person.[12]

Interpreted in this way, Tagore sees Buddha as providing a different rationale for an ethical life than many of his peers. Buddha developed his notion of dharma or good behavior while remaining within "the human sphere." Thus, Tagore believes it is a mistake to identify Buddha's ethical teaching with a cosmic philosophy or doctrine like the one found in the Upanishads. Buddha offered an empirical and experiential ethic, not a creation narrative.

A LINE OF REASONING

Tagore's interpretation of Buddha's epistemology is revealing. In Tagore's view, Buddha not only initiated a social movement founded on the freedom and equality of all persons in Asia; the method Buddha used to establish these ethical ideas is also distinctive. The importance of observations and experiences that are available to all persons is the foundation of Buddha's ethical teaching. I should also point out that Sen makes a similar argument when discussing Buddha's ideas. In *The Argumentative Indian*, Sen states:

> Indian texts include elaborate religious expositions and protracted defense. They also contain lengthy and sustained debates among different religious schools.

But there are, in addition, a great many controversies between defenders of religiosity on one side, and advocates of general skepticism on the other. These doubts sometimes take the form of agnosticism, sometimes that of atheism, but there is also Gautama Buddha's special strategy of combining his theoretical skepticism about God with a practical subversion of the significance of the question by making the choice of good behavior completely independent of any God—real or imagined.[13]

In this passage Sen describes Buddha's approach to ethical obligation through a comparison with other forms of debate and argument present in the subcontinent during the early Indian classical period.[14] In particular, Sen notes that Buddha's approach to ethical obligation involves an intentional choice to completely disaggregate the account of ethical obligation from debates about the presence or absence of a god or gods. These and other speculative ideas like them are not needed to justify a moral and legal code.

Interpreted in this way, Sen—like Tagore—sees in "The Shorter Discourse of Malunkyaputta" the basic starting point in Buddha's analysis of ethics, society, and political life. It is the decision to consciously and explicitly refrain from certain types of speculative questions that distinguishes Buddha's approach to human obligation from other thinkers. Even more: Sen not only claims that Buddha's strategy was unique in the early Indian classical period. Sen also believes this strategy continues to be among the most viable approaches to human obligation now. In the essay "The Contemporary Relevance of Buddha," Sen states:

Buddha's demonstration that moral ideas need not originate in any specific invoking of divinity remains extremely important today. This is not just because there are many non-believers in the world, but also because people belonging to different faiths and distinct religions can still find agreement on moral codes of conduct if morality is not seen as entirely parasitic on a particular view of divinity.[15]

To Sen, the decision to disaggregate ethical claims from religious disputes is as relevant now as it was 2,500 years ago. Buddha has made a lasting contribution to practical reasoning in Sen's view.

VIOLENCE AND GOVERNMENT

I have now sketched out a few of the overarching points Tagore and Sen make regarding the figure of Buddha. Buddha's approach to practical reasoning—and the social movement Buddha set in motion in India and Asia—is of lasting importance to both thinkers. As Sen notes in *The Argumentative*

Indian, "The spread of Buddhism from India to nearly half the world is one of the great events of global history."[16] It is a mistake to neglect this history when studying the idea of justice or the field of practical reasoning in Sen's view. But what are some of the specific ways in which Buddha's reasoned approach to ethics, society and political life are relevant today—in the views of Tagore and Sen? And how can these ideas help solve problems in the contemporary world?

One area of application has already been discussed. The foreign policy internationalism of Tagore and Sen leads with a critique of state strategies of violence. In the view of both thinkers, the decision to rapidly expand a nation's military arsenals—as well as the decision to invade another people—sets in motion a series of counter-responses that make everyone worse off. Buddha's idea that "fear is born from arming oneself" is central to Tagore and Sen's analysis of the international system.[17] But another important area where Tagore employs Buddha's analysis of violence is found in his reflections on British controlled India. The need to maintain nonviolent norms within society is repeatedly emphasized in Tagore's accounts of the British colonial period.

Consider, in this context, a passage from Tagore's "The Disease and the Cure"—an essay from 1908. Tagore states:

> Right at the beginning, we must remember a truth. For whatever reason or through whatever means, if we try to retaliate against the English, then they certainly will do something about it. The consequence of their action will not be beneficial to us.[18]

The form of social and political analysis evident in this passage is highly significant. It may seem like a strategy of taking up arms and violently resisting British occupation would strengthen the standing of Indian persons in their relations with the British.[19] By harming or retaliating against the British rulers of India some measure of agency would be achieved by Indian persons. But in making this point Tagore also draws attention to the inevitable response. The British authorities in India would not ignore the strategy of armed insurrection. They would do something about it. In Tagore's view, the British would retaliate in a proportionate way—or possibly even in a disproportionate way—if the Indian resistance movement adopted these goals. And if the British did respond to violent Indian resistance with further acts of aggression, is it accurate to argue that Indian persons had gained from their initial strategy? Would Indian persons truly benefit from armed rebellion?

In the passage from "The Disease and the Cure," a strategy of violent resistance is criticized as making everyone worse off. Indian persons living under British rule would not improve their standing in India through armed insurrection. Buddha's claim that "fear is born from arming the self" is active in this passage from "The Disease and the Cure."[20] Tagore's letter to Lord Chelmsford is informed by a similar logic. Tagore did not advocate Indian persons taking up arms against the British Raj after the Amritsar massacre of 1919. Instead, he criticized the decisions of the British military commander who ordered the killings. Tagore states:

> The enormity of the measures taken by the government of the Punjab for quelling some local disturbances has, with a rude shock, revealed to our minds the helplessness of our position as British subjects in India. The disproportionate severity of the punishments inflicted upon the unfortunate people and the methods of carrying them out, we are convinced, are without parallel in the history of civilized governments, barring some conspicuous exceptions, both recent and remote. *Considering that such treatment has been meted out to a population, disarmed and resourceless, by a power which has the most terribly efficient organization for destruction of human lives, we must strongly assert that it can claim no political expediency, far less moral justification.*[21] (italics added)

Tagore's description of the British commander's action in this passage is exact and unsparing. The British commander, Brigadier General Dyer, intentionally targeted a large group of unarmed and nonviolent Indian protesters. At least 379 Indian persons were killed and 1,200 injured by rifle fire in the space of fifteen minutes through the British commander's orders.[22] In doing so, the British commander violated the obligations of power. Persons in positions of power should not use their superiority in power to kill unarmed persons and spread feelings of terror and fear.

The primary claim in Tagore's letter is an expression of moral outrage. The British commander violated basic ethical norms with his decision. There is a very terrible abuse of power evident here. This violent and unjust action, however, also set in motion a wave of shock and anger throughout the Indian populace. Hundreds of thousands of Indian persons condemned this act. And this response, as Tagore notes, undermined British rule. The British commander's decision to kill unarmed civilians had the effect of weakening—not strengthening—the British standing in India.

SUTTA NIPATA

Tagore's letter to Lord Chelmsford describes both the immorality of the British commander's action and its imprudence. The immoral violent act always sets in motion an escalating response. It enraged—it did not calm or quiet—numerous Indian persons. In doing so, Tagore reveals the way a violent strategy of governance diminishes the ruler. The commander harmed his own cause through his orders.

Tagore's reflections on the effects of violence on society—the inevitable escalating tension that is set in motion by a violent strategy of rule or a violent strategy of resistance—lead him to characterize the foundation of society in a new way. Diminishing violent strategies of governance and resistance is an essential step in the development of any civilization in Tagore's view. The need for peaceful transitions of power—accomplished through fair and competitive elections, in a more general context of unfettered public reasoning—informs many of Tagore's political statements. But what are some of the specific ways Sen draws Buddha's ideas into his ethical and political thinking?

As noted earlier, Sen is focused on Buddha's accomplishments in the area of practical reasoning. Sen believes Buddha's method of ethical justification continues to be relevant in the contemporary world. However, Sen also speaks about the content of Buddha's ethical ideas. In a key passage from *The Idea of Justice*, Sen states:

> *The perspective of obligations of power was presented powerfully by Gautama Buddha in Sutta Nipata.* Buddha argues there that we have responsibility to animals precisely because of the asymmetry between us, not because of any symmetry that takes us to the need for cooperation. *He argues instead that since we are enormously more powerful than other species, we have some responsibility towards other species that connects exactly with this asymmetry of power.*
>
> Buddha goes on to illustrate the point by an analogy with the responsibility of the mother towards her child, not because she has given birth to the child (that connection is not invoked in this particular argument—there is room for it elsewhere), but because she can do things to influence the child's life that the child itself cannot do. *The mother's reason for helping the child, in this line of thinking, is not guided by the rewards of cooperation, but precisely from her recognition that she can, asymmetrically, do things for the child that will make a huge difference to the child's life and which the child itself cannot do.*[23] (italics added)

The first paragraph of this quotation is focused on persons and animals. As both Buddha and Sen note, persons with weapons and nets and well-honed powers of reasoning can easily kill an animal if they so choose. But there is no way that an animal can kill an armed group of people under ordinary circumstances. There is a tremendous asymmetry of power between animals and people. Consequently, the obligation to care for animals must be understood in terms of the adult human being. It is the adult who recognizes that animals need protection from human power to grow and develop. The adult human being is the one who can shield the animal from the human power to kill.

Interpreted in this way, the ethical teaching Sen extracts from the Sutta Nipata is centered on the way persons reason about animals. A person sees a weaker form of life but chooses to act in terms of that life's needs. The idea of humans protecting fragile life is the main idea. However, the details of the quotation from *The Idea of Justice*—the use of a caring mother to illustrate the idea of the obligations of power in the second paragraph—further ties this passage in *The Idea of Justice* to the Metta Sutta, an early Buddhist discourse collected in the Sutta Nipata. In this discourse, Buddha states:

> Even as a mother protects with her life her child, her only child,
> So with a boundless heart one should cherish all living beings,
> Radiating kindness over the entire world,
> Spreading upwards to the skies, and downwards to the depths,
> Outwards and unbounded, free from hatred or ill-will.[24] (italics added)

As Sen notes, the moral reasoning in this passage is not founded on the idea of reciprocity. This is not a case of person A and person B giving the same thing to each other. Instead, the ethical idea in this passage is unidirectional. The mother can protect the child—but not vice versa. The adult human being is the source of the obligation to care for the child. In particular, the mother can insure the child is fed and sheltered and protected from dangers. The mother can take actions to ensure that the child will grow and develop.

ASHOKA

In Sen's view, the notion of reciprocity does not accurately capture what Buddha is saying in the Metta Sutta and the Sutta Nipata. The relations between adult and child—or the relation between adults and animals—cannot be understood through a contract or agreement. As a consequence, Sen is opposed to the use of the idea of the social contract to explain Buddha's ethical ideas.[25] Buddha's ethical thinking has a different root.

Sen grounds Buddha's understanding of obligation in asymmetries of power. Reflecting on what the adult can do for children and for animals is the core idea in Buddha's ethics. Moreover, Sen's interpretation of the Metta Sutta informs other passages is *The Idea of Justice*. For instance, in the introduction to the work, Sen states:

> Freedom to choose gives us the opportunity to decide what we should do, but with that opportunity comes the responsibility for what we do—to the extent that they are chosen actions. *Since a capability is the power to do something, the accountability that emanates from that ability—that power—is a part of the*

capability perspective, and this can make room for the demands of duty—what can be broadly called deontological demands.[26] (italics added)

This passage can be interpreted in terms of a continuum. On one end of the continuum is the newly born child. The newly born child cannot take actions to protect other people. The child does not have the power or the capability to act in this way. Consequently, one cannot speak of the obligations of the newly born child towards an adult. A child cannot be held responsible for what the child cannot do. On the other end of the continuum is the adult human being with fully developed capabilities of mind and body. This person *can* protect the child from dangers. An adult is able do things for the child that child cannot do on his or her own. Consequently, one can appropriately speak of the adult's responsibilities in this context. A sense of responsibility emerges from the adult's heightened capacity to act.

To Sen, the growth and development of the child into an adult carries with it a gradual expansion of the person's ethical responsibilities. Adults can be held accountable for their actions in a way children cannot. This point also extends to the roles in society that adults can find themselves in. It is especially applicable to heads of state. Heads of state have the power to wage war or pursue peace. These persons also exert a large amount of control over the resources of society. The head of state can do many things that a civilian or a child cannot. But in Sen's view, these individuals have even greater responsibilities towards human persons precisely because their powers are greater. The head of state has a duty to shield persons from violence. And here again there is a link between Sen's thought and the early Buddhist discourses. In the Cakkavatti-Sihanada Sutta—an early Buddhist discourse that is not collected in the Sutta Nipata—the idea of the obligations of power defines the good ruler. At the beginning of this discourse, a good king states to his son:

> Well then, my dear: depend on what is right (Dhamma), honor and respect it, praise it, revere and venerate it, have Dhamma as your flag, Dhamma as your banner, govern by Dhamma, *and arrange rightful (Dhammika) shelter, protection and defense for your family, for the army, for your noble warrior client-(king)s, for Brahman*[27] *householders, for town-dwellers and country folk, for ascetics and Brahman (-renouncer)s, for animals and birds. Let no wrongdoing take place in your territory; if there are poor people in your territory, give them money.*[28] (italics added)

In this passage, persons and animals should be protected from violence by the powers of the state. It is the duty of the good king to protect his people. Likewise, all persons should be shielded from destitution and the extremes of nature. The king should not use the power of the state to satisfy his greed.[29]

The moral rules for kingship—the notion of dhamma (Pali) or dharma (Sanskrit) defended in this discourse—is an example of the obligations of power. Yes, the ideal Buddhist king has greater powers then the unarmed civilians in this society. But it is the way the king uses these powers that matters to Buddha. The king should use the power of the state to protect the life within his territory. The idea of loving kindness or the obligations of power is active in this Buddhist ideal of the king. Sen also draws attention to the historical figure of the third Mauryan emperor Ashoka in this context. In another passage from *The Idea of Justice*, Sen states:

> (Ashoka) had started as a severe and stern emperor, but underwent a major moral and political conversion after being revolted by the barbarity he saw in his own victorious war against a remaining unconquered territory in India (Kalinga, in what is today's Orissa). He decided to change his moral and political priorities, embraced the nonviolent teachings of Gautama Buddha, gradually disbanded his army, and went about liberating the slaves and indentured labourers, and took the role of a moral teacher rather than a stern strong ruler.[30]

Here Sen describes the change in Ashoka's priorities after his turn to Buddhism. Instead of waging additional wars to advance the territory and the power of the Mauryan state Ashoka reduced the size of the armed forces and embarked on a series of moral reforms. The predatory use of power was replaced by the obligations of power in Ashoka's thinking.

The very dramatic change Sen highlights in *The Idea of Justice* is drawn from the thirteenth "Major Rock Edict" of Ashoka. In a remarkable passage, Ashoka states:

> When he had been consecrated eight years the Beloved of the Gods, the king Piyadassi, conquered Kalinga. A hundred and fifty thousand people were deported, a hundred thousand were killed and many times that number perished. Afterwards, now that Kalinga was annexed, the Beloved of the Gods very earnestly practiced Dhamma, desired Dhamma, and taught Dhamma. On conquering Kalinga the Beloved of the Gods felt remorse, for, when an independent country is conquered the slaughter, death, and deportation of the people is extremely grievous to the Beloved of the Gods, and weighs heavily on his mind. What is even more deplorable to the Beloved of the Gods, is that those who dwell there, whether brahmans, *sramanas*, or those of other sects, or householders who show obedience to their superiors, obedience to mother and father, obedience to their teachers and behave well and devotedly towards their friends, acquaintances, colleagues, relatives, slaves, and servants—all suffer violence, murder and separation from their loved ones. Even those who are fortunate to have escaped, and whose love is undiminished [by the brutalizing effect of war], suffer from the misfortunes of their friends, acquaintances, colleagues and

relatives. This participation of all men in suffering, weighs heavily on the mind of the Beloved of the Gods.[31]

Here Ashoka attempts to measure the scale of the suffering caused by the war in Kalinga. He notes that several hundred thousand people were killed by the fighting and its aftermath. He also notes that everyone in the society lost loved ones or knew persons who lost loved ones. It is clear from Ashoka's account that the war with Kalinga was a calamity for the conquered people.

At the most basic level, the thirteenth "Major Rock Edict" is an unflinching account of the consequences of war from the perspective of its victims. All persons in Kalinga suffered violence, murder, and the separation of loved ones. This description of the war with Kalinga, however, is also the entryway into a moral reflection. Ashoka grieved for the death and suffering he had caused. He also began to look for alternatives. In particular, Ashoka decided to use the power of the state to protect civilians from war. To this end, he tried to convince his own descendants and the surrounding heads of state in the region to give up on wars of territorial expansion. Ashoka also diminished the size of the Mauryan army. And if one asks the question "Why did Ashoka do these things?" one answer is the following: if every state in the region gave up on territorial expansion the possibility of war between states would diminish. An international approach to foreign policy is the most effective way to shield people from the violence of war. Moreover, it seems that Ashoka did pursue this type of foreign policy in the second part of his reign. Ashoka sent envoys to other heads of state in the region in order to teach dhamma. Ashoka also wanted to persuade his male descendants to view wars of self-defense as a last resort.[32]

PEACE AND DEMOCRATIC SOCIETY

To Sen, the life of Ashoka shows the great political potential inherent in Buddha's message. Instead of seeing an asymmetry of power as an invitation to invade the weaker state, Ashoka began to think in terms of the obligations of power. Using the power of the state to protect fragile life became Ashoka's core idea.

The discussion of Ashoka in *The Idea of Justice* further develops Sen's account of Buddha's ethical ideas. The idea of the obligations of power is at the center of Sen's thinking about the state as well as the relations between adults and children, or persons and animals. The ubiquity of asymmetries of power in nature and society reveal the fundamental importance of this idea. But another area of Sen's interest in the idea of the obligations of power is focused on sectarian violence. How, exactly, do the obligations of power diminish sectarian violence, in Sen's view?

Sen's analysis of sectarian violence is rooted in his experience of the British colonial period. Sen grimly notes that "thousands upon thousands" of persons were killed as a result of the sectarian violence in the subcontinent during the period leading up to the end of British control.[33] As Sen notes, the British Raj failed to maintain the rule of law in India during the 1940s. But the grim starting point in Sen's analysis is not the last word. After the turn to democracy in 1950, the amount of violence between sects in India has declined greatly.[34] Sen indicates that there has been nothing on the scale of the sectarian violence of the 1940s in India in the decades that followed.

In Sen's analysis, the turn towards democracy in India played an important role in diminishing sectarian violence in the country. The creation of democratic institutions—and especially the maintenance of the rule of law, where there is zero tolerance for murder—is an inflection point when it comes to the question of human security in India or in any society.[35] In the absence of a policy of zero tolerance for murder, the escalating quality of the violent act can quickly fragment a society into different groups. But it is also clear from Sen's discussion that Sen believes the institutions of democracy by themselves are not enough to explain the decline in violence that has occurred within Indian society since 1950. There are other factors at work here.

The need to go beyond the existence of democratic institutions and the rule of law when thinking about violence is discussed in Sen's essay "Violence and Civil Society"—which is collected in the volume *Peace and Democratic Society*. In this text, Sen notes that in 2005 "The average incidence of murder in the 35 cities of India is 2.7 per 100,000 people—2.9 for Delhi." In Calcutta, however, there were 0.3 murders for every 100,000 persons during the same period.[36] The murder rate in Calcutta was much, much lower than the rest of India in 2005. But why should this be? What was it about Calcutta that made it so much less violent than the other large, democratic, urban areas in India during this year? Sen also places this point into a broader context. Sen states:

> In 2005, Paris had a homicide rate of 2.3 [per 100,000 persons], London of 2.4, New York of 5.0, Buenos Aires of 6.4, Los Angeles 8.8, Mexico City 17.0, Johannesburg 21.5, Sao Paulo 24.0, and Rio de Janeiro an astonishing 34.9.[37]

Each of these urban areas have democratic institutions. The holding of periodic elections—which gives the electorate the capability to remove incumbents—is central to the way power is expressed in all these societies. Each of these urban areas also has a justice system. The instruments of the rule of law are operational in these places. And yet there are very wide discrepancies between the homicide rates in these cities. Paris, London, New York,

Buenos Aires, Los Angeles, Mexico City, Johannesburg, Sao Paulo, and Rio De Janeiro do not have the same achievements in the area of human security. Nor are these democratic urban areas remotely close to the achievements of democratic Calcutta, with its homicide rate of 0.3 per 100,000 persons in 2005. Again: what is it about Calcutta that made it so much less violent than its global peers during this period?

Sen is careful when discussing these observations. It is, Sen notes, very difficult to make empirical generalizations about violent crime. There is a need for "humility" in the social sciences on this point, he says.[38] The question of "how do we know?" is a big problem in this context. But these cautions do not stop Sen from making a suggestion. Sen states:

> The prevailing politics of Calcutta and of West Bengal, which is very substantially left of center, has tended to concentrate on deprivation related to class and, more recently, to uses and abuses of political power. That political focus, which is very distinct from the religion and religion-based community, has made it much harder to exploit religious differences for instigating riots against minorities, as has happened, with much brutality, in some Indian cities, for example Bombay (or Mumbai) and Ahmedabad.[39]

The basic idea in this passage is clear. The existence of the formal institutions of democracy are not enough to explain the variations in each democratic society's homicide rate. It is the kind of norms persons are choosing to vote for that matters most in this context. More precisely, persons in Calcutta and West Bengal made voting decisions based on alleviating extreme deprivation and diminishing abuses of power. Concurrently, political parties and elected officials in Calcutta and West Bengal have responded to this voting behavior. It is the responsiveness of parties to the demands of the voting public that has sustained these ethical and political norms.

Interpreted in this way, each person's need for food and shelter and protection from abuses of power is not only publicly acknowledged by political leaders in the city. This need is also acted upon in a way that convinces persons in the city that political leaders care about their lives. The creation of a more inclusive ethical and political identity is central to Calcutta's low homicide rate.[40] And within this context Sen draws attention to the kind of public reasoning used to sustain this identity. In particular, Sen notes that the disaggregation of ethical and political ideas from religious ideas in the public reasoning of Calcutta has contributed to Calcutta's extremely low homicide rate. By refusing to ground important ethical and political norms in "religion-based community," Calcutta has avoided a resurgence of sectarian violence in the recent past.

Sen's argument in "Violence and Civil Society" stands on its own. It is based on an understanding of the history of Calcutta since Independence. Several features of Calcutta's ethical, social, and political life have worked in concert with each other to produce such a low homicide rate. Studying the recent history of this Indian city can shed some light on the problem of violence in any society. But I should also point out that Sen's analysis of the low homicide rate in Calcutta is also compatible with the themes that have been under discussion in the preface and introduction. In particular, the Buddhist idea of the obligations of power—which requires individuals in positions of power to (1) protect persons from abuses of power, and (2) protect persons from extreme deprivation, while (3) disaggregating religious identity from ethical and political argumentation and debate—is central to Sen's discussions in *The Idea of Justice* and *The Argumentative Indian* as well as *Identity and Violence: The Illusion of Destiny*, "The Contemporary Relevance of Buddha" and "Violence and Civil Society."[41] The same ethical framework is present in all these texts. And this, to my mind, is revealing. When Sen states that "Buddha's demonstration that moral ideas need not originate in any specific invoking of divinity remains extremely important today"—and that "people belonging to different faiths and distinct religions can still find agreement on moral codes of conduct if morality is not seen as entirely parasitic on a particular view of divinity"—he is not only stating his personal belief.[42] He is stating a view that has empirical support. In Sen's analysis, something like the Buddhist idea of the obligations of power was a norm in the city of Calcutta in 2005. The urban area with the lowest homicide rate in the world shares many of the same priorities as Buddha's ethic.

THE HUMAN DEVELOPMENT REPORT

In Sen's view, the idea of the obligations of power is an important factor in the achievement of less violent social relations *from an empirical point of view*. The fact that Calcutta had the lowest homicide rate in the world—by quite a lot—in 2005 says something about the idea of the obligations of power in relation to other prominent ethical and political ideas.

Personally, I know of no other contemporary ethical theory that invokes this particular type of empirical support in defense of its leading assumptions. The use of a comparative empirical analysis of the homicide rate in every large urban area of the world to justify the idea of the obligation of power has no analogue that I am aware of. Certainly, different forms of religious communitarianism as well as the social contract tradition of ethical and political philosophy do not justify their leading ethical ideas in this way. Nor do contemporary forms of act and rule utilitarianism lead with this idea.[43] In this sense, the way Sen argues for the ethical idea of the obligations of power is unique. But the last point I would like to make in this context involves another passage from Sen's essay "The Contemporary Relevance of Buddha." In an interesting biographical comment, Sen states:

> I remember thinking immediately of Buddha in 1989 when my friend, the visionary thinker Mahbub ul Haq, wanted me to join him in initiating his great brain child, the *Human Development Report*, which became an annual publication of the United Nations from 1990 onward. . . . In creating the index, Mahbub ul Haq wanted to change the concentration of development studies in general, and development economics in particular, away from such distant indicators of good living as the gross domestic product and toward more direct indicators of the quality of individual human lives, and of the substantial freedoms that people can enjoy to lead the kinds of lives they have reason to value. The human development approach concentrates on indicators such as longevity, education, removal of abject poverty, and other concerns that have an uncanny closeness to the problems that had engaged the attention of young Buddha twenty-five hundred years ago."[44]

As Sen notes here, the *Human Development Report* calculates or estimates life expectancy, number of years of education, per capita income, and much else—including the homicide rate—for most societies in the world. The ethic of development and a truly universal form of social empiricism are melded together in this annual report. But a second aspect of this passage is its focus on Buddha. In Sen's analysis, many of the concerns that animated Buddha's public reasoning also animate the *Human Development Report*. Buddha was an early defender—if not the earliest defender—of a development ethic.

From this point of view, Sen is not only trying to infuse the theory and practice of democracy with something like Buddha's ethical ideas. Sen does not limit his focus to peace and democratic societies in his writings. Instead, his goal is to infuse every society with something like Buddha's concerns. The *Human Development Report* brings Buddha's focus on longevity, the diminution of extreme poverty, and human security into every society, regardless of regime type. All heads of state have an obligation to promote human development in this way of thinking. The obligations of power is a universal ethical idea in Sen's view. I should also point out that Sen's foreign policy internationalism is grounded in this idea. When Sen advocates for nuclear disarmament, the capping of conventional arsenals, the reduction of the arms trade, the redirection of scientific talent away from militarist goals, and other related objectives he is not doing so from the perspective of defending the nation state or the democratic regimes. Instead, he is trying to make the argument that the persons living in all societies are made better off through these endeavors. In particular, the human security of every person is enhanced through a coordinated draw down in military capacity. Every person on the planet will benefit if every nation with nuclear weapons disarms their nuclear arsenals. Sen also notes that less military spending will free up more resources for education, health care and the access to food and shelter, among other urgent humanitarian concerns.[45] By putting limits on each country's military spending, the growth and development of all persons can become a more widespread global norm.

PLAN OF THE BOOK

As can be seen from this discussion Tagore and Sen do not limit themselves to a historical investigation of Buddha's ideas. They also draw on Buddha's ideas in their own reflections on contemporary events. Buddha's analysis of violence—as well as Buddha's concern with the growth and development of persons—is central to the ethical and political philosophies of Tagore and Sen.

The importance of Buddha to Tagore and Sen have shaped the plan of this book. In what follows, I develop the idea of the obligations of power in the writings of Tagore and Sen in a more systematic way. In part I, I present Tagore and Sen's interpretation of the early Buddhist discourses and the Ashokan inscriptions in greater detail. The goal is not to provide an exhaustive commentary on these texts from the early Indian classical period and there are many, many ideas from these texts that I will not engage with or discuss. Rather, the goal is to focus on the texts attributed to the statements of Buddha and Ashoka that Tagore and Sen refer to—or appear to refer to—in their writings. In this way, the basis for Tagore and Sen's own ethical, political and epistemological ideas can be better understood.

Part I examines passages from the early Buddhist discourses and Ashokan inscriptions that are important to Tagore and Sen. Part II focuses on the way Tagore and Sen draw the ideas of Buddha and Ashoka into their own analyses of contemporary events. I discuss the themes of education, human development, human security, and self-defense in the writings of Tagore and Sen and show how these themes are related to their interpretation of the Buddhist idea of the obligations of power. I conclude with a comparison of the social contract tradition of ethical and political philosophy with the foreign policy internationalism of Tagore and Sen. I argue that Tagore and Sen have a much less permissive attitude towards state violence than is found in the social contract tradition—in part because both thinkers draw on Buddha's critique of violence in their works. I also argue that the idea of a democratic peace is an insufficient approach to human security. Finding ways to diminish the conflict between the democratic and the authoritarian regimes must be part of the wider project of promoting the human security of persons in the world.

SOME DIVERGENCES

A goal of this text is to describe the idea of the obligations of power in the thought of Tagore and Sen through a discussion of the texts in the early Indian classical period that Tagore and Sen refer to—or appear to refer to—in their writings. In this way a deeper understanding of the ethical, social, and political ideas of the two thinkers can be better understood. But the final point I would like to make in this introduction concerns the relationship between Tagore and Sen. What are some of the similarities—and what are some of the differences—between their projects?

In the preface and introduction, I have talked about Tagore and Sen in terms that stressed the commonalities between the two thinkers. When Tagore speaks about the Amritsar massacre in the "Letter to Lord Chelmsford," or notes in *Nationalism* that "things that are living are so easily hurt; therefore they require protection" he is drawing on the ethical standard of the obligations of power articulated in the early Buddhist discourses. Sen, meanwhile, notes that "the perspective of obligations of power was presented powerfully by Gautama Buddha in the Sutta Nipata."[46] He also develops an ethical theory in *The Idea of Justice* based on Buddha's ideas. From these passages and others like them, one can conclude that both thinkers are in alignment when it comes to the core content of Buddha's ethical thinking. Equally important, Tagore and Sen also draw attention to the method Buddha used when clarifying his ethical ideas. Buddha's disaggregation of ethical questions from religious disputations in the Cula-Malunkyaputta Sutta are highlighted by both Tagore and Sen. Tagore and Sen also have a similar appreciation for the early history of Buddhism in Asia. They both interpret this history in terms of an ethical movement that advocated for the freedom and equality of all persons. In all these ways, the commonalities between the two thinkers are very strong.

In reflecting on this similarity of interpretation it is tempting to speak about causes. Sen states that he was introduced to Buddha's teaching when he was given a book of early Buddhist discourses by his grandfather while attending Tagore's school at Shantiniketan. Sen also notes that he was "bowled over" by these Buddhists texts.[47] Clearly, Sen's thinking about Buddha can be traced back to his time as a student in Tagore's school. Nevertheless, it is a mistake to claim that Sen and Tagore have an identical understanding of Buddha and the history of Buddhism. There are points of divergence between the two. For instance, Sen notes that persons living in North India did not simply give up all their preexisting beliefs and ideas if they adopted Buddha's perspective. The expansion of Buddhism in North India was not a one-way process. Instead, Sen indicates that the expansion of Buddha's message in North India also involved the substantial evolution of many of Buddha's teachings.

In particular, Sen draws attention to Ian Mabbett's observation that "from the beginning, Buddhism had to come to terms with the population's belief in special beings and special powers."[48] The evolution of Buddhism after Buddha's death was affected by this fact. Ideas and beliefs that were incompatible with Buddha's skepticism about God merged with his ethical and social teachings during this period of expansion in early Buddhism.

From this point of view, Sen's reflections on Buddhism in the subcontinent retain a sharper sense of its internal diversity than is found in Tagore's writings. As Sen points out, several different traditions of thought and practice grew up around the early Buddhist discourses in the subcontinent that did not strictly adhere to the teachings of the Cula-Malunkyaputta Sutta or the Sutta Nipata. Another point: Tagore speaks about *a different variant* of the idea of the obligations of power in the Upanishads. This variant combines the idea of the obligations of power together with the idea that a living essence is in all things and in all persons. Tagore seems to accommodate this perspective within his ethical thinking. Sen, on the other hand, insists on the need to disaggregate ethical thinking from religious ideations and does not draw attention to the ethical teachings of the Upanishads. This is an important difference between the two thinkers.

This point can be expanded. At 1.14.11 in the Brhadaranyaka Upanishad, the Upanishadic thinker offers a description of *Brahman* or divinity. The passage states:

> In the beginning this world was only *brahman*, only one. Because it was only one, *brahman* had not fully developed. It then created the ruling power, a form superior to and surpassing itself, that is, the ruling power among the gods— Indra, Varuna, Soma, Rudra, Parjanya, Yama, Mrtyu, and Isana.[49]

This section of the passage is a speculative narrative of some kind or another: the Upanishadic thinker is articulating a view about the initial state of the world—"In the beginning there was only *brahman*" is the framing idea.[50] There is no equivalent narrative in the Cula-Malunkyaputta Sutta or the Sutta Nipata. But this not all: the Upanishadic thinker goes a step further and articulates a legal standard that is grounded on this conception of *Brahman* or divinity. The Upanishadic thinker continues:

> [Brahman] still did not become fully developed. So it created the Law (dharma), a form superior to and surpassing itself. And the Law is here the ruling power standing above the ruling power. Hence there is nothing higher than Law. *Therefore, a weaker man makes demands of a stronger man by appealing to the Law, just as one does by appealing to a king.*[51] (italics added)

In this passage, Brahman, the ruling power, has created the Law or dharma—and this creative act is a primary reason why persons have an obligation to follow it. The Law has a divine origin and must be observed by all persons. Moreover, the function of this divinely created Law is to protect "a weaker man" from "a stronger man." The Law created by Brahman prohibits abuses of power in this Upanishad.

From this point of view, the difference between the Upanishadic narrative and the Cula-Malunkyaputta Sutta is not limited to the presence or absence of Brahman; the way the concept of Brahman is used to justify a legal standard is also at issue. The kind of justification in the two texts is distinct. I should also point out that the Upanishadic thinker goes on to explicitly frame his ethical thinking in terms of this speculative narrative. The Upanishadic thinker states:

> When he provides food and shelter to human beings, he becomes thereby a world for human beings. When he procures fodder for livestock, he becomes thereby a world for livestock. When creatures, from wild animals and birds down to the very ants, find shelter in his houses, he becomes thereby a world for them.[52]

To the Upanishadic thinker, persons in positions of power have an obligation to promote the growth and development of other living things. These persons must give food and shelter to persons and other forms of life when it is feasible to do so. Moreover, when persons in positions of power act on this understanding they make a more abundant world within the world. They create a world that is "superior to and surpassing" itself.

Understood in this way, there is some overlap between Buddha and the Upanishadic thinker when it comes to the content of a person's ethical obligations. The injunction to avoid abuses of power and protect other living things is common to each. The Metta Sutta and the creation narrative in the Brhadaranyaka Upanishad are not wholly alien to each other. And this overlap in ethical teachings is a point Tagore picks up on. In his book *Sadhana: The Realization of Life*, Tagore states:

> When we define a man by the market value of the service we can expect of him, we know him imperfectly. With this limited knowledge of him it becomes easy to for us to be unjust to him and to entertain feelings of triumphant self-congratulation when, on account of some cruel advantage on our side, we can get of him much more than we pay for. *But when we know him as spirit we know him as our own.* We at once feel that cruelty to him is cruelty to ourselves, to make him small is stealing from our own humanity, and in seeking to make use of him solely for personal profit we merely gain in money or comfort what we lose in truth.[53] (italics added)

In this passage, Tagore has used the word "spirit" as a translation of atman (the manifestation of Brahman in the person). There is a spirit of growth and development and creation in all persons. But this description of the person is also combined with an ethical claim. Since every person is a manifestation of the same spirit every person should be treated with the same respect and dignity. Equality of treatment follows from the idea that all persons are spirit. As a consequence, a stronger man should not take advantage of a weaker man. The stronger man should not steal from or exploit another manifestation of atman.

Tagore's use of the Upanishads is an important feature of his English language works. The text *Sadhana: The Realization of Life* in particular has many references to Upanishadic passages and teachings. Tagore is intimately familiar with the Isa Upanishad among other Upanishadic texts. However, the fact that Tagore describes the ideas of the Upanishads—or for that matter, the ideas found in the Christian Gospels—does not displace the importance of Buddha in his thought. Rather it shows that Tagore believed many religious traditions resisted abuses of power, both "western" and "eastern." Tagore believed it was important for his English language audiences to be aware of this fact.

Interpreted in this way, Tagore's desire to promote conversations across the so-called divide between "east" and "west" lead him to engage with the ethical teachings of many different religious traditions. Tagore was pursuing a kind of international educational project in his English language writings. But this does not mean that Tagore personally identified with any one of these traditions. Tagore never called himself a Hindu or a Muslim or a Christian or the member of any other sect. And Tagore is explicit about the reason why. In a passage from *The Religion of Man*, Tagore states:

> I was born in a family which, at that time, was earnestly developing a monotheistic religion based upon the philosophy of the Upanishad. Somehow my mind remained coldly aloof, absolutely uninfluenced by any religion whatsoever. It was through an idiosyncrasy of my temperament that I refused to accept any religious teaching merely because people in my surroundings believed it to be true. I could not persuade myself to imagine that I had a religion because everybody whom I might trust believed in its value.
>
> Thus my mind was brought up in an atmosphere of freedom—freedom from the dominance of an any creed that had its sanction in the definite authority of some scripture, or in the teaching of some organized body of worshippers.[54]

Tagore clearly emphasizes the idea of freedom in this passage. The "atmosphere of freedom" that permeated his mental and emotional life as a child and young adult was more important to him than the Upanishadic monotheism of his family.

The conclusion I draw from this discussion, then, is as follows. Tagore wanted to promote conversations between persons with different religious identities across the boundaries of "east" and "west." To this end, Tagore points out that, for instance, both the Upanishads and the Christian gospels speak about the need to avoid abuses of power. Likewise, the Upanishads and the Christian gospels also speak to the importance of love in the conduct between persons. There are many ethical commonalities between these two—and many other—religious traditions in Tagore's view. Moreover, this point of ethical contact between various religious traditions is what Tagore means by the title of his book *The Religion of Man*. In Tagore's words:

> It is significant that all great religions have their historic origins in persons who represented in their life a truth which was not cosmic and unmoral, but human and good.[55]

To Tagore, the religion of man promotes an ethical message. Sen, however, takes a different tack on this question. Sen does not disagree with the idea that there are important points of ethical contact between different religious traditions. The Upanishads and the Christian gospels are also discussed in Sen's works.[56] But in Sen's view, it is important for all persons, both religious and nonreligious, to disaggregate their ethical ideas from their various other religious and nonreligious beliefs. It is the ability to ground norms of nonviolence in purely human terms that has led to the largest reduction in violence in society *from an empirical point of view*.

Interpreted in this way, the main difference between Tagore and Sen can be traced back to Sen's more developed form of social empiricism. In Sen's view, the comparative use of social statistics in the *Human Development Report* and other investigations has revealed an important truth about human society—one that aligns with Buddha's ethical ideas. In Sen's view, much can be gained through further study of the obligations of power.

NOTES

1. Amartya Sen, "The Contemporary Relevance of Buddha" *Ethics and International Affairs* 28, no. 1, 15–27.

2. Ibid.

3. Amartya Sen's grandfather Kshiti Mohan Sen and Tagore were colleagues and fellow teachers at Tagore's school in Shantiniketan. Amartya Sen grew up attending Tagore's school and described the experience as "totally remarkable": "I am

personally rather partial to seeing Tagore as an educationalist, having been educated myself at Shantiniketan. There was something totally remarkable about the ease with which discussions in the school move from Indian traditional literature to contemporary as well as classical western thought to China, Japan and elsewhere." Krishna Dutta and Andrew Robinson, eds., with a foreword by Amartya Sen, *Selected Letters of Rabindranath Tagore* (Cambridge: Cambridge University Press, 1997), xxiv.

4. Amartya Sen, *The Argumentative Indian: Writings on Indian History, Culture and Identity* (New York: Picador), 23.

5. Ibid., 23, 89–120.

6. Rabindranath Tagore, *The Religion of Man* (New York: Macmillan, 1931), 152–53.

7. Rabindranath Tagore, *Nationalism* (New York: Macmillan, 1917), 75–76.

8. "Attadanda Sutta: Arming Oneself" (Sn 4.15), trans. Andrew Olendzki, *Access to Insight* (BCBS Edition), November 2, 2013. https://www.accesstoinsight.org/tipitaka/kn/snp/snp.4.15.olen.html.

9. Tagore, *The Religion of Man*, 154.

10. "Cula-Malunkyaputta Sutta" ("The Shorter Discourse to Malunkyaputta"), trans. Thanissaro Bhikkhu. https://www.dhammatalks.org/suttas/MN/MN63.html.

11. Ibid.

12. Ibid. Note that the cosmological point that Tagore makes—do not ask questions about the immortality of the soul or the world, focus on the removal of suffering—is an inference on Tagore's part. Within Buddha's parable of the arrow, a wounded man asks questions about where the archer is from or who made the arrow instead of removing the arrow from his body.

13. Sen, *The Argumentative Indian*, 23.

14. Upinder Singh notes that "The term 'classical Sanskrit' refers to the language whose rules were codified by the 5th/4th century BCE grammarian Panini in his *Ashtadhyayi*." Upinder Singh, *A History of Ancient and Early Medieval India: From the Stone Age to the 12th Century* (Noida: Pearson, 2017), 17. The term "the early Indian classical period" used in the title and the text is meant to roughly correspond with this time period—basically the sixth through the third century BCE. I am not providing a comprehensive account of this immense and highly diverse period of Indian history.

15. Sen, "The Contemporary Relevance of Buddha," 15–27.

16. Sen, *The Argumentative Indian*, 354. Sen draws attention to the work of H. Brechert and Richard Gombritch, *The World of Buddhism: Buddhist Monks and Nuns in Society and Culture*, in this context.

17. See note 8 above.

18. Fakrul Alam, and Radha Chakravarty, eds., *The Essential Tagore: Rabindranath Tagore* (Cambridge, MA: The Belknap Press of Harvard University Press, 2011), 141.

19. Tagore is referring to the Swadeshi program of boycotting foreign goods and schools in this passage in the "Disease and the Cure" among other possible courses of action.

20. See note 8 above.

21. Dutta and Robinson, *Selected Letters of Rabindranath Tagore*, 223.

22. Pletcher, Kenneth. "Jallianwala Bagh Massacre." Encyclopedia Britannica, April 6, 2021, https://www.britannica.com/event/Jallianwala-Bagh-Massacre. Accessed January 20, 2022.

23. Amartya Sen, *The Idea of Justice* (Cambridge, MA: The Belknap Press of Harvard University Press, 2009), 205.

24. "Karaniya Metta Sutta: The Buddha's Words on Loving-Kindness" (Sn 1.8), trans. The Amaravati Sangha, *Access to Insight* (BCBS Edition), November 2, 2013. https://www.accesstoinsight.org/tipitaka/kn/snp/snp.1.08.amar.html.

25. For more on Sen's critique of the social contract tradition of ethical and political philosophy, see chapter 9.

26. Sen, *The Idea of Justice*, 19.

27. Readers should note that the term "Brahman" (or "Brahmin") is spelled and capitalized differently by different translators, including those quoted in this book. In my writing, "Brahman" refers to the deity and "Brahmin" refers to the social class of priests in the varna system.

28. Steven Collins, *Nirvana and other Buddhist Felicities: Utopias of the Pali Imaginaire* (Cambridge: Cambridge University Press, 1998), 604.

29. At a later point in the narrative of the Cakkavatti-Sihanada Sutta, the degeneration of society begins when a king refuses to give money to the poor: "And so, monks, the king had ministers, councilors, etc. called together and asked them about what the noble turning of a Wheel-turning king. He listened to [what they said] and arranged rightful shelter, protection and defense—but he did not give money to the poor." Steven Collins, *Nirvana and other Buddhist Felicities*, 606.

30. Sen, *The Idea of Justice*, 77.

31. Romila Thapar, *Ashoka and the Decline of the Mauryas* (Oxford: Oxford University Press, 1997), 255–56.

32. These ideas will be developed in more detail in chapter 5.

33. Amartya Sen, *Identity and Violence: The Illusion of Destiny* (New York: W. W. Norton and Company, 2006), 172. For more discussion of these points, see chapter 8.

34. The Indian constitution—which established a federal system of parliamentary rule—was adopted on the 26th of November, 1949 and came into effect on January 26th, 1950. Independence from Britain was achieved on the 15th of August, 1947.

35. For more on the critical importance on the ability to remove incumbents in Sen's discussion of democracy, see *Development as Freedom* (New York: Anchor Books, 1999), 18.

36. Amartya Sen, *Peace and Democratic Society* (Cambridge: OpenBook Publishers), 17–18.

37. Ibid., 18.

38. Ibid., 19.

39. Ibid., 19.

40. Ibid., 20. Note that Sen does not claim that left of center economics and politics is the *only* path to a lower homicide rate. Instead, he claims that there are many different potential pathways: "If identities related to left-wing politics and class have had the effect of vastly weakening violence based on religious divisions and community

contrast in the Indian part of Bengal, a similar constructive influence can be seen in the other part of the border, in Bangladesh, coming from the power of identities of language, literature and music, which do not divide Hindu and Muslims into different—and exploitably hostile—camps."

41. Compare the passage on dhamma from the Cakkavatti-Sihanada Sutta—with its injunction to protect persons from violence and extreme destitution, while avoiding appeals to God or divinity—with Sen's discussion here.

42. See note 16.

43. I discuss areas of overlap between the rule utilitarian argument for the principle of noncombatant immunity in Stephen Nathanson's book *Ethics and the Terrorism of War* and the foreign policy internationalism of Sen and Tagore in chapter 9.

44. Sen, "The Contemporary Relevance of Buddha." 15–27.

45. For more discussion of the economic effects of reducing a country's military spending see Leavitt, *The Foreign Policy of John Rawls and Amartya Sen*, chapter 9.

46. See preface, notes 1 and 2.

47. Sen, "The Contemporary Relevance of Buddha," 15–27.

48. Sen, *The Argumentative Indian*, 23.

49. Olivelle, *Upanishads*, 16. (Verse 1.4.11)

50. This passage in the Brhadarnayaka Upanishad appears to build on an analogy with a king's consolidation of power, thereby implying the idea of conquest. On this interpretation, the way a king consolidates power over lesser rulers is to build up an army that is stronger than the independent rulers. Likewise, the way Brahman consolidates his rule over the lesser nature gods is to create a "ruling power" that is more powerful or "above" them. More generally, Upinder Singh suggests that "the speculative mysticism of the Upanishads was inspired by the idea of absolute and universal kingship of the Rigvedic hymns" and that analogies between kingship and Brahman occur throughout the Upanishads. (Upinder Singh, *Political Violence in Ancient India* [Cambridge, MA: Harvard University Press, 2017], 24).

51. Patrick Olivelle, trans., *Upanishads* (Oxford: Oxford University Press, 1996), 16 (Verse 1.4.14).

52. Ibid., 17 (Verse 1.4.17).

53. Rabindranath Tagore, *Sadhana: The Realization of Life* (New York: Macmillan, 1913), 109–10. Note the similarity between Tagore's treatment of the theme of spirit or atman in the Upanishads and the Christian injunction to "Love your neighbor as yourself." In both cases, the ability to identify oneself with other people is the key to ethical conduct.

54. Tagore, *The Religion of Man*, 90.

55. Ibid., 69.

56. See, for instance, Sen's discussion of the Christian gospels in The Idea of Justice (p. 170–72) and the Chandogya Upanishad in *The Argumentative Indian* (p. 68–69).

PART I

Buddha and Ashoka

Chapter 1

Violent Conduct

The goal of part I is to describe Tagore and Sen's interpretation of the early Buddhist discourses and the Ashokan inscriptions in more detail. While Tagore and Sen do not use the same language in all particulars there are many similarities in their treatment of these figures. Both thinkers argue that Buddha did not appeal to divinity when justifying his ethical ideas. Instead, they claim Buddha founded his ethical claims on experiences and perceptions that all persons could have. A form of social empiricism informed Buddha's claims about human obligation, not an article of faith. The question of "How do we know?" is central to their accounts of Buddha's thinking. And while there are many other ways of interpreting Buddha's ethical ideas—the history of Buddhism is vast and richly varied—it says a great deal about Tagore and Sen's project that they focus on this question and not others. Tagore and Sen do not, for instance, speak about "the fourfold path" in their discussions of the early Buddhist discourses.[1] Nor do they attempt to reconstruct Buddha's thinking by appealing to contemporary ethical theories that are centered on the idea of virtue or the social contract.[2] Instead, they focus on the way Buddha reasoned in public within their interpretations. Buddha's commitment to public discussion and public reasoning is emphasized by Tagore and Sen.

Since this book is focused on Tagore and Sen's interpretation of Buddha and its implications for contemporary ethical and political debates, I will not develop alternative accounts of the early Buddhist discourses in this work. The question of whether Tagore and Sen's interpretation of Buddha is "the best interpretation" or "better than all other existing interpretations" is not one I will take up. First of all, this question is not one I am capable of answering. Second, this question is also, I believe, antithetical to Tagore and Sen's intention in discussing Buddha. At no point do Sen and Tagore claim to offer an exhaustive account of all the things Buddha and Buddhism has and can be. Indeed, Sen makes this point explicit in another passage from "The Contemporary Relevance of Buddha." Sen states:

Anchored in the "here and now," Buddha's thinking proceeded also toward more transcendental reflections—toward a metaphysical understanding of the world. *I shall not, however, go into that aspect of Buddha's thought here, and will concentrate instead on his reasoned approach to worldly problems.* Since Buddhism is often taken to be a very unworldly religion, what I am trying to do here is present an account and analysis of "another Buddha"—one who is no less real than the one who has been revered (and sometimes deified) by the dominant schools of Buddhism for the past two thousand years.[3] (italics added)

Here Sen notes that he is trying to enliven a perspective that emphasizes Buddha's commitment to public reasoning. It is Buddha's "reasoned approach to worldly problems"—and not metaphysical or transcendental notions like the idea of "dependent origination"—that Sen and Tagore both home in on in their interpretation of this figure.[4] In what follows, I will focus on the way Sen and Tagore treat these ethical and social themes while leaving aside much else.

The discussion of part I, then, is very narrow in scope. Following Sen, I discuss Buddha's reasoned approach to worldly problems in the Sutta Nipata. In particular, I examine the way Buddha reasons about violent conduct and sectarianism in chapter 1. In chapter 2, I examine Buddha's critique of hereditary hierarchy. In chapter 3, I examine Buddha's reflections on persons and animals, while chapters 4 and 5 discuss Ashoka's response to the problem of violence between states in the international system. The goal is to further characterize the Indian ethical tradition Tagore and Sen draw on in their writings.

THE YOUNGER BUDDHA

As noted in the introduction, both Sen and Tagore describe the inherently escalating nature of the violent act in their writings. Individuals will respond to the threat of violence emanating from other people. I would like to begin this discussion of the early Buddhist discourses, then, with a few comments on the Attadanda Sutta. This discourse—which, in the view of the scholar and translator H. Saddhatissa, belongs to the "oldest stratum of the Sutta Nipata"—presents Buddha's thoughts about violent conduct (*attadanda*) and is a good entry point into Tagore and Sen's interpretation of Buddha's ethical teachings.[5]

The Attadanda Sutta—unlike many other texts in the Sutta Nipata—does not begin with a description of the context of its narrative. The occasion for the discourse is not made explicit. Instead, one has the feeling of entering into a conversation at a key moment. Buddha begins with an exclamation:

1 Fear results from resorting to violence—just look at how people quarrel and fight! But let me tell you now of the kind of dismay and terror that I have felt.

2 Seeing people struggling, like fish, writhing in shallow water with enmity against one another, I became afraid.

3 At one time, I had wanted to find some place where I could take shelter, but I never saw any such place. There is nothing in this world that is solid at base and not a part of it that is changeless.

4 I had seen them all trapped in mutual conflict and that is why I had felt so repelled. But then I noticed something buried deep in their hearts. It was—I could just make it out—a dart.

5 It is a dart that makes its victims run all over the place. But once it had been pulled out all that running is finished and so is the exhaustion that comes with it.

6 These are the things we can learn from this: The bonds of the world should not be pursued. Disenchanted with all sense pleasures one should train one's self in calmness (*Nibbana*).[6]

There are many comments one can make about this passage. It is full of interesting ideas and language and provides a window into some of Buddha's main teachings. But the point I would like to begin with involves the auto-biographical quality of these verses. In this passage, Buddha is reflecting on his own past. The "I" or first-person singular is a prominent feature of this part of the sutta. And it is clear from the passage that Buddha's past was full of upheavals. The younger Buddha seems to have been disoriented by many of his experiences. He felt terror and dismay at much of what he saw and did not immediately know what to do.

The autobiographical layer of the Attadanda Sutta is significant. The younger Buddha did not begin his life teaching the doctrine of calmness. Instead, Buddha has gone through his own process of growth and develop-ment. His understanding of nibbana (Pali) or nirvana (Sanskrit) only emerged after a period of searching.[7] And this, as Sen notes, made Buddha a "very approachable" figure.[8] It is easy for persons to relate to Buddha's teaching in part because Buddha presents himself as a fallible human being.

THE SOCIAL EFFECTS OF VIOLENCE

The Attadanda Sutta offers a humanizing portrait of the Buddha. The younger Buddha's vulnerability and the intensity of his feelings is a prominent part of his lesson. He felt terror and dismay when reflecting on what he saw. Buddha responds to the threat of violent conduct with all his being. But why, exactly, did Buddha feel such strong emotion when perceiving violent conduct? What is causing Buddha so much difficulty here?

The answer to this question is presented in the first verse. In many descriptions of violence attention is focused on the victim. A person—or an animal—is shot with an arrow or pierced with a knife or sword. And if the wound is severe enough the victim will suffer greatly and may eventually die. In this sense, violent conduct can permanently rob a living being of its capacity to act. But in Buddha's understanding, the effects of a violent act are not limited to the individual life that suffers and dies. Instead, violent acts irreversibly harm the victim and create fear in the lives of other people. The violent act changes the way the persons around the victim think and feel. And it is this emotional reverberation—the fear persons experience in response to the violent act—that sets in motion new quarrels and fights.

In Buddha's description, violent actions harm the victim and construct situations in which new acts of violence become more likely. Individuals will not stand idly by if they believe their lives are endangered by other people. The murder of a person can lead to more acts of killing. But even this description of a violent act under-describes the situation. A violent act harms the victim and unleashes a powerful set of destructive emotions. Persons can feel fear or terror in response to a threat. But as Buddha notes elsewhere violent conduct also changes the character of the violent agent. A person who kills once is more likely to kill again. The future actions of the person are affected by their previous decisions. Buddha's description of "the outcaste" focuses on the behavior of persons who have developed a habit of acting in a violent manner.[9] A violent act can also lead, Buddha's says, to the "wrong view" that it is good to kill without cause.[10] And this wrong view most definitely constructs new acts of violence. In Buddha's thinking, ideas and attitudes that mistakenly justify violence towards other living beings are especially dangerous.

COMMUNICATING EMOTION

Buddha has a complicated and nuanced understanding or "model" of the effects of a violent act on society. He knows acts of violence are harmful to the victim and can lead to violent responses. He has seen violent conflict recreating itself in society again and again. And this knowledge and experience is affecting the way he responds to his perceptions. The younger Buddha felt a very strong upsurge of thought and feeling when he saw violent conduct.

From this point of view, Buddha's feelings of terror and dismay are bound together with many interconnected beliefs. The idea that "Fear results from

resorting to violence"—or the idea that "Fear is born from arming oneself,"
which is Olendzki's translation of the first verse of the Attadanda Sutta—
is distinctive.[11] However, the specific challenge Buddha is facing in the
Attadanda Sutta is the challenge of a teacher. Buddha wants other people to
learn from his experience. He needs the persons in the audience to understand
his beliefs and the emotions they sustain—which is not an easy thing to do.
How exactly does Buddha go about accomplishing this?

Buddha responds to this challenge with a series of short and highly evocative descriptions. Buddha's rhetoric in the Attadanda Sutta is also distinctive.
And the first rhetorical device Buddha uses to explain his feelings and beliefs
to the audience involves the use of an analogy. He states:

> 2 Seeing people struggling, like fish, writhing in shallow water with enmity
> against one another, I became afraid.[12]

The idea presented in this verse is founded on Buddha's experience of fear.
Buddha sees people fighting with each other again and again and becomes
afraid. From this point of view, the second verse reinforces the claim made
in the first verse. However, Buddha presents this point in terms of a comparison. Conflict in human society is similar to the world of the fighting fish.[13]
Struggle is something that can characterize the human and the nonhuman
world. Struggle is not limited to the world of people.

On one level, Buddha's analogy with the fish broadens the scope of his
thinking. Violent conflict is evident in nature as well as human societies.
Violent conflict is not restricted to the human world alone. But why, exactly,
are the fish fighting? Was this a very common perception in the lives of the
persons listening to Buddha? What is Buddha getting at here?

To answer this question, it will help to look to another discourse in the
"Chapter of the Eights" of the Sutta Nipata. In the Guhatakka Sutta—the
discourse on the cave—Buddha says the following:

> 6 Look at those who struggle after their petty ambitions, *like fish in a river that
> is fast drying up*.[14] (italics added)

The analogy in this verse is akin to the analogy made in the Attadanda Sutta.
Both persons and fish can struggle and fight. What is different about the
Guhatakka Sutta, however, is the way Buddha has expanded the analogy. The
fish are struggling because there has been a change in the environment. The
river that had sustained their lives is disappearing.

When viewed through this lens, the image of the fish struggling with
enmity with each other in the Attadanda Sutta is in fact a highly compressed
narrative. In earlier times, when the river was large, it could support the

unrestricted movement of many fish. But when a large river rapidly shrinks to a puddle due to the absence of rain or some other cause it constricts the movement of the fish to such an extent that they struggle to swim. The capacity of the fish to freely move is undermined.[15] And this change in the overall environment makes the performance of simple tasks exceedingly difficult for the fish to do. The fish are forced to fight with each other just to move and eat.

Interpreted in this way, the image of the fish fighting with each other in the river is in fact a description of calamity. The fish are collectively miserable and very near death. And if one transfers this understanding to the realm of people, the image of the fish in a drying river becomes a powerful way of describing the effects of violent conduct in human life. When persons or families or societies are caught up in feelings of fear, punctuated by recurring episodes of violence and killing, the result is a massive constriction of human freedom. Existence itself becomes an intense struggle for these persons.

NO SHELTER

The description of the fish in the rapidly drying river is highly evocative. It establishes a firm sense of misery and impending death. And whether the analogy with human life is meant to describe sectarian conflict or interstate war or a struggle over scarce resources or class conflict or some other painful social division—the abstract nature of the analogy allows it to encompass all these types of discord, and others too—one can see why Buddha would feel terror and dismay at this sight. In Buddha's experience, persons are recreating calamity again and again.

The image of the struggling fish introduces a new theme into the discourse. In Buddha's view, violent conduct restricts human freedom in a terrible way. And this understanding of the effects of violence on persons and society seems to carry over into the third verse of the sutta. Buddha states:

> 3 At one time, I had wanted to find some place where I could take shelter, but I never saw any such place. There is nothing in this world that is solid at base and not a part of it that is changeless.

The description of a world without shelter—like the analogy of the fish—requires interpretation. Taken literally, a shelter is a physical human construction that protects one from rain and wind and the cold and the sun. Shelter shields the human body from the extremes of nature. In the context of the sutta, however, it seems clear that the shelter Buddha is looking for is shelter from violent human conduct as well as the emotions of terror and dismay. Buddha is looking for a place that is safe from other people as well as the extremes of nature. And it is this type of shelter—shelter from violent human conduct and the emotions it creates—that Buddha is unable to find.[16] There is no place in the world that is safe in this sense.

Interpreted in this way, the description of the world lacking in shelter is a way of describing Buddha's inability to find a nonviolent community that is stable and lasting. Violent conduct is a feature of all the societies Buddha could see and examine. And if one asks the question "Why?" Buddha's answer seems to be something along the lines of "things change." Human relationships—and especially social and political relationships—can vary in unpredictable ways. The social norms that shield persons from violent conduct can quickly erode.[17]

THE DART

The verse on the lack of shelter in human life emphasizes instability in the natural world and in the world of persons. The younger Buddha was unable to escape this aspect of the human condition. Moreover, this way of thinking about the third verse is also in line with the teaching of the second verse. The way the world changed for the fish—the sudden drying of the river that had sustained their lives and freedom—is something that can happen to any human society. Social and political realities can abruptly shift.[18]

The description of the world without shelter reinforces the image of the struggling fish. Mutual conflict is diminishing the freedom of persons in all of the societies Buddha has seen and experienced. Persons are recreating calamity again and again all over his world. But the culminating description in this sequence of verses involves the image of the "dart lodged in the heart of persons." What is Buddha getting at with this image here?

Buddha's description in this verse draws on the perceptions of war. After a battle in Buddha's time one could see the bodies of many persons pierced with darts or arrows. And while many of these persons were killed by their wounds, there might be many people who participated in the battle who were wounded but still survived. It is this in-between state of living with the suffering caused by violence that Buddha's image seems to express.[19]

Taken in this way, the image communicates the general idea of living in suffering. An existence wounded by violent conduct is the basic idea. And the form this incapacity takes in Buddha's description is revealing. When persons are caught up in fear and thoughts of harming others they are alive but their life is drained by this condition. These persons are pushed into a state of unending agitation by their beliefs and their feelings. And here again there is an echo of an earlier verse. Like the fish struggling in the drying river, the persons with darts lodged in their hearts—the persons who are moved by intense feelings of terror or fear—are exhausting themselves in an almost meaningless struggle.

KEEPING CALM

The image of the dart, the image of the world without shelter, and the image of the fish in the drying river reinforce each other. In the Buddha's view, violent conduct diminishes the ability of persons to act freely in society. It traps persons in patterns of behavior that are destructive and exhausting. And given the content of these descriptions one can see why Buddha would be unable to identify with the world as it is. To Buddha, there is something repulsive about a social world that is continually creating new victims. The unending renewal of violent conflict in human life is a difficult sight to behold.

The story Buddha tells in the first five verses of the Attadanda Sutta focuses on the suffering and lack of freedom violent conduct creates. Violent conduct has a way of trapping persons in relationships of fear. Violent conduct is a mistake. The last point I would like to make in this context, however, involves the way Buddha concludes this part of the narrative. The fish are unable to escape the condition of mutual conflict and struggle. They are powerless to change the drying river. Persons, however, are not bound to this fate. In particular, the individual can make a choice about the kind of life they are going to lead. Persons, unlike the fish, are characterized by a broader form of agency and individual freedom. The person *may* allow their mental and emotional life to continue to be dominated by fear and thoughts of violent retaliation; the person can respond to quarrels and fights with more acts of killing. In Buddha's view, however, the person is also capable of diminishing or avoiding these responses. The individual who has thought carefully about the effects of violent conduct on persons and societies can make a better choice. This person may strive to remain calm in fearful and terrifying situations.

Sectarianism

The Attadanda Sutta shows Buddha communicating with his followers. Buddha wants others to understand some of the experiences he had before his decision to train himself in calmness. But the nature of Buddha's experience is such that it is open to others. The repetition of phrases that are centered on perception—"*look* at how people quarrel and fight," "*seeing* people struggling," "I *never saw* any such a place," "I *noticed*," "I *could just make it out*"—are especially prominent in Buddha's narrative. Moreover, Buddha's focus on perception is not meant to emphasize the uniqueness of his own experience. The person's perceptions do not isolate the individual in Buddha's account. In fact, just the opposite notion is apparent: Buddha's recommendation of calmness to the listeners grows out of experiences that can be confirmed by other people. The idea of *corroborating perceptions* or *corroborating experiences* is central to Buddha's discussion in the Attadanda Sutta. The fact that different people can make the same observations about the effects of violence on persons and societies—the fact that persons can experience the same feelings of fear and terror in response to violent acts—is central to the way Buddha develops his point of view in this discourse.

Buddha's attempt to engage his audience by retelling his own story is revealing. He does not place himself above the people he is speaking too. The persons in the audience also have access to the experiences Buddha is speaking about. As Sen points out, Buddha's social empiricism is part of what makes him so approachable. But in other parts of the "Chapter of the Eights"—the section of the Sutta Nipata that includes the Attadanda Sutta—Buddha broadens his point of view. Buddha also establishes a contrast between sectarian speech and his own public reasoning in the Sutta Nipata.

The contrast between Buddha's public reasoning and the hostile speech of the sectarian is made explicit in the Pasura Sutta. In the beginning of this discourse, Buddha states:

1 They say that purity is theirs alone: they do no say that there is purity in the teachings of others. Whatever teaching they have devoted themselves to, they claim that as the most excellent and thus separately hold diverse truths.

2 The debaters, having entered into the gathering, start disputes, calling each other fools; since they are depending on certain teachers, they seek praise, calling themselves the experts . . .[20]

The problem in this passage is clear. There are respected persons who call themselves experts and who start disputes at public gatherings. These persons are trying to foment divisions with their public statements. In particular, these persons are trying to advance the views of their teachers or their religious or nonreligious schools of thought through aggressive and insulting speech. The idea of corroborating perceptions or corroborating experiences—and the more general concern with inclusiveness that characterizes Buddha's public reasoning—is absent from the sectarians' public statements. Notice also Buddha's observation about the way these persons fragment the notion of truth in the passage. When two persons from different schools adopt the same hostile procedure towards each other—when each person heaps ridicule on the other's beliefs in the name of "the truth"—the result is both division and uncertainty about how to proceed. What standard should a person cling to when the concept of truth itself has become a vehicle for scorn and derision?

The epistemological procedure of the debaters turns truth into a weapon. The debater's conduct makes the concept of truth almost useless to the public. And it is in response to this real-world problem that Buddha adopted the view that it is necessary to disaggregate ethical ideas and religious debates. The "special strategy of combining his theoretical skepticism about God with a practical subversion of the significance of the question" that Sen finds in Buddha's words can be traced back to Buddha's experience of the hostile speech of the various religious and nonreligious sects he was aware of.[21] Buddha also draws attention to the issue of bias in this context. In the Dutthatthaka Sutta, Buddha states:

> 6 It is hard to go beyond preconceived ideas reached by passing judgment in regards to doctrines. Therefore with regards to these views he rejects one and grasps another.[22]

In this passage, Buddha notes that it is difficult to "go beyond" or get outside of one's past intellectual commitments. Achieving an impartial attitude towards one's own ideas is difficult to do. But the hostile speakers are not concerned with the problem of bias; they are not willing to take up a skeptical stance towards their own beliefs. As a consequence, the past intellectual decisions of the hostile speakers—the teachers they chose, the schools they belonged to—is distorting the way the hostile thinkers act towards other people. The sectarian speaker, Buddha indicates here, is too quick to reject.

The lack of concern with the problem of bias—the uncritical way the sectarian speakers think about their own mental and emotional life—affects the way these persons are interacting with other members of their community. Nonexistent or underdeveloped epistemology has significant ethical implications in this passage. And one of the possible negative outcomes Buddha draws attention to in this context is the problem of violent conduct. In the Mahaviyuha Sutta, Buddha states:

> 18 The sage, being free from worldly ties, remains peaceful among the restless. He is indifferent among sectarian squabbles, not embracing them whilst others remain attached.[23]

In this passage, the wise person "remains peaceful" while the sectarians are "restless" or not at peace. The wise person does not act violently or encourage others to act violently when speaking in public.

In Mahaviyuha Sutta, the wise person is characterized by a refusal to participate in "sectarian squabbles." He will maintain a calm attitude when speaking in public. But the description of the sectarians as "restless" is also a highly suggestive. From the sectarian's point of view any person who does not practice a certain rite or affirm a particular religious belief is a potential object of contempt and invective. Whatever differs from the sectarian's own religious views is offensive to him. And since societies are always characterized by a diversity of ideas and points of view, the sectarian will always find a person or a group of people to be angry at—or fear. The sectarians' restlessness is directly connected to their intolerant attitude towards diverging beliefs. And here there seems to be a reference to the Attadanda Sutta. As noted earlier, Buddha describes the persons with darts lodged in their hearts as restless. They are constantly running around and live in a state of exhausting agitation. Are the persons who have darts in their hearts suffering from sectarian ideas? Is sectarianism the specific form of violent conduct Buddha is warning against in the Attadanda Sutta?

Buddha does not explicitly make this identification in the Attadanda Sutta. He does not say, for instance, that the persons with darts in their hearts are suffering from a form of religious intolerance based on a false concept of purity. However, Buddha's description of the mental and emotional life of the intolerant sectarian is compatible with all the descriptions presented in the first six verses of the Attadanda Sutta. When sectarian intolerance is widespread in society there is a very large loss of freedom. Everyone is harmed in this situation. But perhaps the strongest explicit expression against sectarianism in the "Chapter of the Eights" of the Sutta Nipata occurs in the Culaviyuha Sutta. In this discourse a person approaches Buddha, talks about a problem in his community, and then asks a question:

2 So, having thus got into arguments, they dispute (amongst themselves). They say "the other person is a fool and not an expert." Since one and all are expert talkers, which is the true statement out of these?

Here the questioner is again asking Buddha to reclaim the concept of truth from the trained hostile speakers who are abusing it. Which of the many doctrines expressed is the true one here? In response to this question Buddha says the following:

3 If one who does not tolerate another's view is a fool, a dolt and stupid, then all of them are fools without understanding because of all of them abide by their own views only.[24]

The edge of Buddha's language in this passage is exceedingly sharp. The persons who foment division and call each other fools are the worst fools of all. They have no sense of their own fallibility.

DIMINISHING INTOLERANCE

The passages on sectarianism in the Sutta Nipata are revealing. Buddha's understanding of public speech and reasoning can, in part, be understood as a repudiation of persons who believe they are speaking the truth but have venom in their words. In Buddha's view, the public speech of the person should not divide society by inciting hatred and fear. One also gets the impression that the problem of divisive public speaking must have been quite significant in Buddha's time. Many passages in "The Chapter of the Eights"—the section of the Sutta Nipata that includes the Attadandanda Sutta, the Pasura Sutta, the Dutthatthaka Sutta, the Culayvihuya Sutta, and the Mahavihuya Sutta which have been cited in this chapter—are devoted to the harmful effects of divisive public speaking. The problem of sectarian speaking keeps coming up to the surface of Buddha's words in this chapter.[25]

The recurring nature of Buddha's criticism of hostile public speech and sectarianism in the "Chapter of the Eights" speaks to the special importance of this problem. Encouraging violence in the name of a sectarian doctrine is a highly destructive form of human mistake.

NOTES

1. For more discussion of "The Four True Realities for the Spiritually Ennobled" see Peter Harvey, *An Introduction to Buddhism Second Edition: Teachings, History and Practices*, Second Edition (Cambridge: Cambridge University Press, 2013), 50–87.

2. In Harvey's view, "moral virtue is the foundation of the spiritual path" in Buddhism (Harvey, *An Introduction to Buddhism*, 264–86). For a discussion of the possibility that Buddha used the idea of the social contract in his ethical and political thinking see: Andrew Huxley, "The Buddha and The Social Contract." *Journal of Indian Philosophy* 24, no. 4 (1996): 407–20. http://www.jstor.org/stable/23448397.

3. Amartya Sen, "The Contemporary Relevance of Buddha," *Ethics and International Affairs* 28, no. 1, 15–27.

4. A key question Sen leaves open in this passage is what, exactly, he means by the expression "metaphysical reflections." Sen notes at a later point in this essay that Buddha had an atheistic or an agnostic understanding. So whatever Sen is referring to with the expression "metaphysical reflections" it should not be understood as a commitment to god, the immortality of the soul, and other similar doctrines. In the text I note that it is possible that Sen is referring to the doctrine of "dependent origination," but the phrase may extend to other ideas as well.

5. H. Saddhatissa, ed. and trans., *The Sutta Nipata* (Abingdon, Curzon Press, 1994), 4. The dates of Buddha's life and death are a source of debate. As Upinder Singh notes, the "uncorrected long chronology" identifies Buddha's death—the *paranibbana*—with the time period of 544/543 BCE. Theravada Buddhist communities in

South and Southeast Asia use this framework. The "corrected long chronology" places Buddha's death somewhere between 486 and 477 BCE while the "short chronology" identifies Buddha's death with the year 368 BCE. In Singh's discussion of this issue, she notes that "the Ahraura version of Ashoka's minor rock edict" suggests that Buddha's death occurred sometime before 483 BCE. Singh also notes that Buddha was commonly understood to have lived about 80 years. Since the dates of Ashoka's inscriptions are known with more confidence than any other text from this time period, Singh gives priority to this piece of evidence. In Singh's line of reasoning Buddha was born in or around 563 BCE and died in or around 483 BCE (Upinder Singh, *A History of Ancient and Early Medieval India: From the Stone Age to the 12th Century* [Noida: Pearson, 2017], 257, 267).

6. Saddhatissa, *Sutta Nipatta*, 109. I mostly use Saddhatissa's translation of the "Chapter of the Eights" of the Sutta Nipata throughout chapter 1. Also, note that the themes of fear and calmness in the Attadanda Sutta are also treated in the Brhadaranyanka Upanishad, for instance, in the statements of Yajnavalkya to the king of Videha: "Who knows this and has found peace, he is the lord of himself, *his is a calm endurance, and calm concentration.* In himself he sees the Spirit, and he sees the Spirit as all." (italics added) Juan Mascaró, trans., *The Upanishads* (London: Penguin Books), 142–43. However, the achievement of calm concentration and calm endurance is gained through an apprehension of "Spirit" or the "Atman" in all things in this passage and is thus conceptually distinct from Buddha's discussion.

7. K. M. Sen also draws attention to this aspect of Buddha's life: "Buddha was born in the sixth century BC, as Gautama Siddhartha, the son of a king from the Sakya clan, at the foothill of the eastern Himalayas. The tragedies of human existence made him restless and he left the palace in search of truth some time after his first son was born." K. M. Sen, *Hinduism* (London: Penguin Books), 54.

8. Sen, "The Contemporary Relevance of Buddha," 15–27.

9. The Vasala Sutta is discussed in more detail in chapter 2.

10. The Brahmanadhammika Sutta is discussed in more detail in chapter 3.

11. Olendzki's translation emphasizes both the act of picking up a weapon and the blow itself: "Fear is born from arming one's self—Just see how many people fight!" Olendzki also notes that: "The basic image here is that of picking up a stick, *danda*; the stick being a common symbol in Indian literature for both violence and punishment." See introduction, note 8.

12. See note 6. For Olendzki's translation of the first verse of the Attadanda Sutta, see introduction, note 8.

13. The idea articulated in this verse can be compared with the idea of the "law of the fish" described in *The Laws of Manu* and invoked by Sen in *The Idea of Justice* (p. 20–21). Tagore's ethical teaching in *Sadhana: The Realization of Life* (p. 43) is also at one point presented in terms of the way a person responds to a fish.

14. Saddhatissa, ed. and trans., *Sutta Nipata*, 92. This discourse is also part of the "Chapter of the Eights"—the "oldest stratum" of the Sutta Nipata in Saddhatissa's view.

15. Buddha often uses the restricted movement of animals as a metaphor for the lack of freedom caused by anger or hatred. See, for instance, the first verse of the

Dhammapada: "What we are today comes from our thoughts of yesterday, and our present thoughts build our life of tomorrow: our life is a creation of our mind. If a man speaks or acts with an impure mind, suffering follows him as the wheel of the cart follows the beast that draws the cart" (Juan Mascaró, trans., *The Dhammapada* [London: Penguin Books], 35).

16. A similar metaphor is used in the first chapter of the Dhammapada: "Even as rain breaks through an ill-thatched house, passions will break through an ill guarded mind" (Mascaró, *The Dhammapada*, 36).

17. The idea that the norms that protect life from nonviolence can quickly erode will be discussed in the context of a reading of the Brahmanadhammika Sutta in chapter 3.

18. This theme is developed at length in chapters 8 and 9.

19. See, for instance, the description of the aftermath of the battle of Kurekshetra in the Mahabharata: "Meanwhile, out on the darkened battlefield, wounded men, located by their groans, were carried to camp, where surgeons tended them. Men were running to and fro, collecting arrows and other weapons, stripping corpses of their armor and accoutrements to be used again. It was bloody work." After the battle between Bhisma and Arjuna—where Arjuna pierces Bhisma's body with many arrows from the bow Gandiva but Bhisma lives on—there is the line "Surgeons came, skilled at removing arrows" (Carole Satyamurti, ed. and trans., *Mahabharata; a Modern Retelling* [New York: W. W. Norton and Company], 429, 467).

20. Saddhatissa, *Sutta Nipata*, 97.

21. For more on this point, see the introduction, page 6.

22. Saddhatissa, *Sutta Nipata*, 93.

23. Ibid., 106.

24. Ibid., 103.

25.The Paramatthaka Sutta, the Jara Sutta, the Tissametteyya Sutta, the Magandiya Sutta and the Kalahavivada Sutta—which are collected in "The Chapter of the Eights" section of the Sutta Nipata—also contain verses that treat the problem of sectarianism and divisive public speaking in society.

Chapter 2

A Legal Code

Chapter 1 examined several important themes in the Sutta Nipata. Buddha criticized violent conduct both in terms of its effects on the victim and its emotional impacts on society. The idea of a cycle of violence—in which a violent action leads to fear and then possibly a violent response—is a key teaching of the Attadanda Sutta. Buddha was also concerned with the effect of sectarian disputes on society. He criticized the venomous nature of many public debates. But one thing that is absent from Buddha's discussion in these passages is any notion of divinity. The ideas of Atman and Brahman or the living essence that pervades all things—ideas that are central to the teachings of many Upanishads—are not found in the "Chapter of the Eights."[1] Instead, Buddha's reasoning in the "Chapter of the Eights" stays within the human sphere. He confines his reflections to what can be perceived and observed by other people.

To Tagore and Sen, the absence of language about divinity in the Sutta Nipata is highly significant. Buddha untangled moral ideas from sectarian doctrine and other forms of speculative belief. Buddha based his claims on perceptions and experiences that all persons can have. Sen especially emphasizes the consensus-building quality of Buddha's argument. Sen states:

> Indeed, Buddha's demonstration that moral ideas need not originate in any specific invoking of divinity remains extremely important today. *This is not just because there are many non-believers in the world, but also because people belonging to different faiths and distinct religions can still find agreement on moral codes of conduct if morality is not seen as entirely parasitic on a particular view of divinity.*[2] (italics added)

In this passage, Sen indicates that a potential source of division between "believers" and "non-believers" is diminished by Buddha's approach. Persons can agree on the description of violent conduct even when holding very different religious doctrines—or no doctrine at all.

43

Sen and Tagore pick out a specific set of ethical and epistemological ideas in their interpretation of Buddha. The importance of a public empiricism—where reasoning together is founded on what all persons can see and experience—is emphasized in their accounts.[3] In this chapter, I further develop what Sen calls Buddha's reasoned approach to ethics, society and political life by examining Buddha's discussion of the outcaste in the Vasala Sutta.[4] Buddha draws on his nondenominational critique of violent conduct to reform existing ethical and legal codes in this discourse.

THE OUTCASTE

Unlike the Attadanda Sutta, the beginning of Buddha's discourse on the outcaste—the Vasala Sutta—involves a short vignette. Buddha leaves a monastery in a forest and enters the town of Savatthi to ask for alms. He walked around and eventually came to the house of the Brahmin Aggika-Bharadvaja. The Brahmin—who is, according to the discourse, about to perform a ritual sacrifice—sees Buddha and says: "Stop there, shaveling; stop there, wretched ascetic; stop there, outcaste."[5]

Aggika clearly does not want Buddha to come near his house. However, the reason for Aggika's exclamation is not made explicit. The discourse states that Aggika is about to perform a ritual sacrifice. Perhaps Aggika believes Buddha is an "impure" person, someone who will somehow pollute the ritual—and Aggika's house or Aggika's hearth—by his presence? The identifications made in Aggika's exclamation are also revealing. He calls attention to Buddha's physical appearance—a "shaveling" (that is, a person with a shaved head)—his way of life—an "ascetic" (an unmarried man without a house or fields)—and his social status—an "outcaste" (a person who cannot live in the house of the Brahmin, Kashitriya, Vaisya, or Sudra social classes as a slave or servant)—as if these three words were synonyms. He clearly has a low opinion of Buddha's way of living and believes Buddhist persons should remain physically distant.[6]

Aggika's initial statement shows how a person's mental and emotional life can create a barrier or an obstacle in the relationship between two different people. Aggika, the wealthy Brahmin householder, sees Buddha and, based on Buddha's appearance alone, calls Buddha an outcaste. In this situation, the idea of religious impurity is creating a wall between two persons out of thin air.[7] Buddha's response to the Brahmin's statement, however, is interesting. Buddha does not insult Aggika. Nor does he run away. He asks a question: "Do you know, brahman, [what] an outcaste [is], or the things that make an outcaste?"[8] Can Aggika really identify an outcaste based on a person's appearance alone?

Buddha's question here is an example of his open-mindedness. Buddha does not assume Aggika is wrong. Instead, he asks Aggika to explain his claim. He treats Aggika as a person who might have something to teach. In particular, he treats Aggika as a person who has thought carefully about epistemology. "Do you, Aggika, have an objective or impartial way of identifying an outcaste?" is another way of glossing Buddha's question here. And it seems clear from the next line that Aggika realizes he made a mistake. Aggika suddenly identifies Buddha as "Gautama" and presents a very respectful air. "I do not know, Gautama, [what] an outcaste [is], or the things that make an outcaste" he tells Buddha.[9] He then asks Buddha to teach him about this matter.

Aggika's about-face with Buddha reveals a second feature of his mental and emotional life. Aggika looks down on persons with a certain appearance and way of living. Ascetics are not Brahmins, and they own no land and possess no houses of their own. They are an impure and inferior group of people in Aggika's eyes. But as soon as Aggika recognizes Buddha he changes his tune. He respects Buddha's learning and his reputation in society even though Buddha is an ascetic. We also learn something new about Buddha's mental and emotional life from this interaction. In particular, the way Buddha responds to Aggika's insults gives a concrete example of what it means to remain calm in the face of another person's derisive speech. In this passage, remaining calm is a precondition of public discussion and consensus-building.

THE DEED

Buddha, despite being initially insulted, agrees to Aggika's request. The narrative depicts Buddha as somewhat sternly generous to Aggika, as well as open minded. At any rate, Buddha goes on to develop his understanding of the outcaste through a series of nineteen short descriptions. Here are five examples of Buddha's statements to Aggika:

117 Who[ever] in this world harms living creatures, whether once born or twice born, who[ever] has no compassion for a living creature, him one should know [to be] an outcaste.

118 Who[ever] destroys or besieges villages and towns, [and] is notorious as an oppressor, him one should know [to be] an outcaste.

119 Who[ever] in a village or a forest takes by theft what has not been given to him [and is] cherished by others, him one should know [to be] an outcaste.

120 Who[ever] indeed because having contracted a debt, when urged [to repay it] absconds, saying: "[I have] no debt to you," him one should know as an outcaste.

121 Who[ever] indeed because of his desire for some trifle strikes a person going along the road and takes the trifle, him one should know [to be] an outcaste.[10]

This basic idea in these verses is clear. In Buddha's analysis, a person becomes an outcaste through the unjust or violent nature of their deeds. Unjust and violent conduct is the real ground for being cast out of society in Buddha's view. Moreover, the unjust and violent actions of this person have been repeated so many times that they have become apparent to the other members of society. When Buddha states that the person "who destroys and besieges towns *is notorious as an oppressor*" (italics added) the idea of many different observations of the outcaste's behavior is informing the claim. Buddha's public criteria of perception and knowledge is invoked here.

Buddha establishes the outline of his standard of the outcaste through a series of examples. Is the person frequently destructive or aggressive? Is the person frequently stealing or lying to avoid a debt? Does the action involve killing a person and then a petty theft? If the answer to these questions is "yes," the person is an outcaste in Buddha's eyes. However, the clarity of Buddha's examples does not necessarily mean Buddha's criterion is more objective or impartial than Aggika's criterion. Buddha's ideas are different—that is for sure—but that does not mean they are better. Why is Buddha's criterion an improvement on Aggika's criteria and not just another view?

Buddha's answer to this question is interesting. Basically, Buddha defends his criterion of the outcaste by noting its neutrality towards the different classes in the varna system—as well as the persons who are outside of this system (like the forest dwellers). Buddha's approach to this problem disregards a person's hereditary social status when evaluating legal conduct. To give an example: if a member of the Brahmin class kills a person on the road to steal a trinket they are an outcaste in Buddha's view. Likewise, if a Kashitriya or a Vaisya or a Sudra or a forest dweller kills a person on the road to steal a trinket, they are judged to be an outcaste by Buddha.[11] The criterion yields the same result when applied to all these cases. However, when a person thinks about an outcaste in terms of the varna system the situation is different. The fact that a person is born into a Brahmin or a Kashitriya or Vaisya or a Sudra or an outcaste family suddenly takes on very great importance. For instance, a Brahmin may harm a forest dweller—a Brahmin might physically assault a person who is outside of the varna system—but in the eyes of Aggika or someone like him this harm may be understood as a less offensive action. But if a forest dweller harms a Brahmin in the same way—if a forest dweller physically assaults a Brahmin person—it is considered a more egregious offense.[12] The same deed would be evaluated in different ways depending on the family and social class each person was born into.

Interpreted in this way, Buddha believes Aggika's criterion systematically distorts his understanding of the outcaste. A person born into a Brahmin family is going to be treated differently in many cases. And if something like Aggika's thinking informed the legal system of a community—if notions of crime and punishment were organized around Aggika's criterion of the outcaste—the bias evident in Aggika's thinking would create a permanent underclass of persons in society. It would systematically discriminate against all non-Brahmin individuals.

In Buddha's view, blending notions of social class and heredity with concepts of moral superiority harms society in multiple ways. It is an example of a "wrong view" that should be discarded and replaced with a new idea. Indeed, the way Buddha frames this point towards the end of the sutta clearly indicates that he is trying to replace Aggikka's criterion of hereditary hierarchy with something better. He states:

136 Not by birth does one become an outcaste, not by birth does one become a brahman. By [one's] action one becomes an outcaste, by [one's] action one becomes a brahman.[13]

In Buddha's view, a person becomes an outcaste through the reality of their actions, not the social class of their parents.

COMPASSION

A key feature of the Vasala Sutta is the notion of impartiality Buddha introduces into the discussion of the outcaste. In Buddha's view, the same actions must be judged in the same way, all other things being equal. The actions of a Brahmin or a Kashitriya cannot be judged on different scales from everyone else.

Buddha's introduction of a more impartial way of evaluating the actions of the person has significant ethical and legal implications. The social status and religious identity of a person's mother and father should be irrelevant to the judgments people make about theft and murder. A second feature of Buddha's description of the outcaste—and this also really stands out in the narrative—is connected to the way the outcaste *reasons*. The idea of an abuse of power is a prominent feature of Buddha's descriptions of the outcaste.[14]

This aspect of the sutta is most apparent in the verse on the treatment of nonhuman species previously cited:

117 Who[ever] in this world harms living creatures, whether once-born or twice born, who[ever] has no compassion for a living creature, him one should know [to be] an outcaste.[15]

The basic idea in this verse is clear. A person with a bow and arrow, or a knife, or a net, or a trap can destroy other forms of life. Human beings have the power to act in this manner. However, there is no way a deer ("the once born") or a fish or a bird or an insect ("the twice born") is going to kill a human being under ordinary circumstances.[16] There is a very large asymmetry of power between an armed human being and a deer or fish. But what Buddha is also drawing attention to in this verse is the way the person responds to this asymmetry of power. How is the person choosing to act in this situation? What is the person's response to the perception of a weaker being? And Buddha's idea here is to create a continuum. On one end of the continuum is the outcaste. The outcaste's killing of animals is not motivated by the need for food or self-defense. Instead, the outcaste responds to this asymmetry of power by killing weaker species without cause or reason. The outcaste has destroyed life without a justifiable cause many times.[17] On the other end of the spectrum is the person with compassion. The compassionate person does not want other living things to suffer and die or live in oppression. Killing another living being without cause is anathema to the compassionate person. Instead, the compassionate person understands the fragility of a life and, based on this understanding, refrains from harming it. The compassionate person will not abuse or misuse their power to act.

Interpreted in this way, the difference between the outcaste and the compassionate person is not found in each person's perceptions. An animal will look and sound the same to both these individuals. Nor is the difference between the outcaste and the compassionate person found in each person's ability to harm—both the outcaste and the person with compassion are physically capable of ending a life. Instead, the difference arises in the way the outcaste and the compassionate person responds to their perceptions. The outcaste and the compassionate person do not reason and feel about animals in the same way. And this point—as Sen has articulated so clearly in *The Idea of Justice*—is crucial for understanding Buddha's ethical teaching.[18] To Buddha, an ethical life manifests itself in the way the person *reasons* about how to use their powers or capabilities. The compassionate person sees another life and then reasons—and feels—in terms of that life's needs.

THE BUDDHIST LAITY

In the verse on other species, Buddha articulates a contrast between an out-caste and a person with compassion. These two persons are on the opposite ends of Buddha's ethical continuum. Moreover, the contrast between the out-caste and the person with compassion seems to underlie many other verses in the sutta. The individual who is a vandal or thug, the individual who steals, the individual who lies about his debts, and the individual who kills a man on the road for a trinket cannot be described as compassionate persons. These individuals are using their powers or their capabilities to intentionally harm other people without cause or justification.

Interpreted in this way, the Vasala Sutta is making two basic kinds of claims about the ethical and legal codes of society. The first is that the actions of all persons should be evaluated independently of the social status of the persons involved. It is the unjust nature of the act—and not the social class of the mother and father of the agent—that defines the outcaste. The second claim, however, involves the concept of an abuse of power. Ethical and legal systems should be on guard against abuses of power wherever they occur. Both the ethical and the legal norms in society must impartially restrain abuses of power in Buddha's view. And while Buddha's ideas on these points did not have binding status in the society at large they did define membership in the society of Buddhists. In particular, Buddha's rules for the laity in the Dhammika Sutta—which are distinguished from the rules for the sangha of monks—include these ideas. Buddha states:

> 394 Laying aside violence in respect of all beings, both those which are still and those which move, in the world, he should not kill a living creature, nor cause to kill, nor allow others to kill.[19]

In this passage, compassion and the obligations of power are identified as a central feature of Buddhist identity. It is the way persons respond to asymmetries of power—in particular, it is the repudiation of the predatory mentality in the life of the person, where a person sees in all weakness an invitation to attack—that defines membership in the Buddhist laity in the Dhammika Sutta.

Interpreted in this way, there is a fundamental continuity in perspective between the Dhammika Sutta and the Vasala Sutta. Both discourses repudiate the human tendency to abuse superior power. Persons in a position of power have a duty to act with compassion towards both the strong and the weak. Equally important, Buddha includes a concern with *the public reasoning* of the Buddhist laity within his ethical code. In particular, the passage from the Dhamikka Sutta cited above notes that the members of the Buddhist laity should not "allow others to kill." Persons should not support the idea that it is good to kill without cause in their speech and reasoning. Rather, members of the Buddhist laity should resist the intention to kill emanating from other people. Publicly speaking against the intention to kill is part of Buddha's moral code. In this way, Buddha further distinguishes members of the Buddhist laity from the violent sectarian. A subsequent passage in the Dhammika Sutta extends this idea to the way the person reasons in a government forum. Buddha states:

> 397 When gone to the audience hall or assembly, he should not speak falsely to a single person, nor cause to speak, nor allow [others] to speak. He should avoid every untruth.[20]

In this passage, Buddha is establishing a norm for public reasoning in political contexts. In Buddha's view, it is very important for the members of the Buddhist laity to tell the truth in these settings. And if one asks the question "Why?" the answer is clear: lying or intentionally misleading persons in positions of power (in the assembly or the audience hall) was understood by Buddha to have a large range of negative effects. The lie can lead to wrongful punishments or distorted policy. The lie—when accepted by others—can become the basis of bad decision making. The slandered individual or group will also feel fear and anger towards the wrongful accuser. The lie puts the lives and the livelihoods of innocent people in danger. For these reasons, it is unjust to falsely accuse a person or a group in society of murder or the intention to kill. False public statements in political contexts are highly divisive for society. In Buddha's view, lying in public must be avoided.

THE EXPANSION OF BUDDHISM
WITHIN THE SUBCONTINENT

As can be seen from this discussion, Buddha did not exempt the Buddhist laity from his ethical claims. Buddha did not create a new version of the varna system with Buddhists on top. Instead, his ideas are framed in a way that clearly applies to all people. No one is above the claims made in these passages, including the society of Buddhists. All persons should cultivate the mental and emotional attitude of compassion and the ethical standard of the obligations of power. Persons should think and reason in terms of another life's needs when it is feasible to do so. Likewise, the public reasoning of the Buddhist laity should reflect these norms. The members of the laity should not lie to others or encourage others to kill.

Interpreted in this way, Buddha attempted to introduce a more impartial form of ethical reasoning into North India. The ethical and legal codes of society needed to change. And this point—the way Buddha treats all persons in the same way within his ethical and legal codes—is central to the way Tagore and Sen understood the appeal of Buddhism. The expansion of early Buddhism in the subcontinent is directly connected to the impartial quality of Buddha's ethical thought in their writings.

This claim can be made more precise. Sen—in *The Argumentative Indian*—notes that both Buddhism and Janism:

> included a "leveling" feature that is not only reflected in the message of human equality for which these movements stood, but is also captured in the nature of the arguments used to undermine the claim to superiority of those occupying exalted positions. Substantial parts of the early Buddhist and Jain literatures contain expositions of protest and resistance.[21]

Sen's comment here is directly applicable to discourses like the Vasala Sutta and the Dhamikka Sutta. Buddha argues that the same action should be treated in the same way—no matter who performs it. If a man kills a stranger on the road for a trinket, the man is an outcaste. The social standing of the man's parents is irrelevant in the moral or ethical assessment of this person's acts. But in commenting on this issue, Sen brings out the underlying focus that animates Buddha's approach. The Vasala Sutta and the Dhammikka Sutta, Sen suggests, are part of a larger expression of resistance to Brahmin and Kashitriya superiority in the varna system. Buddha wanted to diminish the false sense of superiority of persons like Aggika.

Sen interprets the Sutta Nipata in terms of the broader goal of resisting false notions of superiority through more careful public reasoning. In this way, Buddha hoped to create a social movement for reform centered around the freedom and equality of all persons. Sen also notes in this context that the large number of persons who were comparatively underprivileged under the varna system might help explain "the class basis of the rapid spread of Buddhism, in particular, in India."[22] Here Sen suggests that the outcastes, as well as the members of the Sudra and the Vaisya social classes, might have been especially open to the teaching of Buddha given their lower position within the varna system.

The comments Sen makes about the expansion of Buddhism in India reveal an important aspect of Sen's thinking about this social movement. To Sen, the decision of the third Mauryan emperor Ashoka to embrace Buddhism after the war with the Kalinga in the third century BCE is not enough to explain the rapid expansion of Buddhism in the subcontinent that occurred after Buddha's death. Instead, it is the way Buddha's message of equality stood out against the social hierarchy of the varna system that best explains the initial rapid expansion of Buddha's ideas in the subcontinent, in Sen's view.

I should also point out that Sen's focus on the class basis of the expansion of Buddhism also frames the role of Ashoka in the expansion of Buddhism in a different way. When Ashoka explained his turn to Buddhism in the first "Minor Rock Edict," the decision is framed in entirely personal terms.[23] Ashoka does not speak about anything other than his own growth and development as a person in this inscription. However, Ashoka's turn to Buddhism was also a response to existing realities on the ground. In this interpretation, a broader social change predated—and made possible—the choice of the Mauryan king. Another point to consider in this context involves the role of merchants and traders in the spread of Buddha's ideas. In particular, Sen points out that merchants and traders—that is, members of the Vaisya social class—might have had a particularly significant role in expanding Buddhism across the subcontinent, given the way these persons traveled between cities, villages, and other settlements.[24]

Sen emphasizes the impartial ethical dimensions of Buddha's thought when discussing early Indian Buddhism's class appeal. Buddha wanted to free persons from abuses of power and his teaching argued for the equality of all persons. Ultimately, it is the persuading power of these ethical ideas that set in motion the Buddhist social movement in India, in Sen's view. But the last point I would like to make in this context is focused on the similarity between Sen and Tagore. Many of the ideas Sen stresses in his account of early Indian Buddhism are also found in Tagore's *The Religion of Man*. To recall the passage discussed in the introduction, Tagore states:

> We must never forget to-day that a mere movement is not valuable in itself, that it may be a sign of a dangerous form of inertia. We must be reminded that a great upheaval of spirit, a universal realization of the true dignity of man once caused by Buddha's teachings in India, started a movement for centuries which produced illuminations of literature, art, science, and numerous efforts of public beneficence. This was a movement whose motive force was not some additional accession of knowledge or power or urging of some overwhelming passion. It was an inspiration for freedom, the freedom which enables us to realize dharma, the Truth of eternal Man.[25]

The "true dignity of man" is Tagore's way of speaking about human equality. The life of all persons mattered to Buddha. No life could be discounted because of the status of their family in society in Buddha's view. Likewise, the "inspiration for freedom" Tagore mentions in the passage is connected to the idea of diminishing abuses of power in society. All persons in society should be free from abuses of power in their daily lives. Protecting persons from oppression is central to Tagore's understanding of Buddha's teachings. Tagore also draws attention to the rapid spread of Buddhism in this passage. The ideas of equality and freedom in the Sutta Nipata and other early Buddhist discourses led to an "upheaval of spirit" in the subcontinent and beyond. Tagore, like Sen, frames Buddha's message in terms of the social movement it helped to create.

NOTES

1. For more on this point see the end of the introduction and chapter 1, note 6.

2. See introduction, note 16.

3. For an invaluable discussion of developments in thinking about the theme of perception in later Buddhist traditions see Bimal Krishna Matilal, *Perception: An Essay on Classical Indian Theories of Knowledge* (Oxford: Oxford University Press, 1986).

4. Upinder Singh notes that "According to Buddhist tradition, the Sutta and Vinaya Pittakas were recited at the first council of monks at Rajaghriha immediately after the Buddha's death, and 100 years later at the second council at Vaishali. But their composition must have extended over several centuries, up to the time of the third council in the 3rd century BCE during the reign of Ashoka. The basic core of the Pali Tipitaka can therefore be placed between the 5th and 3rd centuries BCE." Singh also notes that the "Sutta Nipata also belongs to this period" (Upinder Singh, *A History of Ancient and Medieval India: From the Stone Age to the 12th Century* [Noida: Pearson, 25], 258). If this is true, the Vasala Sutta—like the Attadanda Sutta and the rest of the Sutta Nipata—has its origins in a process of oral composition or recomposition that can be traced back to the early Indian classical period.

5. K. R. Norman, trans., *The Rhinoceros Horn and Other Early Buddhist Poems: The Group of Discourses*, Sutta Nipata, vol. 1 (London: The Pali Text Society Oxford, 1996), 15.

6. Romila Thapar describes the outcaste as having a lower social standing than slaves *during the Mauryan period*. Romila Thapar, *Asoka and the Decline of the Mauryas* (Oxford: Oxford University Press), 92. Whether or not something like these social norms and rules existed in Buddha's time is difficult to say. Another difficulty involves the relationship between varna and jati. Upinder Singh notes that "*Varna* and *jati* (caste) are both hereditary classifications and the two did come to be related, but they are not the same thing. There are many differences between them, and the nature of these differences themselves has changed over time" (Singh, *A History of Ancient and Medieval India*, 293). What seems clear from the text is that Aggika views Buddha as an impure person who should remain physically distant from Aggika's house and hearth.

7. For more discussion of this image in Tagore's writing, see Tagore's "Letter to Gandhi" discussed in chapter 6.

8. Norman, trans., *The Rhinoceros Horn and Other Early Buddhist Poems: The Group of Discourses*, Sutta Nipata, vol. 1, 15.

9. Ibid., 16.

10. Ibid., 16.

11. Ibid., 16.

12. McClish and Olivelle draw attention to this type of distortion in the legal code described in the *Arthashastra*: "In matters of verbal assault, as in other suits, social standing matters. Classical South Asian society, like many traditional societies, was acutely aware of the relative stature of the individuals in social exchange. We see that fines for abuse were doubled if an inferior insulted a superior and halved in the reverse case." Likewise, "In assessing the punishment for a given assault, the court took into consideration the relative status of the attacker and victim" (Mark McClish and Patrick Olivelle, eds., *The Arthasatra: Selections from the Classic Indian Work on Statecraft* [Oxford: Oxford University Press], 91–92). The Vasala Sutta indicates that something like this way of thinking about ethical and legal norms was also a reality during Buddha's life.

13. Norman, *The Rhinoceros Horn and Other Early Buddhist Poems: The Group of Discourses*, Sutta Nipata, vol. 1, 18.

14. For more discussion of the theme of protection in ethical and legal philosophy anchored in a different philosophical tradition, see Robert E. Goodin, *Protecting the Vulnerable: A Reanalysis of Our Social Responsibilities* (Chicago: University of Chicago Press, 1985).

15. See note 5.

16. Tagore also alludes to theme of the "twice born" in his discussion of the Upanishads. But in this context, the theme of the "twice born" speaks to the idea of rebirth: "In Sanskrit, the bird has been called the twice born. So too the man who has gone through the ceremony of the discipline of self-restraint and high thinking for a period of twelve years: who has come out simple in wants, pure in heart, and ready to take up all the responsibilities of life in a disinterested largeness of spirit. He is considered to have had his rebirth from the blind envelopment of self to the freedom of soul life; to have come into living relation with his surroundings: to have become one with the All." Rabindranath Tagore, *Sadhana: The Realization of Life* (New York: Macmillan, 1913), 14.

17. In the Kalama Sutta, Buddha describes greed as a mental and emotional attitude that can lead to violent conduct: "What do you think, Kalamas? When greed arises within a person, is it to one's benefit or detriment?" "To one's detriment, sir." "So Kalamas, does this greedy person, being overpowered by greed and having lost control of his mind, kill living beings, take what is not given, go with another's wife, tell lies, and encourage others to do the same, which things are to his detriment and suffering for a long time?" "Yes, Sir" (John J. Holder, trans., *Early Buddhist Discourses* [Indianapolis, IN: Hackett Publishing Company: 2006], 21).

18. For more on this point see the introduction and chapter 9.

19. Norman, *The Rhinoceros Horn and Other Early Buddhist Poems: The Group of Discourses*, Sutta Nipata, vol. 1, 48.

20. Ibid., 48.

21. Sen, *The Argumentative Indian*, 10.

22. Ibid., 10.

23. For more discussion of the First "Minor Rock Edict" and thirteenth "Major Rock Edict" see chapter 4.

24. Sen, *The Argumentative Indian*, 10.

25. See introduction, note 6.

Chapter 3

Persons and Animals

The last two chapters focused on the way Tagore and Sen interpret Buddha's ethical and legal thought. In the view of both thinkers, Buddha wanted to diminish violent conduct in society and protect living things from abuses of power. He also wanted to free the ethical and legal codes of society from the concepts of religious purity and class bias. Buddha initiated a social movement founded on the freedom and equality of all persons in India and beyond. Moreover, in the process of developing these ideas, I have paid special attention to the epistemological aspects of Tagore and Sen's interpretation. Both thinkers emphasize the way Buddha stays within the human sphere when advancing his ethical arguments.

In this chapter, I further develop the ethical themes of the Sutta Nipata by focusing on Buddha's discussion of the treatment of animals in the Brahmanadhammika Sutta. I also discuss the themes of loving kindness and the protection of persons and animals in the Metta Sutta. To Tagore and Sen, the most important ethical ideas in the Sutta Nipata are found in the Metta Sutta.

A FALL

The Brahmanadhammika Sutta begins with an introductory narrative in which the relationship between Buddha and Brahmin persons is center stage. In particular, the discourse states that several elderly and wealthy Brahmins sought out the Buddha's company, "exchanged the customary friendly greetings" with Buddha and sat at his side.[1] It is clear that these elderly Brahmins respect Buddha and have no problem at all being near Buddha's body.

On the surface, this introductory narrative might seem to communicate innocuous details. The idea of a "customary greeting" implies that a form of politeness was a widespread social norm in Buddha's society. Countless greetings like this took place in daily life. However, this friendly greeting between

Buddha and the Brahmins also contrasts greatly with the commanding insults of Aggika in the Vasala Sutta. Aggika's first words to Buddha—"Stop there, shaveling; stop there, wretched ascetic; stop there, outcaste"—is clearly hostile when compared with the elderly Brahmins in the Brahmanadhammika Sutta.[2] And while it is impossible to know whether the encounter with the elderly Brahmins or Aggikka is true in the sense of "actually happened in the historical world" it is interesting that the Sutta Nipata retains a sense of diversity when discussing the mental and emotional lives of Brahmin persons. Aggikka and the elderly Brahmins are not the same.

The presence of the friendly Brahmins in the Sutta Nipata introduces complexity into this text. In the Sutta Nipata, the Brahmin tradition is not monolithic. And it is important to note, in this context, that Amartya Sen speaks about the heterodox interpretation of Hinduism advanced by his grandfather—Kshiti Mohan Sen—in *The Argumentative Indian*. In particular, Amartya Sen notes that his grandfather's book *Hinduism* "brought out with great clarity the heterodoxy of beliefs that Hinduism allowed, with a rich variety of well-developed but diverse religious arguments. Kshiti Mohan identified an overarching liberality as being part and parcel of the basic Hindu approach."[3] From this point of view, Kshiti Mohan Sen might have understood the friendliness of the elderly Brahmins towards Buddha as a precursor of this more heterodox and liberal form of Hindu belief. There were curious and open-minded Brahmins who were interested in Buddha.

The introductory narrative communicates the idea that Buddha and some Brahmins were on friendly terms. A second noteworthy aspect of the introductory narrative, however, involves the intellectual interests of these Brahmins. Basically, the elderly Brahmins at a certain point in the discussion invite Buddha to reflect on their own tradition. In particular, the elderly Brahmins ask Buddha to compare the lives of the Brahmins as they are "now" with the lives of "the Brahmans of old." Do the Brahmins observe the same "brahmanical lore" as before?[4]

Buddha's response to this question is interesting. Basically, Buddha presents a narrative in order to respond to the question of the Brahmins. He describes a society in a "Golden Age" and then goes on to narrate a "Fall" from this state. Important norms of nonviolence have been lost over time in Buddha's story: the society became more violent towards animals during this period.

OUR GREAT FRIENDS

Buddha's story begins with an account of the distant past. And within these descriptions—which are extensive and cover a variety of topics—Buddha draws attention to the conduct of this society towards a specific animal, the cow. In the distant past, this society treated the cow in a respectful way. Buddha states:

296 Like a mother, father, brother, or other relative too, cows are our best friends, in which medicines are produced.

297 They give food, strength, good complexion, and likewise happiness—knowing this fact, they did not kill cows.[5]

In this verse, the ancient Brahmins acknowledged the many good things the cows gave to them through the formulation of an ethical rule. Do not kill the source of your own food, strength, beauty, and health (or medicine). Respect the animals who are so similar to you, and which sustain your life.

Framed in this way, the attitude towards cattle expressed in this older society blends a form of enlightened self-interest together with an expansive concept of familial obligation. You are harming yourself—you are harming a family member who supports your life—when you harm cattle. Do not harm yourself by killing these animals. But a second condition of this respectful attitude towards the cattle was the Brahmins' more general belief in the value of learning:

285 The Brahmans had no cattle, no gold, no wealth. They had study as their wealth and grain. They guarded the holy life as their treasure.[6]

In this description, the ancient Brahmins lived in a kind of self-imposed poverty. They did not want to possess cattle or any other source of material wealth. Instead, they spent their lives devoted to learning. The Brahmins' own mental and emotional development as persons was their main concern.

In this situation, the society in the "Golden Age" experienced a kind of steady state with regards to the cattle. Everyone had an enlightened attitude towards the lives of these animals. However, the reasons informing this respectful attitude seemed to vary across groups. The persons who possessed cattle as property saw the cattle as a source of milk, strength, beauty, and health. The Brahmins' attitude towards the cattle included this idea, too. The Brahmins understood the importance of cattle for individual persons as well as for society. Importantly, though, the Brahmins also had an additional reason for holding this view. The Brahmins were concerned with their own growth and development and learning, not the accumulation of property and material wealth. Their concern for the truth—not just the benefits the society gained from cattle—was another basis for their behavior.

RELATIVE INEQUALITY

In Buddha's story, the ancient society contained different standards of valuation. Some persons in this society were motivated by (1) norms of enlightened self-interest, and (2) an expansive sense of familial obligation while (3) valuing learning and the pursuit of truth. It is all these factors together that sustain the norm of nonviolence towards the cattle.[7] But as Buddha's narrative moves forward, things began to change. The society was stable and peaceful and the persons who did possess homes and fields and cattle began to prosper. The king of this society also became enormously wealthy. Meanwhile, the ancient Brahmins—who were rich in learning but unmoved by material wealth—remained in their initial condition. That is to say, the relative inequality between the Brahmins and the rest of the society had increased.

The introduction of higher levels of economic inequality in the narrative might appear unrelated to the attitude of the Brahmins towards the value of learning. Why, exactly, should these two things be connected to each other? In Buddha's narrative, however, this development is critical. The increase in economic inequality in this society—the greater distance between the materially impoverished Brahmins and the wealthy householders plus the king—led to a change in the mental and emotional life of the Brahmins. They lost confidence in their views about the intrinsic value of learning and the importance of truth. Instead of valuing learning as the most important thing in life they began to seek out wealth and property of their own. In particular, some Brahmins used their learning to "compose hymns" and approached King Okkaka, asking for a portion of his wealth. King Okkaka agreed and gave these Brahmins many goods.[8]

The exchange of song for wealth described in this verse might seem inconsequential. Like the development of relative inequality in society, it is not initially clear why the Brahmins' decision is a problem here. Freely exchanging what one has for what one wants is a basic human activity. What, exactly, is so wrong with this swap? But in the narrative, this is also a significant transformation. The Brahmins no longer saw learning as intrinsically valuable. Instead, they used their learning to get what they wanted from the king. They see their learning as a means to satisfy their newfound desire for wealth and pleasure. Their priorities and way of evaluating actions have changed. And once they begin to see learning as an instrument to accumulate their own wealth—and to experience the variety and intensity of pleasures that this wealth brings—they lose all sense of perspective. They wanted more and more wealth from the king. The story continues:

306 And they, receiving wealth there, found pleasure in hoarding it up. Overcome by desire, their craving increased the more. Having composed hymns for this purpose, they went up to Okkaka again.

307 "As are water, earth, gold, wealth, and grain, so are cows to men. For this is a requisite for living creatures. Sacrifice, [for] your wealth is much."

308 And then the king, the lord of warriors, induced by the Brahmans, had many hundred thousand cows killed in sacrifice.

309 Not by their feet, nor by their horns, nor by anything [else] had the cows harmed [anyone]. They were like sheep, meek, giving pails of milk. [Nevertheless] the king, seizing them by the horns, had them killed with a knife.[9]

The key event in passage is the last step in the erosion of an ethical and social norm. The Brahmins once believed the cows should be protected from violent conduct, however, their desire to possess wealth became so strong that their views changed. Instead of seeing the cows like friends or a family members— as a mother or father or a living being not unlike themselves—the Brahmins started to think of the cows as no different from the water, the earth, gold, or grain. The cows became an unfeeling thing in the Brahmins' minds.

The narrowing of the Brahmins' way of thinking about the cows in the passage is revealing. The cows can feel pain and pleasure. They grow and develop. They are living beings. Identifying the cows with things that cannot feel, grow, and develop is a mistake. Cows are not like the water, the earth, gold and grain. But certain individuals—because of their covetousness or their greed—lost their concern with describing the cattle in a truthful way. They present a false way of thinking about cattle to King Okkaka.

INJUSTICE

In Buddha's narrative, a concern with truth and learning—a sense of the search for truth as intrinsically valuable—is essential to the maintenance of an ethical and social norm. If persons lose their concern with seeking the truth the reasons or justifications behind a social norm can begin to erode. In this case, the Brahmins use the power of their speech to advance a wrong view about cattle. But a second feature of Buddha's narrative here is the way it further develops the concept of an abuse of power. The actions of the violent outcaste discussed in the last chapter are bad for the unfortunate forms of life that are in the outcaste's way. But when a norm governing the asymmetry of power erodes in society the result is a calamity for the weaker being. The cows that were formerly protected from violence are now subject to it. In the narrative, many hundred thousand cows are killed at once.

The significance of this point cannot be stated strongly enough. In Buddha's view, ethical and legal norms must guard against abuses of power. The discussions from the Vasala Sutta and the Dhammika Sutta in the last chapter make this clear. But if the ethical and legal codes of society fail in this task, the results are catastrophic for the weaker form of life. The human capability to think and reason as well as construct tools and weapons will be brought to bear on the members of the unfortunate group. These animals will be suddenly and totally exposed to violent conduct with no countervailing constraint.

In the narrative, the erosion of norms protecting an animal from violent conduct is a calamity for the weaker being. The violence unleashed by this process is extraordinarily large. Nor, Buddha indicates, is it particularly easy to reestablish a norm that restrains violent conduct once that norm has eroded. The mental and emotional life of the different groups in society must go through a process in which they regain an understanding of the significance of the norm prohibiting violent conduct. There must be a wide-scale shift in the attitudes in society for both the erosion and the formation of nonviolent norms.

The difficulty of recreating a nonviolent norm is emphasized in the last part of Buddha's narrative. After King Okkaka seizes the cows and had them killed by the knife there is a sudden interjection:

310 And then the devas and the fathers, Inda, asuras and rakkhasas cried out: "[This is] injustice," when the knife fell on the cows.[10]

The cry of Brahmin tradition and the pantheon in this passage is both highly emotive and connected to reason. When a king or a head of state uses their superiority in power to kill a weaker being for the wrong reason—when a leader responds to an asymmetry of power by using violence to satisfy their greed or, in this case, to appease the greed of a powerful group—the action is unjust. It is a violation of a person's duties or their obligations to use power in this way. However, the shout of injustice in this passage—the collective cry of tradition—did not effect a change in this ancient society. The narrative continues: "This injustice of using violence has come down [to us] as an ancient practice. Innocent [cows] are killed; the sacrificers fall away from justice" (312).[11] The norm prohibiting violence towards these animals has not yet been restored.

THE METTA SUTTA

The Brahmanadhammika Sutta develops the human relationship with a particular animal, the cow, in greater detail. In the ancient Brahmins' view, a friendly and compassionate attitude should be extended to this animal. The ethical norms in society should not reflect the false view that cows are unfeeling things. Moreover, it is clear from the narrative that Buddha believes there are ethical points of contact between Brahmin lore and his own ideas. The importance of restraining abuses of power—and the importance of telling the truth—are common to each.

The points of ethical contact between Brahminism and Buddha's ideas are interesting. Is it possible that Buddha was aware of the passage in the Brhadaranyaka Upanishad, discussed in the introduction, where the person is directed to provide fodder to livestock? Is there a textual basis informing this commonality? To recall, the passage from the Brhadaranyaka Upanishad states:

> When he provides food and shelter to human beings, he becomes thereby a world for human beings. *When he procures fodder for livestock, he becomes thereby a world for livestock.* When creatures, from wild animals and birds down to the very ants, find shelter in his houses, he becomes thereby a world for them.[12] (italics added)

Unfortunately, there is no way to know with certainty whether Buddha was aware of something like this passage in the Brhadarnayaka Upanishad. It may be that this point of ethical contact was incidental. Cows were, after all, a very important animal to the society of the Upanishads, the Rig Vedas, and, even earlier, the Yamnaya, the pastoralists who migrated out of the area north of the Black Sea towards the subcontinent.[13] Taking care of cattle is bound to be an important task to the people who were so economically dependent on them. Buddha may be thinking about the economic reality of the cattle to Brahmin persons in this story without any specific knowledge of the Brhadaranyaka Upanishad or the Vedas. It is important to note, however, that Kshiti Mohan Sen—Amartya Sen's grandfather—*did* think it likely that Buddha was influenced by the Upanishads. Kshiti Mohan Sen states: "The date of the Upanishads is uncertain, but probably most of them were composed about 800 BC or after, but before Buddha, for he seems to have been strongly influenced by them."[14] Amartya Sen likewise defends this view. In *The Argumentative Indian*, Sen notes that "Buddhism is arguably as much an inheritor of the earlier Indian traditions of the Vedas and the Upanishads as Hinduism is, since both the religious traditions drew on these classics."[15] I should also note that Tagore advanced a similar idea. In *Sadhana: The*

Realization of Life Tagore indicates that Buddha "developed the practical side of the teaching of Upanishads."[16] Sen, his grandfather, and Tagore believed there was a line of influence between the earliest Upanishads and the early Buddhist discourses, including the Brhadaranyaka Upanishad cited above.

In the view of Tagore, Sen's grandfather, and Sen, the ethical points of contact between the Upanishads and the early Buddhist discourses—coupled with the assumption that the earliest Upanishads predate Buddha—are enough to establish the claim that Buddha was influenced by the Upanishads. Other scholars take a different tack.[17] But however this may be, it is clear that Buddha's understanding of the relation between persons and animals in the Metta Sutta communicates a very strong ethical teaching that is akin, in some ways, to the teaching in the Brhadaranyaka Upanishad. There is a moral duty to care for these and other animals in this early Buddhist discourse.

This point can be made more precise. At the core of the Metta Sutta is a poem that wishes "ease" to all living things. The poem states:

> Whatever living beings there may be,
> Whether they are weak or strong, omitting none,
> The great or the mighty, medium, short or small,
> The seen and the unseen,
> Those living near and far away,
> Those born and to-be-born,
> May all beings be at ease![18]

This poem goes to the heart of Buddha's message. A living thing, Buddha notes, may be strong or weak. There are differences in size and capability and power throughout the living world. Asymmetries of power are ubiquitous in nature and society. But the existence of these asymmetries of power is irrelevant to the attitude Buddha is trying to communicate in the poem. To Buddha, all beings—both the weak and the strong—should live a life free from terror and fear. Instead of living in terror and fear, all living things should be at ease.

The poem—which is addressed to the listener, but which lacks a reference to a god or gods—articulates a hoped-for future. It would be better if all living things can live a life of ease, free from terror and fear. A reality free from terror and fear is a highly desirable thing in Buddha's view.[19] The next part of the Sutta, however, moves from the realm of hope or wish to a more concrete focus on what human beings can do to contribute to the lives of persons and living things. There is a shift to a more agent-oriented perspective in the verses that follow the poem. Buddha states:

> Let none deceive another, or despise any being in any state,
> Let none through anger or ill will wish harm upon another.[20]

In this passage, despising another person or another form of life is a mindset one should strive to avoid. The agent is asked to diminish the hostile thoughts and feelings that arise within their person. Training oneself in calmness will help diminish suffering in the world.

Interpreted in this way, the verse in the Metta Sutta is akin to the teaching of the Attadanda Sutta discussed in chapter 1.[21] The individual should calm or quiet the hostile emotions that arise in their person. As such, the idea of nirvana or nibbana is informing this statement.[22] But what is distinctive about the Metta Sutta is the way the text goes on to supplement the idea of training oneself in calmness with a second kind of standard.[23] The person should not only diminish the hostile thoughts that arise in their person. The person should also think and feel in terms of what other forms of life need to grow and develop. The person should cultivate friendly feeling in their life. Buddha states:

> Even as a mother protects with her life her child, her only child,
> So with a boundless heart one should cherish all living beings,
> Radiating kindness over the entire world,
> Spreading upwards to the skies, and downwards to the depths,
> Outwards and unbounded, free from hatred or ill-will.[24]

In the passage, Buddha indicates that a mother can use her powers—her abilities or her capabilities broadly considered—to protect another life. The child benefits greatly from the mother's care and attention. But this is not all. Buddha indicates that *any* adult can cultivate the attitude of metta in their person, not just adult women with children. The attitude of metta is a fundamental human possibility, not a gendered construct. Moreover, the attitude of metta can be extended to any living being that can experience terror and fear, not just persons. The cherishing of fragile life is the core idea in this verse.

TAGORE'S METTA SUTTA

The Metta Sutta indicates that a person can reason and feel in terms of the growth and development of other living beings. The individual can become an agent who enhances the life around them in their thought and—when feasible—their action too. But the last set of points I would like to make in this context concerns Tagore and Sen's interpretation of the Metta Sutta. How do Tagore and Sen understand this early Buddhist discourse?

Tagore offers an extensive set of comments on the Metta Sutta in his book *The Religion of Man*. And part of the way Tagore presents this early Buddhist discourse in this text is through a translation of his own. Tagore states:

Do not deceive each other, do not despise anybody anywhere, never in anger wish anyone to suffer through your body, words or thoughts. Like a mother *maintaining* her only son with her own life, keep thy immeasurable loving thought for all creatures.[25] (italics added)

Note that Tagore emphasizes the idea of the mother *maintaining* her child in his translation, which is an interesting choice. The term maintaining refers to all the actions the mother takes to keep the child alive—including the action of protecting the child from danger.[26] The sense of a mother feeding her child and bathing her child and speaking to her child and playing with her child are all signaled by this term.

Tagore's translation emphasizes the way the mother changes the trajectory of the child's life through her speech and decisions. By maintaining the child, the mother helps the child to grow and develop. Sen also emphasizes this point in his interpretation of the Metta Sutta. In Sen's view, the mother "recognizes that she can, asymmetrically, do things for the child that would make a huge difference in the child's life and that the child itself cannot do."[27] It is the mentality of the adult intervening in the life of the child that is so important to Tagore and Sen.

Interpreted in this way, both Tagore and Sen draw attention to the idea of the obligations of power in their discussions of the Metta Sutta. As Sen points out, the basis for the mother's care of the child is not grounded in the notion of a contract or agreement. Another interesting feature of Tagore's interpretation of the Metta Sutta, however, is connected to the link Tagore establishes between Buddha's understanding of nibbana (or nirvana) and metta. In *The Religion of Man*, Tagore states:

Buddha's teaching speaks of Nirvana as the highest end. To understand its real character we have to the know the path of its attainment, which is not merely through the negation of evil thoughts and deeds but through the elimination of all limits of love.[28]

Here Tagore speaks about nibbana or nirvana in terms of the metaphor of a path or journey. There are steps—there is a path—the individual must take to calm or quiet the hostile emotions in their person. The individual does not start out in this condition. But the steps in this journey are mental and emotional steps, not just a physical climb of the mountain: it is the inner life of the person that must grow and evolve. More precisely, a person makes progress towards nibbana or nirvana when they learn to respect and protect and maintain the life around them in a more expansive way. In Tagore's view, diminishing hostile thoughts and feelings is one part of the greater process of cultivating love.

Tagore sees the theme of calming or quieting the self in the early Buddhist discourses in terms of the mental and emotional attitude of loving kindness it helps to create. Removing hostile thoughts and feelings is part of this journey. And the basic idea behind Tagore's interpretation is clear. A person cannot think in terms of the growth and development of another life when they are caught up in hostile attitudes towards that life. Hatred and anger are incompatible with the attitude of metta in Tagore's view. This general point, however, can also be understood in terms of the discourses examined in part I. The sectarian speakers are, for instance, too caught up in their own animosity towards persons with different religious views to develop the attitude of loving-kindness towards these persons. The mental and emotional life of the angry or fearful sectarian is incompatible with metta. Or again: the outcaste who destroys life without cause does not think and reason in terms of his victim's needs, while the mind of the greedy person is overwhelmed by the desire to possess and consume. In Tagore's view, these persons have developed qualities of mind or habits of reasoning that are incompatible with metta.

Tagore understands Buddha's thoughts about loving-kindness partly in terms of the attitudes it rules out. Violent sectarians, outcastes, the greedy person—in Buddha's view, these persons exhibit mental and emotional attitudes that prevent the development of metta. Some change is needed in the life of these persons to set in motion a process of inner reform. In the absence of this process of inner change, these persons will be unable to cultivate the more universal form of love that Buddha is espousing. I should also point out that the link between nibbana and metta is also advanced in Tagore's book *Sadhana: The Realization of Life*. Tagore states:

> In his sermon to Sadhu Simha Buddha says, *It is true, Simha, that I denounce activities, but only activities that lead to the evil in words, thoughts, or deeds. It is true, Simha, that I preach extinction, but only the extinction of pride, lust, evil thought, and ignorance, not that of forgiveness, love, charity or truth.*[29]

The claim in this passage is highly significant. Nibbana or nirvana is often associated with the negation of the self. For instance, the Oxford English Dictionary entry on nirvana states that nirvana is "the extinction of individual existence and absorption into the supreme spirit, or the extinction of all desires and passions and attainment of perfect beatitude."[30] Tagore's passage, however, indicates that nibbana or nirvana does not involve an absolute or comprehensive extinction of the self. Instead it involves a selective type of extinction. The person cannot be controlled by pride, lust, evil thoughts, or ignorance. The person must extinguish or diminish these realities in their minds and emotions. Forgiveness, love, charity and truth, however, are not negated. Instead, they are cultivated through the process of calming the mind.

Interpreted in this way, nibbana or nirvana, the highest goal of Buddha's teaching, is *practical* or *ethical* in Tagore's view. Nibbana or nirvana is a practice, a daily training, that ultimately helps one to love.

DIFFERENT LANGUAGE

Tagore sees the process of gaining control over the hostile thoughts and feelings that arise in one's person as a step on the path to the cultivation of a broader and more universal form of love. Extinction does not mean—it cannot mean—the elimination of all the tendencies of the person's life and feelings.[31] But the last point I wish to make in this context is a comparison. What are some of the similarities in Tagore and Sen's interpretation of the Metta Sutta? And how do these interpretations diverge?

As can be seem from this discussion—as well as the discussion in the preface and introduction—Tagore and Sen both interpret the Metta Sutta through the idea of the obligations of power. The existence of asymmetries of power calls forth the need to protect fragile life from abuses of power. This is a central ethical theme in their writings. It is clear, however, that Tagore also engages with the idea of nibbana in his writings on Buddha in a way that Sen does not. The idea of nibbana is not mentioned in *The Idea of Justice* or *The Contemporary Relevance of Buddha* or *The Argumentative Indian*.

The absence of the idea of nibbana from Sen's interpretation of Buddhism is interesting. It may be that Sen understands the idea of nibbana to be a part of Buddha's metaphysical understanding of the world. In this case, the idea of nibbana is a part of Buddha's teaching that Sen has decided to bracket in favor of the more empirically reasoned aspects of Buddha's project.[32] Also, Sen never says that the human power to love is infinite or knows no bounds—a point that Tagore makes in his discussion of "living in the infinite."[33] Instead, Sen states that a strong emotion of any kind should be the basis of more thought and reflection. Emotion is always an invitation to more reasoning, in Sen's view.[34] On these two points, Sen and Tagore seem to diverge.

The areas of separation between Tagore and Sen regarding the Metta Sutta may or may not be that significant. As noted in the introduction, I view these differences mainly through the distinct type of projects Tagore and Sen are pursuing. Sen's more developed form of social empiricism may lead him to avoid an engagement with some of Buddha's (and Tagore's) ideas. The key point for the discussion that follows, however, is that both thinkers find the obligations of power in the Metta Sutta. In particular, when Sen states that an adult "can do things that would make a huge difference to the child's life which the child itself cannot do"—and when Tagore speaks of the way the mother can maintain and protect the life of the child—they are drawing attention to an ethical idea of enormous importance. If one person adopts the obligations of power it can alter the trajectory of a child's life. And if many persons adopt this idea entire societies can be transformed. Individuals can promote the growth and development of other living things if they so choose.

NOTES

1. K. R. Norman, trans., *The Rhinoceros Horn and Other Early Buddhist Poems: The Group of Discourses*, Sutta Nipata, vol. 1 (London: The Pali Text Society Oxford, 1996), 35.

2. See chapter 2, note 5.

3. Amartya Sen, *The Argumentative Indian: Writings on Indian History, Culture and Identity* (New York: Picador, 2005), 46.

4. Norman, *The Rhinoceros Horn and Other Early Buddhist Poems: The Group of Discourses*, Sutta Nipata, vol. 1, 35.

5. Ibid., 37.

6. Ibid., 36.

7. Olivelle and McClish note that "The early Vedic literature depicts society as divided into three groups: the priests (Brahmans), the warriors and nobility (Kashitriyas), and the people of the tribe." Olivelle and McClish also note that the priests had a distinctive role within this society: "As composers of the sacred hymns, masters of the sacred language of Sanskrit, and performers of powerful ritual, the Brahmanas positioned themselves as the keepers and defenders of Aryan culture. Control of access to these cherished institutions helped the Brahmanas evolve into a powerful intelligentsia" (Mark McClish and Patrick Olivelle, *The Arthasatra: Selections from the Classic Indian Work on Statecraft* [Indianapolis, IN: Hackett], xxiv, xxv). The significance of this similarity—if any—is unclear.

8. Norman, *The Rhinoceros Horn and Other Early Buddhist Poems: The Group of Discourses* Sutta Nipata, vol. 1, 38. In the Ambattha Sutta, King Okkaka is identified as an ancestor of Buddha's and the founder of the Sakyas clan. See Rhys Davids, Ambatha Sutta, 112–33.

9. Ibid., 38.

10. Ibid., 38.

11. Ibid., 38. Upinder Singh notes that the Jain concept of time is framed in terms of symmetrical phases of progress and decline (Upinder Singh, *History of Ancient and Early Medieval India: From the Stone Age to the 12th Century* [Noida: Pearson, 2017], 313). In the Brahmanadhammika Sutta, however, there is a decline without any hint of future progress. The Brahmanadhammika Sutta does not follow the Jain form of time. The Cakkavatti-Sihanada Sutta, on the other hand, *is* figured in terms of symmetrical phases of decline and progress. The reason for this difference in conceptions of time in the early Buddhist discourses is not clear.

12. See introduction, note 3.

13. David Reich, *Who We Are and How We Got Here: Ancient DNA and the New Science of the Human Past* (New York: Vintage Books, 2019), 123–54.

14. Kshiti Mohan Sen, *Hinduism* (London: Penguin Books, 2005), 42.

15. Sen, *The Argumentative Indian*, 56.

16. Rabindranath Tagore, *Sadhana: The Realization of Life* (New York: Macmillan, 1913), 17.

17. See, for instance, Johannes Bronkhorst's book *Greater Magadha: Studies in the Culture of Early India* (Leiden: Brill, 2007). Bornkhorst argues that "Greater Magadha, roughly the eastern part of the Gangetic plain of northern India, has so far been looked upon as deeply indebted to Brahmanical culture. Religions such as Buddhism and Jainism are thought of as derived, in one way or another, from Vedic Religion. This belief is defective in various respects."

18. "Karaniya Metta Sutta: The Buddha's Words on Loving-Kindness" (Sn 1.8), trans. The Amaravati Sangha. *Access to Insight* (BCBS Edition), November 2, 2013. https://www.accesstoinsight.org/tipitaka/kn/snp/snp.1.08.amar.html.

19. The ease communicated in the poem of the Metta Sutta is the inverse of the terror and fear Buddha describes in the Attadanda Sutta. Other links between these two early Buddhist discourses will be described below.

20. "Karaniya Metta Sutta: The Buddha's Words on Loving-Kindness."

21. The Attadanda Sutta is discussed in chapter 1.

22. The first verse refers to nibbana: "This is what should be done by one who is skilled in goodness/And who knows *the path of peace*" (italics added). The last clause of the first stanza also invokes this idea: "*Peaceful and calm*, and wise and skillful, not proud and demanding in nature" (italics added). "Karaniya Metta Sutta: The Buddha's Words on Loving-Kindness."

23. Upinder Singh stresses the importance of friendship or loving-kindness in her book *Political Violence in Ancient India*: "The prohibition against violence was accompanied by an emphasis on the positive quality of friendship or loving kindness (*metta*) that should be followed by all beings, an attitude that is considered as having enormous power" (Singh, *Political Violence in Ancient India* [Cambridge, MA: Harvard University Press, 2017], 27).

24. See introduction, note 25. The Terigatha—which contains songs of renunciation voiced by women—also draws attention to the concern a mother can have for a child. But in one dialogue between Buddha and a woman Ubbiri, the emphasis is on coping with the death of her daughter. [Buddha:] "Mother, you cry out 'O Jiva' in the woods. Come to yourself, Ubbiri. Eighty-four thousand daughters all with the name 'Jiva' have burned in the funeral fire. For which one do you grieve?"

[Ubbiri] "I had an arrow in my heart and he took it out—that grief for my daughter. The arrow is out, the heart healed of hunger. I take refuge in the Buddha-sage, the Dharma, the Sangha" (Singh, *A History of Ancient and Medieval India*, 25).

This dialogue or poem composed of two songs helps to further define the concept of Metta. The idea of protecting life in the Metta Sutta also requires letting go of a life that is gone.

25. Rabindranath Tagore, *The Religion of Man* (New York: Macmillan, 1931), 68.

26. In the translation of the Metta Sutta from Tagore earlier work *Sadhana: The Realization of Life* (p. 106) *did* use the term protection: "He shall have measureless love for all creatures, even as a mother has for her only child, whom she *protects* with her own life" (italics added). There seems to have been a subtle shift in Tagore's thinking about this verse from the Metta Sutta between the two texts.

27. See introduction, note 52.

28. Tagore, *The Religion of Man*, 68.

29. Tagore, *Sadhana: The Realization of Life*, 31–32.

30. Quoted in Steven Collins, *Nirvana: Concept, Imagery, Narrative* (Cambridge: Cambridge University Press, 2010), 51. Note that Collins states that the Oxford English Dictionary definition "is about 50 per cent correct, although even the second definition needs commentary."

31. "He asked the lamp to give up its oil. *But purposeless giving up is a still darker poverty which he could never have meant.* . . . The path Buddha pointed out was not merely the practice of self-abnegation, but the widening of love. And therein lies the true meaning of Buddha's preaching" (italics added). Tagore, *Sadhana: The Realization of Life*, 76–77.

32. For more on the relationship between Tagore and Sen, see the last section of the Introduction.

33. For Tagore's interpretation of "living in the infinite" see *The Religion of Man*, 67–68.

34. Amartya Sen, *The Idea of Justice* (Cambridge, MA: The Belknap Press of Harvard University Press, 2009), xvii, 39.

Chapter 4

From the Ethical to the Political

In the Metta Sutta, the person is directed to create a world of loving-kindness within the broader violence of nature and the conflicts between people. The person can become an agent of growth and development in the world. However, the Metta Sutta does not speak about the actions or decisions of heads of state when discussing these themes. The idea that a king or the political leaders of society can use the power of the state to create a world of loving-kindness within their territory is not examined.

The Metta Sutta is framed in terms of the ethical theme of protection in abstraction from the reality of kings and their armies. "As a mother protects her child, her only child" is the image put forward by Buddha. However, in the Cakkavatti-Sihanada Sutta—a longer early Buddhist discourse that was not collected in the Sutta Nipata—the situation is different. In this discourse, a king enumerates the basic duties of the head of state to his son, the prince. In doing so, the king explicitly draws the theme of protecting life into the political sphere. The king states:

> Well then, my dear: depend on what is right (Dhamma), honor and respect it, praise it, revere and venerate it, have Dhamma as your flag, Dhamma as your banner, govern by Dhamma, and arrange rightful (Dhammika) shelter, protection and defense for your family, for the army, for your noble warrior client-(king)s, for Brahmin householders, for town-dwellers and country folk, for ascetics and Brahmin (-renouncer)s, for animals and birds. Let no wrongdoing take place in your territory; if there are poor people in your territory, give them money.[1]

This passage articulates two duties of the prince. The prince is told to shield the persons and animals living in his realm from violent conduct. Diminishing violent conduct is the first duty of the head of state. The second duty, however, is more economic in nature. The prince is also told to shield the persons living in his realm from extreme destitution. Protecting life in this context means maintaining the economic conditions of every person's growth and development in the kingdom. Moreover, the narrative goes on to describe what happens if a leader fails in this task. When a king does not protect persons from violent conduct and extreme destitution the society suffers; the average life spans of persons living in society decrease. In the Cakkavatti-Sihanada Sutta, state policy has a direct effect on the length and the quality of the life persons can lead.[2]

The Cakkavatti-Sihanada Sutta shows one way the theme of metta took on political significance. The notion that state policy can improve the life expectancy of persons by protecting individuals from violence and shielding persons from extreme deprivation is a new political development that nevertheless seems to draw on the more general theme of protection in the Metta Sutta.[3] I should also point out that the political potential inherent in Buddha's ideas was not confined to the literature that grew out of Buddha's teaching. It also effected a historical regime. When the third Mauryan emperor Ashoka embraced Buddhism after the war with Kalinga, the ethical ideas articulated by Buddha were joined together with the powers of a very large state. The theme of protecting life from war and other forms of deprivation is central to the way Ashoka justifies his actions in the second part of his reign.

The two examples cited here show the great political potential implicit in Buddha's teaching. The obligations of power also apply to the actions and the policies of the head of state. In chapters 4 and 5, then, I discuss some of the inscriptions of Ashoka with special emphasis on the new norms Ashoka tried to create. Ashoka's foreign policy internationalism, his concern with the growth and development of persons and animals, his critique of sectarianism and much else influenced Tagore and Sen.

THE FIRST-PERSON POINT OF VIEW

Vincent Arthur Smith (1848–1920) noted in his book *Ashoka: the Buddhist Emperor of India* that the personal qualities of most rulers in the third century BCE are mostly unknown. There is little evidence that has been preserved about the way these persons thought and felt. In the case of Ashoka, however, Smith claims the situation is different. Ashoka adopted the practice of inscribing important messages to the people on rocks, pillars, and other surfaces throughout his realm. Ashoka was the first known ruler to use writing as a vehicle for mass communication in the subcontinent.[4] And since many of the inscriptions are framed in a personal manner, as if Ashoka was speaking directly to his subjects about himself, his life, his feelings and his motivations, the inscriptions reveal something about the mental and emotional basis of Ashoka's conduct. In Smith's estimation, more is known about the inner life of Ashoka than virtually any other ruler from this period.[5]

Smith's way of understanding the inscriptions sees them as texts that have
gone through a process of editing which nevertheless preserved features of
Ashoka's inner life. "It is impossible" Smith states, "for any student to read
the edicts with care, and not to hear the voice of the king himself."[6] But
part of what makes Ashoka's voice in the edicts so distinctive is his willingness to publicly acknowledge his mistakes and shortcomings. Ashoka—like
Buddha—presents himself as a fallible human being who has gone through a
process of growth and development in the inscriptions.[7]

This point can be made more precise. In the first "Minor Rock Edict"—which
Romila Thapar believes was made public in or around 256 BCE—Ashoka
identifies two phases in his own growth and development. Ashoka states:

> Thus speaks the Beloved of the Gods, Ashoka: I have been a Buddhist layman
> for more than two and a half years, but for a year I did not make much progress.
> Now for more than a year I have drawn closer to the Order and have become
> more ardent.[8]

In this passage, Ashoka's initial choice to become a lay follower of the
Buddha did not lead to a definitive transformation of Ashoka's mental and
emotional life. This description does not emphasize the idea of an immediate and radical inner change. Instead, Ashoka made a sequence of choices
over time that gradually deepened his resolve. Ashoka decided to become a
member of the Buddhist laity and then, after a year, decided to devote himself
more intently to the teachings of Buddha. He seems to have had close contact
with—and perhaps received instruction from—Buddhist monks and nuns.
Moreover, Ashoka is keen to stress the importance of effort and hard work
in this process. Strenuous or ardent exertion—a willingness to focus on difficult goals for a long period of time—seems to have had the greatest effect
on Ashoka's life in his own estimation. In Ashoka's view, the last year or so
of his observance has led to a more substantive personal change.

The "Minor Rock Edict" emphasizes the importance of daily discipline as
the key to reshaping one's mental and emotional life. Ashoka speaks openly
of his own shortcomings and his attempt to overcome them in this inscription.
In the thirteenth "Major Rock Edict"—which Thapar believes was also made
public in or around 256 BCE—Ashoka places his own growth and development as a person within a wider context. Ashoka states:

> When he had been consecrated eight years the Beloved of the Gods, the king
> Piyadassi, conquered Kalinga. A hundred and fifty thousand people were
> deported, a hundred thousand were killed and many times that number per-
> ished. Afterwards, now that Kalinga was annexed, the Beloved of the Gods
> very earnestly practiced Dhamma, desired Dhamma, and taught Dhamma.
> On conquering Kalinga the Beloved of the Gods felt remorse, for, when an

independent country is conquered the slaughter, death, and deportation of the people is extremely grievous to the Beloved of the Gods, and weighs heavily on his mind. What is even more deplorable to the Beloved of the Gods, is that those who dwell there, whether brahmans, *sramanas*, or those of other sects, or householders who show obedience to their superiors, obedience to mother and father, obedience to their teachers and behave well and devotedly towards their friends, acquaintances, colleagues, relatives, slaves, and servants—all suffer violence, murder and separation from their loved ones. Even those who are fortunate to have escaped, and whose love is undiminished [by the brutalizing effect of war], suffer from the misfortunes of their friends, acquaintances, colleagues and relatives. This participation of all men in suffering, weighs heavily on the mind of the Beloved of the Gods.[9]

This passage—like the first "Minor Rock Edict"—shows Ashoka reflecting on his past. Ashoka's father Bindusara Amitraghata died in 273 or 272 BCE, Ashoka's coronation was held in 269 or 268 BCE and the war with Kalinga was initiated in 261 or 260 BCE.[10] But during this period of his rule it seems that Ashoka had not clearly thought through the realities of war from the perspective of its victims. He did not immediately realize or feel the extent of the suffering he could unleash. It is only after the experience of this war that Ashoka fully understood the calamitous nature of his choice in the lives of other people. Ashoka's decision to become a lay follower of the Buddha seems to have originated in this experience.

The thirteenth "Major Rock Edict" places the narrative of the first "Minor Rock Edict" within the broader context of Ashoka's decisions as ruler. The violent death of one hundred thousand persons in battle—as well as the death of many hundreds of thousands of persons through famine and other causes related to the war, in addition to the suffering of the persons who were deported—fundamentally altered the way Ashoka thought and felt. The sense of a single converting moment is stronger in this passage than in the first "Minor Rock Edict." But even in the thirteenth "Major Rock Edict" the way Ashoka presents his response to the war is described as a process. The experience of war and its aftermath led to (1) the practicing of dhamma, and then (2) a "desire" for dhamma, and (3) a willingness to "teach" dhamma. Ashoka identifies a sequence of mental and emotional steps in this passage. Moreover, it is possible that the steps within this process are connected to Ashoka's decision to draw closer to the order of Buddhist monks and nuns described in the first "Minor Rock Edict." If this is true, Ashoka's turn to Buddhism is ultimately founded on a love of dhamma that emerged out of a very terrible war that he initiated.

THE *ARTHASHASTRA*

The narrative of the thirteenth "Major Rock Edict" and the first "Minor Rock Edict" draw attention to key moments in Ashoka's past. Ashoka wanted his subjects to understand the broad contours of his own growth and development. He made a strenuous effort to change the personal basis of his conduct after the war with Kalinga. However, in the process of describing his enlightenment in the thirteenth "Major Rock Edict" Ashoka also draws attention to the way he thought about war in the early part of his reign. The first years of his rule were not informed by a strong mental and emotional regard for the persons living in Kalinga. But a key question here is "Why?" What features of Ashoka's upbringing and education lead him to overlook or downplay this aspect of war? How did this blind spot towards other people emerge in his life?

The Ashokan inscriptions do not directly address this question. Ashoka is silent about the education he received as a child and young adult in the thirteenth "Major Rock Edict." It is therefore impossible to answer this question in any definitive way. Moreover, while the *Arthashastra* of Kautilya might shed light on this question, the date and location of composition of the *Arthashastra* has divided contemporary scholarship.[11] Patrick Olivelle and Mark McClish argue that the *Arthashastra* cannot be used to describe the Mauryan period, while other scholars, including Romila Thapar and Upinder Singh believe the *Arthashastra* can be used as a source of information about the Mauryan period. Amartya Sen also holds the view that the *Arthashastra* can be used to describe the Mauryan period.[12]

The reasoning that informs the view of Thapar, Singh, and Sen is interesting. In Singh's judgment, "There do not yet to seem to be sufficient grounds to abandon the idea that some part of the text was composed in the Maurya period by a person named Kautilya, allowing for later interpolations stretching into the early centuries CE."[13] In her view, information about the Mauryan period can be gleaned from the *Arthashastra*. But in what follows I mainly wish to compare Ashoka's ideas in the inscriptions with some of the ideas articulated in the *Arthashastra*, without making any definite claims about dates and influences. At the very least, a discussion of the *Arthashastra* can provide a sense of contrast with the attitudes Ashoka adopted after the war with Kalinga.

THE CONQUEROR

Keeping these cautions in mind, a defining feature of Kautilya's analysis of foreign policy is its focus on expanding the territory of the state. Kautilya frames his foreign policy advice as guidance for the potential "conqueror" of India. In particular, he wanted a ruler to unify India, overcoming the existing condition of multiple warring states. This assumption in focus, in turn, affected the way Kautilya discusses the decision to go to war. In a key passage from the *Arthashastra*, Kautilya states:

> The would-be conqueror shall judge the relative strengths and weaknesses of the following aspects [of waging a war], as applicable to him and to his enemy, before starting on a military expedition:
>
>   - power:
>
>   - the place [of operations];
>
>   - the time [of the military engagement];
>
>   - the season for marching [towards the battle ground];
>
>   - when to mobilize different types of forces;
>
>   - the possibility of revolts and rebellions in the rear;
>
>   - the likely losses, expenses and gains and
>
>   - the likely dangers
>
>   If, [on balance, after giving due weight to the different factors as explained below], the conqueror is superior the campaign shall be undertaken; otherwise, not.[14]

From the point of view of the thirteenth "Major Rock Edict," an obvious feature of this list is what it leaves out. There is no mention of the soldiers who will die in battle or their parents and families. The way war destroys persons and breaks apart relations of loyalty and love is not discussed. Instead, the defining feature of this list is its focus on an empirical inquiry that is centered on power. Kautilya indicates that the ruler must judge the relative might of his armed forces compared to the armed forces of the opponent. The conqueror should not wage war unless his military and economic power is clearly superior to the military and economic power of the enemy state. Moreover, the idea of the census—which is also a feature of Kautilya's approach to politics—takes on increased significance in this context. By conducting a census of persons and animals in the kingdom, the conqueror obtains a clearer sense of the economic and military power he wields. The ideal king will make better decisions about warfare *if* his decisions are informed by an accurate census.

Kautilya asks the ruler to carefully assess his chances of winning a campaign. "Can the conqueror prevail in war?" is the all-important question in Kautilya's analysis, not the suffering of persons. Kautilya is primarily focused on the economic and military *institutions* of societies in his analysis.[15] It is also important to note the complexity of the calculation Kautilya is calling for in this passage. The factors Kautilya identifies in this list cannot be thought of in isolation from each other. Instead, the factors in Kautilya's list are interdependent with each other. For instance, the conqueror needs to compare his state's military and economic power with the military and economic power of his adversary. The census is one of the tools the conqueror must use to assess this point. But the conqueror must also consider the way the rest of the region will respond to the war he is about to unleash. Will the conqueror's state be attacked "in the rear" by a third state when the conqueror wages war with the enemy? Will the conqueror become vulnerable to the destabilization of his own territory by other powers when he sends his troops to war? Since this is a possibility, Kautilya advises the ruler to leave "a third or a quarter of his army" at home during the invasion.[16] It is always necessary to protect one's state from attacks by ambitious neighboring kings when conducting a war of conquest.

Interpreted in this way, a more precise description of the calculation the ruler should make is as follows: is the economic and military power of the conqueror's state clearly superior to the economic and military power of the adversary—when one third of his armed forces must be left at home? Can the conqueror win the war with two thirds of his forces—considering the dangers and accidents that inevitably follow such an undertaking? And this formulation only considers three or four points on Kautilya's list. Kautilya also asks the conqueror to weigh factors like the time of year when conducting a campaign. Under what environmental conditions will the conqueror's troops have the greatest advantage relative to the troops of the enemy? Are the enemy's troops less effective as a fighting force in the rainy season or in the cold or heat? The answers to these questions all contribute to the conqueror's calculation.

THE CONFLICT BEFORE THE WAR

Kautilya clearly believes undertaking a campaign requires a rigorous empirical analysis of the economies, armies and incentives of all the states in the
region, as well as a thorough knowledge of the land and the seasons. An
exacting investigation must inform the decision to go to war in Kautilya's
view. However, the human costs of the war for the enemy state are not
included in the conqueror's focus. Kautilyan inquiry systematically disregards certain types of evidence, experience, and points of view.

Kautilya asks the ruler to engage in a project of continuous observation
and study. The Kautilyan king must remain in touch with what is happening
in several societies. But Kautilya's advice is not focused on observing and
planning alone. Kautilya also recommends actively weakening the enemy
state before the first battle. For instance, Kautilya encourages the use of spies
to sow dissension in the enemy's territory. By creating internal divisions—
between the king and his counselors, or between the different social and
economic classes in the state, or by some other means—the strength of the
enemy is sapped.[17] Kautilya also recommends disrupting the enemy's food
supply in this context. He notes that the conqueror could time a campaign in
the fall to "destroy the enemy's rainy season crops and to prevent winter sowing." By attacking the enemy when the "food stocks are exhausted" and its
"new stocks are not yet collected" the conqueror diminishes the enemy's ability to create the surplus of food needed to sustain troops on the battlefield.[18]
Kautilya notes that it is also possible to attack in March and April—and
again in May and June—for much the same reason. In Kautilya's view, the
enemy state goes through predictable periods of heightened vulnerability in
the time frame immediately prior to the harvesting of crops. The conqueror's
knowledge of the agricultural calendar of India can increase the conqueror's
effectiveness in waging war.

From this point of view, Kautilya's foreign policy advice, when thought
through in its totality, requires a ruler to consider every possible way of
degrading the enemy state—even when the conqueror and the enemy state
are ostensibly at peace. A large part of the conqueror's mental and emotional
life must remain focused on these objectives. If the conqueror cannot discipline his mental and emotional life along these lines, Kautilya indicates the
foreign policy of the conqueror will not be successful. The personal basis of
the king's conduct is, therefore, also an important topic to Kautilya. And it
is important to note in this context that part of the conqueror's preparation
for war involves the conqueror making war, as it were, with parts of his own
inner life. In Kautilya's view, the conqueror must also overcome the *internal*
"obstacles to achieving gain." In particular, the conqueror cannot be ruled by:

passion, anger, timidity, *compassion [leading to aversion to fighting]*, recoiling from awarding deserving punishment, baseness (not acting like an Arya), haughtiness, a forgiving nature, thinking of the next world, being too pious, meanness, abjectness, jealousy, contempt for what one has, wickedness, distrust, fear, negligence, inability to withstand harsh climate (cold, heat or rain) and faith in the auspiciousness of stars and days.[19] (italics added)

This list is quite long—Kautilya clearly liked lists—but it is significant that Kautilya believes compassion is a weakness in the ruler. The head of state cannot focus on the suffering his actions cause in the lives of people living in neighboring domains. For Kautilya, the ruler must cultivate a mental and emotional blind spot to the life, growth and development of many persons when he considers foreign policy.

THE KAUTILYAN AND THE BUDDHIST KING

The Kautilyan approach to neighboring states can be described as one of unrelenting observation and careful planning. The empirical quality of Kautilya's advice—the ruler must gain an accurate and timely sense of what is happening both in his own land and in the land of other people—really stands out. But Kautilyan foreign policy empiricism is informed by an assumption of violent conflict, not compassion. Degrading the enemy state is the chief Kautilyan concern.

The Kautilyan approach to enemy states required the conqueror to refashion his mental and emotional life in the direction of minimal sensitivity to the suffering of foreign persons. An opportunistic and predatory mentality towards the enemy state is a Kautilyan virtue. From this point of view, the distance between the thirteenth "Major Rock Edict" and the section on foreign policy in the *Arthashastra* is remarkably large. Ashoka's turn to Buddhism— with its emphasis on the obligation to protect all persons from war, as much as is feasible—diverges quite radically from Kautilya's views.[20]

KAUTILYAN WELFARE

The foreign policy of Kautilya is framed in terms of violent conquest and the absence of compassion when considering war. But Ashoka's foreign policy after his turn to Buddhism is framed by the attitudes of compassion and an aversion to war. There are few divides in political life as great as this. In reflecting on the relationship between Kautilya's principles and the Ashokan inscriptions, however, it is important to avoid oversimplifying Kautilya's ideas. The *Arthashastra* is not completely devoid of ethical principles and points of view. Rather, the ethical principles Kautilya affirmed did not apply to the relationship with enemy states. The section on domestic policy and the section on foreign policy in the *Arthashastra* require the ruler to think in two vastly different ways.

The most obvious expression of this difference is found in Kautilya's passage on the goal of economic and political science. In a passage which summarizes the guiding principle of the *Arthashastra*, Kautilya states:

> The source of the livelihood of men is artha (wealth); that is to say, the territory [and the inhabitants following various professions] is the wealth [of a nation]. *The science by which territory is acquired and maintained* is Arthashastra—the science of wealth and welfare.[21] (italics added)

In this passage, Kautilya understands his teachings as contributing to the science of welfare. Improving the prosperity of one's own citizens was Kautilya's—and the ideal Kautilyan ruler's—chief concern. But it is also clear that acquiring territory comes at the expense of one's adversaries. The science of welfare in the *Arthashastra* is defined by the competition between states for more territory and wealth.

The split nature of Kautilya's advice—the ruler must promote the welfare of his own people while undermining the welfare (and thus the power) of the people living in adversary states—is apparent in Kautilya's understanding of the goals of the science of government. The split nature of Kautilya's advice is also evident in many of his specific discussions. As noted earlier, the treatment of agriculture in the section on foreign policy focuses on the best time to destroy the enemy's crops. Attacking the enemy's fields just before the harvest delivers the greatest blow. But in his discussion of food in the section of the *Arthashastra* devoted to domestic policy Kautilya takes an entirely different tack. In this section, Kautilya indicates that the ruler must take steps to enhance the food security of his people and prevent outbreaks of famine. Kautilya states:

> The methods of counteracting the effects of famine are:
>
> > distribute to the public, on concessional terms, seeds and food from the royal stores;
> >
> > undertake food-for-work programmes such as building forts or irrigation works;
> >
> > share out the royal food stocks

commander for public distribution private stocks of food

shift the affected population to a different region

encourage [temporary] migration to another country

move the entire population [with the King and Court] to a region or country with an abundant harvest or near the sea, lakes or rivers;

supplement the harvest with additional cultivation of grain, vegetables, roots and fruits, by fishing and by hunting deer, cattle, birds and wild animals.[22]

The responses Kautilya identifies here reveal a highly nuanced understanding of the causes of famine and the policies that can prevent it. The Kautilyan king has a duty to prevent the starvation of his subjects. And yet this duty is, in Kautilya's mind, entirely compatible with the goal of disrupting the food supply of neighboring states during a military campaign.

LESS DIVIDED

Kautilya's domestic policy recommendations and his foreign policy recommendations are highly divergent. The conqueror must protect his people from famine but can destroy the enemy's crops. The conqueror must promote the wealth and stability of his society while undermining the wealth and stability of his neighbors. Even Kautilya's treatment of ethical norms is split in two. Kautilya asks the ruler—that is, the conqueror—to cultivate a common sense of duty among his people. He states:

Duties common to all: *Ahimsa* (abstaining from injury to all living things); *Satyam* [truthfulness]; cleanliness; freedom from malice; compassion and tolerance.[23]

Compassion, tolerance, truthfulness, and a general injunction to avoid harming all living things, including animal life, are identified here as contributors to *artha*. Society benefits—it becomes more wealthy and powerful—when the people develop these qualities. Something like the idea of "social capital" is expressed in this passage. It is also the case, however, that the personal qualities that are beneficial in the civilian population are considered by Kautilya to be harmful to the conqueror. As noted earlier, compassion is identified as an internal obstacle to the conqueror's ability to successfully wage war.

The preceding comments allow for a more nuanced characterization of the change that accompanied Ashoka's turn to Buddhism. Norms of nonviolence, tolerance, compassion, and the welfare of society are present in the *Arthashastra*—and *may* have informed the early education that Ashoka received. But in addition to these ethical norms, the *Arthashastra* asks the ruler to harm the persons living in enemy states. The Kautilyan ruler must act from the point of view of *ahimsa* and *himsa* in his mental and emotional life. And it is this split perspective—the highly discordant attitudes at the root of Kautilya's advice—that Ashoka is commenting on in the thirteenth "Major Rock Edict." Ashoka could no longer justify such a radical divergence in his attitudes towards human beings. The dualism between "source of power" and "enemy state" gave way, in the thirteenth "Major Rock Edict," to an understanding of the commonalities that all peoples share.

THE CRITIQUE OF NATIONALISM

In this chapter, I discussed the first "Minor Rock Edict" and the thirteenth "Major Rock Edict" of Ashoka in terms of Ashoka's inner change. Initially, Ashoka indicates that his foreign policy focused on the conquest of a new territory. However, after reflecting on the terrible suffering caused by this war, Ashoka began to consider new priorities. A strong aversion to all wars developed in his person, and Ashoka embraced the moral teachings of Buddha. But the last point I wish to make in this context involves Sen and Tagore. How do Sen and Tagore respond to Ashoka's change?

On one level, Ashoka's change informs Sen and Tagore's sense of the history of the subcontinent. As Sen puts it, Ashoka's newfound aversion to war—his adoption of "the non-violent teachings of Gautama Buddha"—draws attention to the political implications of Buddha's message.[24] The aversion to violence that is so evident in the Sutta Nipata informed the actions of a historical king. From this point of view, Buddha's influence was very worldly indeed. The "otherworldly religion" that Sen notes many people have found is Buddhism is not the only way of describing this tradition.[25] But Ashoka's influence on Sen and Tagore goes beyond an episode in the history of Buddhism. Ashoka's aversion to all wars of expansion is also a "root moral norm" in Tagore and Sen's foreign policy internationalism.[26] There is no statement in favor of a war of expansion in the writings of Tagore and Sen.

Understood in this way, the most important influence of Buddha and Ashoka on the foreign policy internationalism of Tagore and Sen—the core moral idea that has been passed down from thinker to thinker—involves the understanding that wars of expansion are immoral and unjust. At no point do Sen and Tagore identify the goal of the state policy in terms of the conquest of others.

The primary ethical idea in Tagore and Sen's foreign policy reflects Ashoka's moral critique of war. A tremendous abuse of power is evident in all expansionist wars. But a second aspect of Ashoka's Buddhist inspired teaching that affects Sen and Tagore is the regard Ashoka showed towards the persons living in other societies after his turn to Buddhism. Ashoka's ethical universalism—his belief that all persons are bound together in relationships of love and loyalty—had a strong impact on Tagore and Sen.

This point can be put another way. In a passage from *Sadhana: The Realization of Life*, Tagore states:

> A band of robbers must be moral to hold together as a band; they may rob the world but not each other. To make a moral intention successful, some of its weapons must be moral. In fact, very often it is our very moral strength which gives us most effectively the power to do evil, to exploit other individuals for our own benefit, to rob other people of their rights.[27]

This passage is speaking about the hostile nationalism of the colonial period. In Tagore's view, the British, the French, the Dutch, the Portuguese, and other European states organized the power of their own people through the ethical ideas of freedom from foreign domination. None of the people living in these European nations wanted to be controlled by another European power. However, these heads of state used this moral power of organization for the most immoral of ends. They robbed the lands of the foreign peoples they conquered in the name of their own security and freedom.[28] As Tagore and Sen point out in many different contexts, India suffered greatly from almost two hundred years of British rule. But the problems inherent in European nationalism—which is not fundamentally different from the problems inherent in Kautilyan foreign policy—also indicate the need for ethical universalism in foreign policy. To Buddha, Ashoka, Tagore, and Sen, the moral critique of violence must inform the foreign policy decisions of every head of state.

NOTES

1. Steven Collins, *Nirvana and other Buddhist Felicities: Utopias of the Pali Imaginaire* (Cambridge: Cambridge University Press, 1998), 604.

2. Ibid., 606.

3. Section twenty of the Cakavatti-Sihanada Sutta describes how the absence of dhamma in the policies of the eighth king eventually led to the destruction of metta in this fictional society. The passage states: "And for those who live for ten years, there will be terrible anger present among them, one toward another, terrible hatred, terrible ill will, terrible thoughts of killing, mother against child, child against mother, father against child, child against father, brother against brother, brother against sister, and

sister against brother—there will be such terrible anger, hatred, ill will, and thoughts of killing among them, one for another." The inversion of the Metta Sutta—with its focus on the mother who protects her child—is evident here. John Holder, *Early Buddhist Discourses*, 186.

4. "When Ashoka set up pillars and massive boulders inscribed with royal edicts around 250 BC, he become the first ruler in ancient India to use writing to communicate to the masses." Jonathan Mark Kenoyer, *Ancient Cities of the Indus Valley Civilization*, 78. Kenoyer also notes in this context that "The recent discovery of Brahmi script on potsherds from Sri Lanka dates to around 500 B.C., but the use of both Kharoshthi and Brahmi on stone edicts in the peninsular subcontinent dates somewhat later, around 250 B.C." The Brahmi script—which was one of the scripts used on the Ashokan pillars—may have entered the peninsular subcontinent through Sri Lanka.

5. Vincent Arthur Smith, *Ashoka: The Buddhist Emperor of India* (Dehli: S. Chand, 1909), 105.

6. Vincent Arthur Smith, *Ashoka: the Buddhist Emperor of India*, 105. Patrick Olivelle's essay "Asoka's Inscriptions as Text and Ideology" in *Reimagining Ashoka* develops the textual aspect of the inscriptions in more detail. Olivelle's notes that careful reflection on the process by which Ashoka's statements came to be inscribed on hard surfaces throughout his realm indicates that his inscriptions are not the "ipssisima verba" of the king. Olivelle also notes that Ashoka was sometimes dissatisfied with the results of this process of textual production.

7. For more on Buddha's own process of growth and development in the Sutta Nipata, see chapter 1.

8. Romila Thapar, *Ashoka and the Decline of the Mauryas* (Oxford: Oxford University Press, 1997), 259.

9. Romila Thapar, *Ashoka and the Decline of the Mauryas*, 255–56.

10. All dates in the text follow Romila Thapar's chronology in *Ashoka and the Decline of the Mauryas*, 15–19.

11. There are two main interpretive camps on this question. In Kangle's judgment, "there is no convincing reason why this work should not be regarded as the work of Kautilya who helped Chandragupta come to power in Magadha" (R. P. Kangle, *The Kautilya Arthashastra*, Part III; A Study, [Dehli: Motilal Banarsidass, 1965], 106). L. N. Rangarajan's translation of the *Arthashastra* also adopts Kangle's chronology and location of composition—see Rangarajan, *The Arthashastra* (Gurgaon: Penguin Books, 1987), 6–8. In this line of reasoning, teachings in the *Arthashastra* are dated to Chandragupta's reign, the teachings originated from within Magadha, and the text can be used to fill in details about the Mauryan Empire. Mark McClish and Patrick Olivelle, however, argue that the *Arthashastra* was not composed in Magadha and did not predate Ashoka's reign. Instead, they cite a range of evidence that indicates the *Arthashastra* was composed between 100 BCE and 100 CE in the region that is now coastal Maharashtra (on India's west coast). McClish and Olivelle, *The Arthashastra: Selections from the Classic Indian Work on Statecraft* (Indianapolis, IN: Hackett, 2012), xix–xx and xlii. McClish's essay "Is the *Arthashastra* a Mauryan Document?" in *Reimagining Ashoka: Memory and History* develops this line of reasoning in more detail.

12. In Sen's view, the *Arthashastra* of Kautilya was "first written in the fourth century BCE though revised and finalized a few centuries later." Amartya Sen, *The Argumentative Indian: Writings on Indian History, Culture and Identity* (New York: Picador, 2005), 166.

13. Upinder Singh, *A History of Ancient and Early Medieval India: From the Stone Age to the 12th Century* (Noida: Pearson, 2017), 324. Singh discusses the Ashokan understanding of kingship and the understanding of kingship in the *Arthashastra* on pages 340–49 of *A History of Ancient and Early Medieval India: From the Stone Age to the 12th Century*.

14. L. N. Rangarajan ed. and trans., *The Arthashastra* (Gurgaon: Penguin Books, 1987), 588.

15. For more on the institutional nature of Kautilya's analysis see Amartya Sen, *The Idea of Justice* (Cambridge, MA: The Belknap Press of Harvard University Press, 2009), 76–77.

16. L. N. Rangarajan, *The Arthashastra*, 590.

17. L. N. Rangarajan, *The Arthashastra*, 598–99, 616–17, 620. See also Rangarajan's discussion of *bheda* (p. 91).

18. L. N. Rangarajan, *The Arthashastra*, 591. Rangarajan summarizes the category of "Vigraha" or hostilities in Kautilya's thought in the following way: "open war, a battle in the normal sense; secret war, attacking the enemy in a variety of ways, taking him by surprise; and undeclared war, clandestine acts using secret agents and occult practices" (L. N. Rangarajan, *Arthashastra*, 513). Destroying the enemy crops just before the harvest could be an "open war" or a "secret war" depending on the context.

19. L. N. Rangarajan, *The Arthashastra*, 597.

20. As will be discussed in the next chapter, the thirteenth "Major Rock Edict" does not advocate for an absolute pacificism. Wars may still be necessary, Ashoka states.

21. L. N. Rangarajan, *The Arthashastra*, 79. The conqueror's concern for the welfare of his people is, however, based on a self-interested motive. The welfare of the people is the basis for the king's power. By increasing the welfare of the people, the conqueror is also enhancing his own strength.

22. L.N. Rangarajan, *The Arthashastra*, 107.

23. L.N. Rangarajan, *The Arthashastra*, 85.

24. See note 30 in the introduction.

25. Amartya Sen, "The Contemporary Relevance of Buddha," in *Ethics and International Affairs* 28, no. 1 (2014): 15–27.

26. This expression is drawn from David A. Reidy's discussion in Reidy and Martin, *Rawls' Law of Peoples: A Realistic Utopia?* (Malden: Blackwell, 2006), 177. Note, however, that Reidy is referring to Rawls's criteria of reciprocity when he invokes this phrase while a root moral norm for Sen and Tagore involves the idea of an abuse of power. This difference will be commented on in chapter 9.

27. Rabindranath Tagore, *Sadhana: The Realization of Life* (New York: Macmillan, 1913), 56.

28. Tagore makes a similar point in *Nationalism* (New York: Macmillan, 1917), 132. He states: "By this device [the creation of a nation] the people which loves freedom perpetuates slavery in a large portion of the world with the comfortable feeling

of pride in having done its duty; men who are naturally just can be cruelly unjust in both their act and their thought, accompanied by a feeling that they are helping the world to receive its deserts; men who are honest can go on blindly robbing others of their human rights for self-aggrandizement, all the while abusing the deprived for not deserving better treatment." In this passage—like the passage from *Sadhana: The Realization of Life* cited in note 27—the heads of state of the European colonial powers are robbers, not arbiters of truth and justice.

Chapter 5

New Norms

Ashoka's turn to dhamma is associated in the thirteenth "Major Rock Edict" with a transformation of his attitudes towards non-Mauryan peoples. Ashoka indicates that he developed compassion—and possibly even loving kindness or metta—towards the persons living in all societies after the war with Kalinga. This shift in the internal basis of Ashoka's conduct, however, also had profound effects on the policies Ashoka pursued in the second part of his reign. Ashoka's foreign policy and his domestic policy moved in a new direction.

In this chapter, I focus on some of the norms and institutions Ashoka attempted to create in the Mauryan Empire and in the larger region after the war with Kalinga in 261 BCE. In particular, I focus on Ashoka's understanding of "conquest by dhamma"—as well as the themes of education, the health of persons and animals, and the dangers of sectarianism—in the "Major Rock Edicts." I also discuss Tagore and Sen's interpretation of the Mauryan ruler in more detail in this context.

SONS AND GREAT GRANDSONS

As noted in chapter 4, one manifestation of Ashoka's internal change after the war with Kalinga is connected to a desire to "teach dhamma." Ashoka's turn to Buddhism is associated with a new concern with the growth and development of all people. But what were some of the concrete ways Ashoka pursued this objective? And who, exactly, were the people Ashoka was trying to teach?

Consider, in this context, the concluding section of the thirteenth "Major Rock Edict." In a very interesting passage, Ashoka states:

This inscription of Dhamma has been engraved so that any sons or great grandsons that I may have should not think of gaining new conquests, and in whatever victories they may gain should be satisfied with patience and light punishment. They should only consider conquest by Dhamma to be a true conquest, and delight in Dhamma should be their whole delight, for this is of value in both this world and the next.[1]

This passage is noteworthy in part because it frames the goal of the thirteenth "Major Rock Edict" in a new way. What began with a discussion of Ashoka's painful growth and development after the war with Kalinga has now morphed into a lesson between father and son. Ashoka wanted his descendants to understand the scale of the suffering caused by the war with Kalinga. Ashoka did not want his descendants to make the same mistakes he made in this campaign.

The primary meaning of the coda is framed in terms of a cautionary tale. "Do not do what I did" and "Learn from my experience" is the overarching theme. On a second level, however, the passage is significant because it establishes a new priority in the conduct of foreign policy. Instead of seeking more territory through violent conduct, Ashoka hoped his descendants would consider an alternative, which he describes as "conquest by dhamma." Convincing his descendants of the truth inherent in dhamma—not organized violence at a societal scale—produces a lasting victory in Ashoka's analysis.

THE ENVOYS

One manifestation of Ashoka's newfound desire to "teach dhamma" in the thirteenth "Major Rock Edict" is directed towards his male descendants. Ashoka wanted his sons and great grandsons to understand war as the last resort of foreign policy.[2] He did not want his male descendants to develop an opportunistic and predatory mentality towards other people. In this sense, the idea of the obligations of power is evident in Ashoka's statements to his children. The head of state has an obligation to protect other peoples.[3] However, a second manifestation of the desire to "teach dhamma" in the thirteenth "Major Rock Edict" is connected to the kind of diplomacy Ashoka conducted with his neighbors. Ashoka notes that he sent "envoys" or ambassadors to several heads of state in the region. These envoys were given the task of explaining the benefits of dhamma to these rulers.

On one level, the Ashokan envoy can be understood in terms of furthering Ashoka's desire to spread dhamma to other lands. Ashoka was clearly interested in pursuing an international education project after his turn to Buddhism. But this description of the Ashokan envoys probably understates their role. In a discussion of the *Arthashastra*, Mark McClish and Patrick Olivelle make the following comment about the Kautilyan envoy. They state:

The Arthashastra tells us that the king would sit and deliberate over foreign affairs regularly with his counselors (1.2) and, once a decision has been reached, they would dispatch an envoy. This gives the impression that *the groundwork for all interstate relations, whether they ultimately ended in peace or war, was laid by the diplomatic corps*. Presumably, then, kings would usually signal an intention or negotiate through envoys before other actions were taken. *The strategic exchange of envoys was at the heart of foreign affairs*.[4] (italics added)

To Kaultilya, the sending of envoys is always a step in a state's foreign policy. The dispatching of the envoy is always a strategic move. And while there is no comparable discussion of the envoys in the "Major Rock Edicts"—Ashoka does not describe the inner deliberations of the Mauryan state apparatus in the inscriptions—there is a good probability that the envoys also fulfilled a similar function in the Mauryan realm.[5] On this reading, the sending of envoys by Ashoka to other heads of state in the region is meant to the lay the diplomatic groundwork for future peace.

Interpreted in this way, the role of the Ashokan envoys is to both teach and lay the foundation for Ashoka's new foreign policy. The envoys are trying to convince foreign heads of state that a more peaceful foreign policy is simultaneously moral and prudent.[6] Having said that, it is important to note that Ashoka was not naïve about the prospects of this approach to foreign policy or the use of violent force. He also notes in the thirteenth "Major Rock Edict" that the decision of one group of people to adopt a violent policy could lead to a violent response. The menacing comment Ashoka directs towards the "forest people"—"And the Beloved of the Gods conciliates the forest tribes of his empire, but he warns them that he has power even in his remorse, and he asks them to repent, lest they be killed"—indicates that Ashoka did believe violent conduct is justifiable in response to the violent actions of other people.[7]

The warning shot Ashoka aims at the forest people is important to keep in mind when reflecting on the Ashokan notion of dhamma—as well as the foreign policy internationalism affirmed by Tagore and Sen. Ashoka did not interpret the prohibition against violent conduct in an absolute way; protecting one's own people from violent conduct is a duty that can entail a military response. And this ambiguity regarding Ashokan dhamma shows the difficulties inherent in moving from an ethical perspective to a political perspective. Military science—which, at its core, is a science of violence—is still a necessary science in Ashoka's view.

Chapter 5

TRUST

The warning aimed at the forest people introduces an important nuance into this discussion. In most cases, the ethic of development and the obligations of power sustain similar recommendations. A general injunction—Sen calls it an imperfect duty—to promote the growth and development of all persons is common to each.[8] However, the idea of the obligations of power also contains within it an extra clause about the use of violent force. Persons in positions of power also have a duty to protect the persons living in their own society from armed aggression. Military campaigns—which are always inherently violent—can be justified in terms of this defensive goal.

The relationship between the ethic of development and the obligations of power will be discussed more in part II. Both Tagore and Sen affirm the general duty to promote the growth and development of persons within the context of a foreign policy that allows for wars of self-defense. Tagore and Sen do not interpret Buddha and Ashoka's arguments against violence in an absolute way. But returning to the theme of the Ashokan envoy, one can say the following: the Ashokan envoy is an interesting figure in part because of the goal the envoy is tasked with pursuing. The envoys are both extensions of Ashoka's desire to "teach dhamma" to other people and conduits of state policy. They are diplomats and international educators at the same time. However, the specific method of the Ashokan envoy is also interesting. Building trust through dialogue—along with the assumption that lasting cooperation between heads of state is both possible and feasible—is central to the project of the Ashokan envoy.[9]

From this point of view, the envoy's diplomacy reveals some of Ashoka's underlying ideas about persons and society. There is nothing about human nature or the international system that prevents the heads of state in the region from agreeing to a common foreign policy. Trust is possible between different heads of state. However, it is also clear that there are many hurdles to building this trust. The Mauryan Empire was, for instance, much larger than all its immediate neighbors to the west. These neighboring heads of state must have been keenly aware of the asymmetry of power that existed between the Mauryan realm and their own. Only a lasting commitment to a defensive foreign policy by Ashoka and Ashoka's descendants could overcome the invasion fears of these neighboring states.

At the most basic level, building trust with the neighboring states in the region required putting to rest the fear of invasion. The neighboring heads of state needed to develop the view that Ashoka's new foreign policy endeavor was genuine and stable in the short and medium term. Any backsliding on Ashoka's commitment to a defensive foreign policy would, to put it mildly, be viewed with deep suspicion. I should also point out in this context that Ashoka's war with Kalinga would have made the task of building trust with these neighboring heads of state more difficult. There was a living memory of Ashoka pursuing an expansionist war in the minds of these persons. The envoys would need to overcome this resistance against Ashoka's foreign policy for "conquest by dhamma" to succeed. But communicating the genuine nature of Ashoka's intentions is just the leading edge of the problem of building trust. It is also the case that the Ashokan envoys needed to avoid arousing suspicion and distrust towards the Mauryan Empire in their daily conduct. In particular, the Ashokan envoys could not sow discord between persons or engage in violent conduct to fulfill their mission. The envoys could not exact a toll on the social capital of the societies they were present in. If the envoys engaged in any of these types of behavior, they would undermine Ashoka's foreign policy project. They would cause alarm instead of building trust between neighboring heads of state.

When understood concretely, Ashoka's new foreign policy required a great deal more than open and honest communication. This policy required a lasting commitment to a difficult project by many people in different societies. It is also required the agents of the Mauryan government to avoid the kind of behaviors exhibited by the Kaultiyan spy discussed in the last chapter. Inflaming the divisions between the wealthy and the poor—and undermining the relationships between the head of state and his counselors—would break apart the new regional norms Ashoka was trying to create.

GREEK AND ARAMAIC

The contrast between the Ashokan envoys who teach dhamma and the Kaultiyan secret agent is very large. Instead of using the powers of the state to foster distrust and hatred between groups, Ashoka wanted to create a new and lasting norm of nonviolence in the relation between the states that he was in contact with. Everyone, Ashoka believed, would benefit from this new endeavor. And this helps to explain why Ashoka went to such great lengths to spread his message. In another part of the thirteenth "Major Rock Edict," Ashoka states:

> The Beloved of the Gods considers victory by Dhamma to be the foremost victory. And moreover the Beloved of the Gods has gained this victory on all of his frontiers to a distance of six hundred yojanas [i.e. about 1,500 miles] where reigns the Greek king named Antiochus, and beyond the realm of that Antiochus in the lands of the four kings named Ptolemy, Antigonus, Magas and Alexander; and in the south over the Colas and the Pandyas as far as Ceylon.[10]

In this passage, Ashoka indicates that kings in North Africa, Europe, Ceylon (Sri Lanka) and the subcontinent have been brought over to dhamma by Ashoka's envoys. Ashoka believed norms of nonviolence between the states in the region were in fact established over a large part of the earth. Moreover, some of the "Major Rock Edicts" located in the western part of the Mauryan Empire were inscribed in Greek and Aramaic.[11] By presenting his ideas in the languages of other peoples, Ashoka hoped the principles expressed in the "Major Rock Edicts" would circulate throughout the societies of the near east, North Africa, and the Mediterranean. Ashoka wanted to initiate broader social change along with his international foreign policy project. And if one asks the question "Why did Ashoka do this?" one answer is the following: building trust at the level of persons also diminishes the potential for war. There would be less domestic support for a new war in non-Mauryan territories *if* the persons in these neighboring societies believed in dhamma.

POLITICAL ECONOMY

Ashoka's new foreign policy placed great importance on discussion and reasoning together. Ultimately, "conquest by dhamma" in the thirteenth "Major Rock Edict" comes down to the success or the failure of an international norm-building project. If all the heads of state in the region came to understand war as the last resort of foreign policy, future conflicts like the war against Kalinga could be avoided. But what I would like to do now is to switch perspectives and focus on Mauryan domestic policy. How, exactly, did Ashoka's foreign policy effect internal developments in the Mauryan state?

To begin with, a foreign policy of nonaggression had implications for the political economy of the Mauryan Empire. As Vincent Arthur Smith noted, the size of the military from the time of Chandragupta to the conquest of Kalinga (321–261 BCE) was large. A substantial amount of wealth and natural resources was needed to sustain the standing army that expelled Alexander's generals from India and then expand the Mauryan Empire to its eventual size.[12] But after Ashoka's turn to Buddhism, the situation changed. Smith notes that "Ashoka's peaceful policy probably required a smaller military establishment."[13] And while Smith indicates that this point is an inference on his part, the basic idea is clear. Fewer troops are needed to defend a territory than to prepare for invasion. This is especially true if the Mauryan leader believed he needed to keep one-quarter or one-third of his troops out of an invasion force. By switching to a more defensive posture, it is possible that Ashoka was able to reduce the military establishment by a substantial amount. And if Smith's inference is correct, there would be many other downstream effects of Ashoka's decision. The officials who focused on planning for new conquests could also shift their energies and abilities to other endeavors; the employment of persons within the Mauryan state could evolve. The shift to a more defensive posture would also decrease the natural resources required by the Mauryan army. This is partly because there would be fewer resources needed to sustain a smaller army. But it is also the case that a much larger quantity of natural resources is required to sustain an army in territories far removed from the Mauryan state—because the supply chain itself must be provisioned and protected. From these points of view, keeping a remnant standing army near home requires less.

PUBLIC WORKS

The change of focus in Ashoka's foreign policy most likely affected the political economy of the Mauryan Empire. It freed up the talents of persons and conserved the natural resources and the wealth of the Mauryan state. But it is not just a matter of resource use foregone. This change also created the opportunity to fund a new series of state initiatives. A large amount of the social product could be directed to other goals. Moreover, it is clear from the testimony of the remaining inscriptions of the "Major Rock Edicts" that Ashoka did spend considerable sums on public works projects throughout the Mauryan realm after his turn to Buddhism. Improving the quality of life of the civilian populace became a central focus of Ashokan policy.

Smith summarizes the references to Ashoka's public projects in the inscriptions—as well as evidence about these projects gathered from other historical sources—in the following way:

> Within (Ashoka's) own dominions he provided for the comfort of man and beast by the plantation of shade-giving and fruit-bearing trees, the digging of wells, and the erection of rest houses and watering places at convenient intervals along the high roads. He devoted special attention to elaborate arrangements for the care and healing of the sick, and for the cultivation of and dissemination of medicinal herbs and roots in the territories of foreign allied sovereigns and as well as within the limits of the empire. Although the word "hospitals" does not occur in the edicts, such institutions must have been included in his arrangements, and the remarkable free hospital which the Chinese pilgrim (Fa-hien) found working at Pataliputra six and a half centuries later doubtless was a continuation of Asoka's foundation. The curious animal hospitals which still exist in Surat and certain other cities in Western India also may be regarded as survivals of Asoka's institutions.[14]

The scale of these projects is significant. The length of the roads that united the different regions of the subcontinent at this time was large; improving their quality would require a significant amount of labor and resources. Likewise, establishing the provision of medical care to persons and animals across the Mauryan Empire as well as the neighboring regions was a formidable challenge. A considerable expenditure of resources would be required to achieve these goals, even in part. But it is not just the sheer size of these projects that makes them so distinctive. The primary way Ashoka justifies these projects in the "Major Rock Edicts" is through the idea of dhamma. A concern with the protection of persons and animals living in the Mauryan realm is evident here.

Interpreted in this way, Buddhist notions of dhamma effected the kind of public projects Ashoka pursued. The life of persons, the life of animals, and the shape of the land itself was changed through these interventions. Ashoka, one might say, hoped to create a landscape of metta in India. Ashoka's focus on the quality of the life of animals is especially noteworthy in this context. Animals—like persons—are vulnerable to dehydration and sickness. Placing wells along the highways relieved animal suffering, as did the creation of animal hospitals and the provision of medicinal herbs. The concern with the quality of life of both persons and animals is evident in these passages. But perhaps the most remarkable expression of Ashoka's concern with animals is presented in the first "Major Rock Edict." Ashoka states:

> Formerly in the kitchens of the Beloved of the Gods, the King Piyadassi, many hundreds of thousands of animals were killed daily for meat. But now at the time of writing of this inscription on Dhamma, only three animals are killed, two peacocks and a deer, and the dear not invariably. Even these animals will not be killed in the future.[15]

The observation Ashoka makes here is startling. The scale of the violence towards animals during a single day in Ashoka's kitchens was comparable to—or larger than—the scale of the violence towards the adversary soldiers during the war against Kalinga. And while it is not certain what exactly Ashoka is referring to in this passage—is he talking about the number of animals killed to sustain the standing army of the Mauryan Empire? Or the entire Mauryan bureaucracy including the royal house as well as the army? Or some other combination?—a substantial change of the daily practice in Ashoka's kitchens would be needed to accomplish this goal at the scale Ashoka is referencing in the inscription. New animal husbandry and agricultural practices must have come into being in response to these changes.

RESPECTFUL DEBATE

As can be seen from this discussion, the change in political economy initiated by Ashoka altered the trajectory of the Mauryan Empire across a range of issues. When Tagore, in *The Religion of Man*, draws attention to the "numerous efforts of public beneficence" set in motion by "Buddha's teachings in India" he is referring to the policies of the Mauryan emperor, among other people.[16]

Ashoka's concern with acts of public beneficence is clear from the inscriptions. Redirecting the energies of a large and powerful state away from war can accomplish a great deal for the persons and other forms of life in that society and the larger region. Much is made possible by a more peaceful foreign policy. But a distinctive form of public beneficence in the inscriptions is connected to Ashoka's thoughts about public reasoning. Ashoka believed improvements in the quality of public reasoning in society also contributed to dhamma. Reforming the way persons deliberated in public was on par with improvements in health care, the public food supply, access to water, access to shade, and the diminishment of violence towards persons and animals in Ashoka's thinking.

This point can be made more precise. Sen, in *The Argumentative Indian*, notes that something like Robert's rules of order are articulated by Ashoka.[17] In particular, Sen notes that Ashoka asked his subjects in the twelfth "Major Rock Edict" at Erragudi to frame their public statements in a particular way. Sen states:

> (Ashoka) demanded, for example, "restraint in regard to speech, so that there should be no extolment of one's own sect or disparagement of other sects on inappropriate occasions, and it should be moderate even on appropriate occasions." Even when engaged in arguing, "other sects should be duly honored in every way on all occasions."[18]

The content of the twelfth "Major Rock Edict" Sen cites in this passage is centered on the public statements of the person. Ashoka asks the speakers at public gatherings to avoid inciting anger and hatred with their words. A kind of neutrality regarding religious group identity or nonidentity is often called for when speaking in public. But this neutrality concerning identity does not mean the speaker must give up argument and debate. Reasoned argument is permitted if it is respectful. A person can criticize a point of view while avoiding inflammatory language.

In the twelfth "Major Rock Edict," the way persons speak to each other creates a background of trust within the foreground of argument and debate. It establishes a sense of respect in the discussion—even as these persons give voice to their beliefs and disagreements. And from this point of view, Ashoka's recommendations appear to echo ideas described in the Sutta Nipata discussed in chapter 1. In particular, Buddha's critique of sectarianism and incendiary public speech seems to inform Ashoka's words. The perspective of the "Chapter of the Eights"—as well as longer discourses like the Kalama Sutta—is active here.[19] I should also point out that Ashoka's recommendations differ from the speech of the Kaultiyan spy who is trying to inflame hatreds and divisions with his or her words. Both the Kaultiyan spy and the sectarian speaker share a venomous rhetoric, even though their underlying intentions and motives are distinct.

Ashoka's twelfth "Major Rock Edict" indicates the need to avoid damaging statements about the different sects living in society. Like Buddha, the disaggregation of public debate from hostile sectarian speech is a key feature of the political culture Ashoka was trying to create. Equally important, in Sen's view, is the way in which Ashoka seeks to establish his claim. Ashoka gives an example of public reasoning in the twelfth "Major Rock Edict," creating a kind of modified dialogue with his subjects in the inscriptions. For instance, at one point in the discussion Ashoka states:

> Depreciation should be for specific reasons only because the sects of other people all deserve reverence for one reason or another.[20]

Here Ashoka indicates that he is opposed to general indictments of a group of people. The notion that a sect is in total error on every subject is both false and harmful. There is a distinction between human fallibility and absolute concepts of sectarian disparagement in Ashoka's thought. Nor is this Ashoka's last word on the matter. Ashoka continues:

> For he who does reverence to his own sect while disparaging the sects of others, wholly in attachment to his own sect, in reality inflicts, by such conduct, *the severest injury on his own sect.*'[21] (italics added)

The ideas presented in this passage are again reminiscent of the Sutta Nipata. Insulting the traditions of other people is harmful in multiple ways. It causes the insulted persons to feel the emotions of anger or fear. However, it also, as Sen notes, causes these insulted persons to lose confidence in the speaker and the sect they belong to.[22] The ability to trust a group is undermined when prominent figures in that group speak in a disparaging way.

The echoes of Buddha's teachings about public reasoning stand out in Sen's discussion of Ashoka. All persons are hurt by sectarian speech—including the speaker. Mutual conflict and hostility are the fruits of this form of conduct. Indeed, part of the reason Ashoka became so horrified with the war against Kalinga is connected to the way Ashoka came to understand the lives of the persons who belong to different religious traditions. This is especially evident in the passage on the horrors of war from the thirteenth "Major Rock Edict" discussed in chapter 4. To recall, Ashoka states:

> What is even more deplorable to the Beloved of the Gods, *is that those who dwell there, whether brahmins, sramanas, or those of other sects*, or household-ers who show obedience to their superiors, obedience to mother and father, obedience to their teachers and behave well and devotedly towards their friends, acquaintances, colleagues, relatives, slaves, and servants—all suffer violence, murder and separation from their loved ones.[23] (italics added)

In this passage, Brahmins, *sramanas* (i.e., "ascetic renunciants" such as Buddhists, Jains, Ajivikis) and the members of other sects are described in terms of their capacity to love and their personal relationships of love and loyalty as well as their vulnerability to suffering. There is a common human-ity that cuts across the boundaries of family, sect, and political territory in this passage.

ASHOKA AND THE FOREIGN POLICY INTERNATIONALISM OF TAGORE AND SEN

In this chapter, I have discussed some of the norms Ashoka attempted to establish in the Mauryan Empire after the war with Kalinga. Ashoka did not follow the path of Alexander the Great and pursue territories in distant lands after his turn to Buddhism. Instead, Ashoka probably maintained an army at a reduced size for defensive purposes only after this change in priorities. Equally important, Ashoka tried to convince future Mauryan leaders to avoid war as much as possible. Ashoka also sent envoys to other heads of state to speak about the benefits of diminishing war. The creation of a more peaceful regional system was part of his goal.

Ashoka's reign brought some of Buddha's teachings into the political domain. When the power of the state is informed by the notion of the obli-gations of power the lives of many persons can be much improved. The suffering that comes with a violent, society-wide, loss of loved ones can be avoided—if all of the heads of state in the region adopt a foreign policy informed by dhamma. However, while making this point it is important to keep in mind the ambiguity about Ashoka's dhamma that was also identified in this chapter. In Ashoka's view, the head of state can resort to violence in order to protect his own people from violent aggression. There is still a place for a standing army and the science of warfare in Ashoka's thinking. Askoka's policy of diminishing war in the wider region described in the "Major Rock Edicts" was compatible with a notion of armed self-defense.

The goal of Ashoka's foreign policy as well as the ambiguity about dhamma that has been identified in the "Major Rock Edicts" will reappear again in the foreign policy internationalism of Tagore and Sen. While both thinkers opposed wars of territorial expansion and supported a coordinated approach to foreign policy, neither thinker advocates for the complete disarmament of a people. As Sen notes, "Tagore was not as uncompromisingly pacifist as Mahatma Gandhi."[24] Nor, for that matter, is Sen. The broader goal of diminishing war in the international system is combined with an understanding of—and a commitment to—a people's self-defense.

NOTES

1. Romila Thapar, *Ashoka and the Decline of the Mauryas* (Oxford: Oxford University Press, 1997), 256–57.

2. For all of Ashoka's innovations, he did not think outside of the confines of a hereditary monarchy when imagining the future in the "Major Rock Edicts": there is no mention of the idea of democracy or anything like it in the inscriptions. Likewise, the idea that women could rule was also outside of the thinking expressed in the "Major Rock Edicts."

3. Consider the Melian dialogue in Thucydides' *History of the Peloponnesian War* (352) in *The Landmark Thucydides: A Comprehensive Guide to the Peloponnesian War* in this context. In this dialogue, the representatives of militarily powerful Athens speak to the militarily weak Melians and say: "right [justice] only exists between equals" and "the strong take what they can and the weak suffer what they must." It is clear from this passage that the Athenian concept of justice depends on the assessment of the military power of several different states, relative to each other. For further discussion of the Melian dialogue, see Leavitt, *The Foreign Policy of John Rawls and Amartya Sen* (Lanham, MD: Lexington Books, 2013), 88–89.

4. Mark McClish and Patrick Olivelle, eds. and trans., *The Arthashastra: Selections from the Classic Work on Indian Statecraft* (Indianapolis, IN: Hackett, 2012), 124.

5. As noted in chapter 4, the relationship between the Arthashastra and the Mauryan period is contested. Sen believes the Arthashastra can be dated back to the fourth century BCE and the beginning of Chandragupta's reign. McClish and Olivelle argue for a much later date of composition. My own thought is that the Mauryan Empire—which itself was very large and could only be held together by an elaborate communication system—also relied on a diplomatic corps for the day-to-day functioning of its foreign policy. The envoys were a part of this foreign policy system, but their exact role within the Mauryan bureaucracy is not known with certainty. Instead, the role of envoys discussed in the text is an inference that is compatible with existing facts.

6. The idea that foreign policy must be moral to also be prudent is strongly defended by Sen in *The Argumentative Indian* and is central to his reading of Tagore's *Nationalism*. For more on this idea, see chapters 7 and 9.

7. Romila Thapar, *Ashoka and the Decline of the Mauryas*, 256.

8. Amartya Sen, *The Idea of Justice* (Cambridge, MA: The Belknap Press of Harvard University Press, 2009).

9. Again, consider the contrast with the Melian dialogue discussed in note 3 on this point.

10. Romila Thapar, *Ashoka and the Decline of the Mauryas*, 256.

11. Ibid., 276–78.

12. Vincent Arthur Smith, *Asoka: the Buddhist Emperor of India* (Delhi: S. Chand, 1909), 102.

13. Ibid., 102.

14. Ibid, 66. The second "Major Rock Edict" is the source for many of these claims.

15. Romila Thapar, *Ashoka and the Decline of the Mauryas*, 250. In the first "Major Rock Edict" Ashoka inverts the action of King Okkaka in the Brahmanadhammika Sutta. It is impossible to know with certainty if Ashoka was aware of—yet alone responding to—this early Buddhist discourse in the inscription.

16. See introduction, note 6.

17. Amartya Sen, *The Argumentative Indian: Writings on Indian History, Culture and Identity* (New York: Picador, 2005), 16.

18. Ibid., 16.

19. For more on Buddha's critique of sectarianism in the Sutta Nipata, see chapter 1.

20. Sen, *The Argumentative Indian*, 18.

21. Ibid., 18. The references to Buddhism in the "Minor Rock Edicts," combined with the lack of references to Buddha in the "Major Rock Edicts," can be explained in terms of Ashoka's injunction to avoid references to sect in the twelfth "Major Rock Edict." If this is the case, Ashoka is also following the rules for public discussion he is asking the people to consider in the "Major Rock Edicts."

22. Sen, *The Idea of Justice*, 75.

23. See introduction, note 31.

24. Sen, *The Argumentative Indian*, 252.

Conclusion to Part I

As discussed in the introduction, a variant of the idea of the obligations of power is presented in the Brhadaranyaka Upanishad. In particular, the idea that persons in positions of power have a special obligation to avoid abuses of power and promote the growth and development of other living things is articulated in this text. However, the Upanishadic thinker justifies this ethical and legal idea through the framework of a speculative narrative about the beginning of the world as well as the legal and social order. According to the Upanishadic thinker, Brahman created the Law or dharma. When persons avoid abuses of power and promote the growth and development of living things, they are creating a new world within the world.

The Upanishadic teacher anchors Law and the obligations of power in the divine creative act. But as Tagore and Sen note, the early Buddhist discourses develop a different approach to these ideas. In the Buddhist formulation, the obligation to avoid abuses of power and promote the growth and development of other living things is founded on perceptions that are available to all human beings. Observation and experience are central to Buddha's thoughts about how to live. As a consequence, Buddha neither affirms nor denies speculative narratives like the one found in Brhadaranyaka Upanishad. Buddha does not ground his ethical thinking in the divine creative act.

To Tagore and Sen, Buddha's ethical and legal thought remained within the human sphere. Moreover, while it is the case that the context of Ashoka's "Major Rock Edicts" is distinct from the context of the Sutta Nipata—Ashoka was the ruler of the Mauryan Empire, a very large and powerful state—the idea of the obligations of power is still evident in Ashoka's inscriptions. The moral critique of war in the "Major Rock Edicts"—as well as Ashoka's efforts to teach dhamma to all people—brought what Sen calls "the non-violent teachings of Gautama Buddha" into the political sphere.[1]

The impression that emerges from the introduction and part I, then, is one of ethical diversity and evolution. There are different variants of the idea of the obligations of power articulated in the early Indian classical period. The Brhadaranyaka Upanishad, the Sutta Nipata, and the Ashokan inscriptions each defend the idea that it is important to avoid abuses of power while

103

promoting the growth and development of living things. However, it is also clear from the discussion in part I that Tagore and Sen elevate the human sphere and human reasoning in their approach to ethical obligation. The empiricism of Buddha—as well as Buddha's reasoned critique of sectarianism, class bias, and abuses of power—is central to Tagore and Sen's ethical thought. The Metta Sutta is especially relevant to both thinkers. Tagore emphasizes the need to cultivate friendly-feeling or loving kindness towards all living things in his reading of the Metta Sutta. Sen likewise finds the notion of a human obligation towards animals and persons in the Metta Sutta. In Sen's reading, the adult human being can do things for a child which the child itself cannot do. For both thinkers, it is the mentality of the adult who promotes the growth and development of persons and other forms of life that Buddha is trying to spread.

NOTE

1. See introduction, note 30.

PART II

A Development Ethic

Chapter 6

Living Reality

Part I examined Tagore and Sen's interpretation of the Sutta Nipata. The idea of the obligations of power—as well as the themes of human equality and freedom—are central to the way both thinkers describe Buddha's ethical teaching. I also emphasized Tagore and Sen's interpretation of Ashoka's "Major Rock Edicts" in this context. The critique of sectarianism in the "Major Rock Edicts"—as well as Ashoka's international educational project, his public work projects, and his focus on the alleviation of human and animal suffering—developed many of Buddha's ethical concerns in a political context. Like Ashoka, Tagore and Sen defend an ethic of development while maintaining the need for societies to pursue collective strategies of self-defense.

Tagore and Sen clearly ground many of their ideas in the early Indian classical period. Buddha and Ashoka are very important figures in their writings. In part II, I speak to some of the ways Tagore and Sen use the ideas of Buddha and Ashoka in their own arguments and analyses, beginning with the theme of education in Tagore's writings. Tagore hoped to initiate a new program of primary schooling for all children living in India and around the world. Like Buddha and Ashoka, Tagore focused on the mental and emotional development of all people.

SHANTINIKETAN

Judging by his own testimony, Tagore had strong ideas about primary schooling from an early age. In the essay "My School," Tagore recounts in some detail the feeling of alienation he experienced when he was uprooted from his home and the environment he was accustomed to and forced into a barren room to listen to teachers who he described as "living gramophones."[1] The procedure of rote memorization, the noninteractive stance of the teachers,

and the lifeless quality of the room all struck the young Tagore as a point-
less imposition.

Tagore's distaste for the kind of instruction he received at an early age
continued into his adulthood. From the age of thirteen onward, Tagore was
mostly self-taught.[2] And yet it is also clear that these initial experiences of
school remained with Tagore throughout his life. When Tagore founded his
own primary school at Shantiniketan (the "place of peace") in 1901 at the age
of forty he vowed it would be quite different from the one he experienced.[3]
Tagore did not want his primary school to simply repeat the mechanical form
of instruction he received as a child.

Tagore indicates in "My School" that he came into his first year of teaching at Shantiniketan with a strong sense of what he wanted to avoid. Both
the setting and the educational methods of his school would diverge from
his earlier experience. In particular, Tagore decided his school should mostly
be "open air" and the specific location for his classes was determined by the
expansive view of the sky it afforded.[4] Tagore also decided to employ an educational method that was participatory in nature and open to improvisation.
In Tagore's words:

> My idea was that education should be a part of life itself and must not be
> detached from it or made abstract . . . in all of their activities I tried to put before
> (the children) something that would be interesting to them. I tried to arouse their
> interests in all things, in nature's beauty and the surrounding villages and also
> in literature, through play-acting, through listening to music in a natural man-
> ner, not through merely class teaching. . . . And this was my method. I knew the
> children's mind. Their subconscious mind is more active than the conscious one,
> and therefore the important thing is to surround them with all kinds of activities
> which could stimulate their minds and gradually arouse their interests.[5]

The idea Tagore describes in this passage is striking. Instead of creating a
room deprived of sensory stimulus in the hope of reducing distractions and
encouraging focus and memorization, Tagore wanted to build his lessons
off the experience of natural beauty and human relation. He put traveling to
nearby villages, interactive play and storytelling into the day while trying to
avoid deadening routine.

Tagore's educational method as described in "My School" is clearly based
on the idea of enriching experience. The practice of imposing austerity on
children is anathema to Tagore.[6] Tagore's comment about the conscious and
subconscious mind of the child in this passage from "My School" is also
interesting. In Tagore's usage, the conscious mind is the person's perceptions
and memories as well as their focus. It is the form of awareness that is most
associated with lasting choices and decisions. The subconscious mind, in

turn, is rooted in the person's health but is perhaps best described as a kind of exuberant curiosity or wonder. The subconscious mind is the sense of interest in the world that is informing the child's awareness. Moreover, when Tagore claims that a child's "subconscious mind is more active than the conscious one" he is stating that the child's exuberant curiosity and desire for play is highly expressed while the long-term goal-forming and goal-pursuing capabilities are less developed. Children also have fewer memories and conceptual habits or models to draw on when they interpret the world.

GITANJALI

Tagore's educational principles were based entirely on his own experience with children, his reading and his conversations with others. Tagore notes that he had no special academic expertise or training to bring to bear on the question of how to teach children.[7] It is clear, however, that Tagore's understanding of the conscious and subconscious mind is nuanced and resistant to overly reductive ideas about learning and development. The mind is not just a storehouse of information in Tagore's description.

Tagore's comments about the conscious and subconscious mind in the passage from "My School" are framed in terms of the life of children. In childhood, the subconscious mind is predominant. Stimulating the child's subconscious mind is the entryway into more careful reasoning about the world. In other texts, however, Tagore speaks to the importance of the subconscious mind in the life of the adult. In his Nobel Prize acceptance speech Tagore notes the way his own subconscious mind was nourished by the experience of teaching children at Shantiniketan. In a moving passage, Tagore states:

> The vigor and the joy of children, their chats and songs filled the air with a spirit of delight, which I drank every day I was there. And in the evening during the sunset hour I often used to sit alone watching the trees of the shadowing avenue, and in the silence of the afternoon I could hear distinctly the voices of children coming up in the air, and it seemed to me that these shouts and songs and glad voices were like those trees, which come out from the heart of the earth like fountains towards the bosom of the infinite sky. And it symbolized, it brought before my mind the whole cry of human life, all expressions of joy and aspirations of men rising from the heart of Humanity up to this sky. I could see that, and I knew that we also, the grown-up children, send up our cries of aspiration to the infinite. I felt it in my heart of hearts . . . In this atmosphere and in this environment I used to write my poems *Gitanjali*.[8]

The set of associations in this passage are numerous and highly interesting. The daily experience of the joy of children—the exuberant curiosity and expressiveness of his students in the context of a beautiful natural setting—entered Tagore's spirit and helped him to create. He drank in the atmosphere of his school and this water nourished his mind. The poems of *Gitanjali* grew out of this daily experience. The symbolism of the tree in the passage is also striking. In Tagore's description the waving and tinkling of the leaves in the wind and the sun is like a bubbling fountain; it is a swaying movement of sound, color, and varying light that bursts out from the earth. But this description of the tree, in turn, is woven into Tagore's understanding of the voices of the children in their singing and Tagore's own voice in *Gitanjali*. A spirit of joyful life is common to each.

THE CLEAR STREAM OF REASON

In the Nobel speech, Tagore indicates that the daily experience of his students in an open-air school made possible new developments in his poetry and music. Tagore's school created the atmosphere within which this work was composed. In his own way, then, Tagore is thanking his students in this passage from the Nobel Prize acceptance speech. His students helped him achieve this award.

Tagore's passage on the origins of *Gitanjali* reveals a great deal about his understanding of the person. Individuals need experiences of beauty and social relation to truly satisfy their personalities and to create. Abstract reasoning by itself is not enough. But in reflecting on this aspect of Tagore's thinking—the great importance Tagore attaches to the subconscious mind in the life of children and adults—it is important to avoid overly narrow characterizations of what Tagore was trying to accomplish in his school. Nourishing the subconscious mind of children is essential to the growth and development of the child. But this connected to Tagore's broader desire to develop his students' capabilities in reading, writing, mathematics and science.[9] He also encouraged the agency of his students and tried to give them the confidence to question ideas and beliefs.

Tagore makes this point in a variety of ways in his writings. The development of every individual's capacity to reason is a recurring theme in Tagore's works. But one of the clearest expressions of this aspect of Tagore's thought is found in *Gitanjali*. In the thirty-fifth poem of *Gitanjali*—which is, in Sen's judgment, the most important poem in this work—Tagore sings:

> Where the mind is without fear and the head is held high;
> Where knowledge is free;

Where the world is not broken up into fragments by narrow domes-
tic walls;
Where words come out of the depth of truth;
Where tireless striving stretches its arms to perfection;
Where the clear stream of reason has not lost its way into the
Dreary desert sand of dead habit;
Where the mind is lead forward by thee into ever-widening thought
and action –
Into that heaven of freedom, my Father, let my country awake.[10]

The thirty-fifth poem of *Gitanjali* does not contain the word "school" or
"university." No specific institution of learning is named. Still, the ideas
articulated in the poem—the focus on knowledge, truth, reason, and a mind
that is both confident and untouched by fear, as well as the poem's emphasis
on a world without walls and confining divisions—can also be associated
with the environment Tagore tried to create at Shantiniketan. The "atmosphere of freedom" Tagore experienced in his open-air school described in
the Nobel speech and the "heaven of freedom" described in this poem from
Gitanjali are closely related. Tagore's use of water as a symbol for new life
in the poem also closely parallels the water imagery Tagore later used in
the Nobel acceptance speech. Tagore believes "the clear stream of reason"
can gradually overcome the static forces of "dead habit" in Indian society.
For Tagore, critical reasoning is like the life-giving waters of a river cutting
through the desert.

The ideas articulated in the thirty-fifth poem of *Gitanjali* further develop
Tagore's thoughts about education. Encouraging persons to reason in freedom—breaking down the "narrow domestic walls" that isolate persons from
each other and from nature—is affirmed in this poem in the strongest of
terms. Like Buddha and Ashoka before him, Tagore believed better reasoning
can improve Indian society in several ways. Equally important, in this context, is the social and political significance Tagore attaches to public debate
and public reasoning at the end of the poem. Tagore hopes the freedom India
will awaken to one day is the freedom of reason. A society where all persons
can pursue knowledge and critically debate together in the open, in public,
is the society Tagore hopes India will become. The discussions Buddha had
with others—as well as Ashoka's attempt to teach dhamma to all Mauryan
persons through the inscriptions—culminates in Tagore's thoughts about
neighborhood schools for all Indian children. Teaching and learning, through
discussion and play, is the bedrock foundation for the India Tagore was trying to build.

BRITISH EDUCATIONAL POLICY

The thirty-fifth poem of *Gitanjali* affirms the idea of reasoning on an individual and a social level. Tagore hopes that India will become a more enlightened society, where persons are encouraged to voice their reasoned criticisms and pursue new endeavors. The importance of public reasoning is clearly expressed in this poem. And while it might be tempting to interpret the last line of the poem as the expression of an impossible or unattainable dream this was clearly not Tagore's intention. The creation of a system of primary schools for all Indian children could bring India a step closer to the freedom Tagore is describing in the last verse. Tagore believed all persons in India should experience the atmosphere of Shantiniketan.

Interpreted in this way, the shift from the present tense to the future tense in the last line of the poem is not meant to be an expression of utopian longing. Instead, it communicates a criticism to the reader. The future Tagore is hoping for in the last line of the poem is within reach, but it is also far removed from India's present. A great many Indian persons have not experienced the type of freedom Tagore is describing in this poem. As such the poem implicitly criticizes British educational policy. The poem opens up a contrast between Tagore's stance towards Indian children and the attitude towards Indian children and Indian persons expressed in the policies of the British Raj.

The social realities Tagore draws attention to in the last line of the poem is only hinted at. As a rule, the moments of criticism in *Gitanjali*—and there are many such moments—are not developed in a sustained way.[11] This does not mean Tagore's implicit criticism at the end of this poem should be dismissed. The educational attainments of Indian persons under British governance at this time were shockingly low. In 1911, 11 percent of all Indian males could read, while the literacy rate for Indian females was 1 percent.[12] Meanwhile, great strides were being made in Britain on the question of literacy during this period. Britain was moving towards universal primary schooling at the beginning of the twentieth century. And this startling division in outcomes in turn poses the key question of "Why?" What belief or set of beliefs encouraged British policymakers to affirm the mental lives of English children while neglecting the mental lives of Indian children? Why, exactly, were British authorities so unwilling to ensure Indian children access to primary schooling? It is this probing question that Tagore points to in the last line of the poem.

Tagore does not directly answer the question the thirty-fifth poem raises within *Gitanjali*. This question is, however, explicitly addressed in *Nationalism*. In a strident passage, Tagore states:

The portion of education allotted to us is so raggedly insufficient that it ought to outrage the sense of decency of a Western humanity. We have seen in these countries how the people are encouraged and trained and given every facility to fit themselves for the great movements of commerce and industry spreading over the world, while in India the only assistance we get is merely to be jeered at by the Nation for lagging behind. While depriving us of our opportunities and reducing our education to a minimum required for conducting a foreign government, this Nation pacifies its conscience by calling us names, by sedulously giving currency to the arrogant cynicism that East is East and West is West and never the twain shall meet.[13]

Here Tagore traces British educational policy in India back to its foreign policy imperatives. The British wanted to control and exploit India to maintain their empire. British officials were mainly concerned with the education of a class of civil servants that made this control and exploitation more efficient. As a consequence, the vast majority of Indian children were ignored by this focus. Tagore also indicates that racial prejudice played an important role in rationalizing this policy decision.

CULTIVATING IGNORANCE

The passage on British educational priorities in *Nationalism* sheds additional light on the thirty-fifth poem of *Gitanjali*. Tagore is drawing on his own experiences at Shantiniketan in this poem. But he is also rejecting the British colonial understanding of Indian children and Indian persons as mentally incapable. An educational policy based on the desire to cultivate ignorance in a population—in order to better control and exploit that population—is highly unjust.[14] The image of the "mind free of fear" and "the head held high" in the first verse of the poem takes on greater significance when understood against the backdrop of the racially charged name-calling of British officials.

The abuse of power inherent in British educational policy in India was appalling to Tagore. British policy makers did not understand themselves as having a duty to promote the capabilities of Indian children or satisfy the Indian child's need for joy and play. The motives of their foreign policy had nothing in common with the international educational project pursued by Ashoka. Instead, Indian persons were mostly understood as a permanent underclass of laborers and soldiers in the Empire.[15] It is, Tagore believes, a violation of the obligations of power to treat persons this way.

PRAYER HALLS

Tagore believed the neglect of the mental and emotional abilities of Indian children amounted to a colossal injustice. The difference between Tagore's understanding of Indian children and, for instance, the British political leader Winston Churchill's understanding of Indian children is extraordinarily large.[16] But Tagore's criticism of British educational policy goes well beyond this point. Tagore thought the failure to educate Indian children in primary schools of good quality also had the effect of strengthening India's internal divisions. The role of caste prejudice and sectarian concepts of impurity in Indian society was enhanced by British rule.

The connection between the British failure to educate Indian persons and the enhancement of India's internal divisions is made in several ways within Tagore's writings. As a rule, themes in Tagore's poetry and his essays and his letters cross-pollinate each other. Similar ideas keep appearing in the different genres of his art and thought. But one especially prominent example of Tagore's concern here is his letter to Mahatma Gandhi in March of 1933. The theme of education is central to this correspondence.

Tagore begins this letter with a comment about the exclusionary aspect of temple worship which Gandhi had asked him about. Tagore states:

> It is needless to say that I do not at all relish the idea of divinity being enclosed in a brick-and-mortar temple for the special purpose of exploitation by a particular group of people.[17]

In this passage, Tagore is critical of the idea of temple worship. Localizing divinity in a specific place—and then excluding many people from access to that place, on the grounds that they are supposedly "impure" or "polluting"—is unjust. It is harmful to Dalit persons (the term Dalit means "untouchable") and reinforces the sense of a caste hierarchy within Indian society.[18] It is also harmful to Muslim persons and members of other non-Hindu religious groups who were also excluded from Hindu temple worship based on the supposed impurity of their bodies.[19]

Tagore's analysis of the effects of temple worship on Indian society was exact and unsparing. Like Buddha before him, Tagore believed the concept of impurity was creating several different types of divisions in Indian society out of thin air. The initial attitude Aggika displays towards Buddha in the Vasala Sutta was still very much alive in the British colonial period.[20] Tagore further develops this point in a subsequent passage. Tagore states:

> The traditional idea of Godhead and conventional forms of worship hardly lay emphasis upon the moral worth of religious practices; their essential value lies

in the conformity to custom which creates in the minds of the worshipers an abstract sense of sanctity and sanction. When we argue with them in the name of justice and humanity it is contemptuously ignored for as I have said the moral appeal of the cause has no meaning for them and you know that there are practices and legends connected with a number of our sectarian creeds and practices which are ignoble and irrational.[21]

The primary intent in this passage is descriptive. When a group of persons perform the same actions in the same space for many years, a common practice or custom is formed. In this situation, the memories of different persons—as well as the expectations these persons develop about the way the future should be—are coordinated around a specific routine. A large part of the person's mental and emotional life becomes centered on the exclusionary practice of temple worship. But a second part of this passage is more comparative in nature; it focuses on what is missing in the rituals of temple worship. In particular, Tagore notes that the actions performed in exclusionary temple worship—and the words recited in exclusionary temple worship—are rarely connected to the idea of the universal worth of all persons. Notions of justice or a common humanity are often absent from these routines. Nor, Tagore states, do the rituals involved in temple worship encourage critical reasoning or an open attitude towards persons whose ideas are different. In Tagore's view, there are important shortcomings and omissions in this approach to the teaching of children and adults. I should also point out in this context that Tagore is responding to the problem of exclusionary temple worship in *The Religion of Man*. When Tagore notes that "It is significant that all great religions have their historic origins in persons who represented in their life a truth which was not cosmic and unmoral, but human and good"—and when Tagore spends so much time describing the teachings of the Upanishads and Buddha in this and other texts—he is also criticizing hostile and exclusionary forms of sectarian worship in India.[22] The theme in the "Letter to Gandhi" is also informing his English language works.

THE REFORMER

The problem Tagore draws attention to in the letter to Gandhi is significant. Sectarian temple worship may seem benign, but Tagore believes it fosters an exclusionary sense of identity that is closed to criticism. "Contemptuously ignoring" the voice of other people is a harmful outgrowth of the attitude of sectarian pride.

The first section of Tagore's letter to Gandhi is briskly stated but its message is stark and somewhat grim. Tagore believes many sectarian practices and doctrines are "irrational and ignoble." And yet there are features of the mental and emotional life of these persons that makes them resistant to change. Tagore indicates that it will take a long time to make headway here. Nevertheless, Tagore does not lose heart on this point. The second part of the letter to Gandhi outlines "the methods" Tagore believes must be employed to effect positive change.[23] In a passage that is important for understanding Tagore's views about social progress, he states:

> A reformer in dealing with such morally wrong traditions cannot adopt coercion and yet as in fighting other wrong and harmful customs he must exert moral force and constantly seek to rectify them. This fight is necessary.[24]

In this passage, Tagore repudiates violence as a response to harmful sectarian traditions. Destroying temples and jailing religious leaders and followers is not the answer. As Tagore puts it in a letter to his friend Charles Freer Andrews: "I am frightened of an abstraction which is ready to ignore living reality."[25] No political program that saw a human life as a thing to violently discard was acceptable to Tagore. This, however, does not mean Tagore believed these traditions should go unchallenged. Tagore indicates that these sectarian practices must be constantly criticized as harmful in public. The idea that any person is "impure"—and that contact with that person is "polluting," either in a temple or in daily life—must be resisted. Becoming aware of a problem is the first step in effecting change.[26]

Like Buddha, Tagore believed the force of public moral argument—and not the threat of violence and the shedding of blood—is necessary when confronting harmful sectarian practices. But Tagore also believed that it was not enough to simply criticize a practice in public; something more positive needed to be put in its place. And in this context Tagore points to some of the practices he developed at his school in Shantiniketan. In particular, he tells Gandhi that the Shantinketan prayer hall "is open to all peoples of every faith."[27] No one is excluded from this space based on his or her family background or their religious or nonreligious beliefs. As such, the prayer hall at Shantiniketan is fundamentally different from the sectarian temple. It creates a common sense of belonging and significance in the lives of children and adults. The services held in the prayer hall also makes explicit the idea that all persons have equal worth. The ideas Tagore discussed in *The Religion of Man*—as well as what Sen calls Tagore's "unusually nondenominational" religious beliefs—could also gain a hearing in this space.[28]

THE INDIAN INDEPENDENCE MOVEMENT

Tagore's comment about the prayer hall in his letter to Gandhi is carefully thought through. Instead of building multiple separate and discrete places for persons to worship, thereby recreating a landscape of exclusion within Shantiniketan, Tagore tried to create a setting where persons of different faiths could mingle together in song and reflection on the moral worth of all persons. Tagore wanted to create a social space that was free from sectarian identity at his school. But even the prayer hall—which Tagore believes is a substantial improvement on the excluding temple—is not without its drawbacks. Tagore notes that:

> Our religious service could as well take place under the trees, its truth and sacredness would not at all be affected but in fact enhanced by such an environment.[29]

Here, Tagore again voices his interest in the idea of "open air" gatherings. The continual impressions of the forest and the sky on the young children and the adult children would nourish each person's subconscious mind in a way no human construction can do. The experience of the swaying trees and the clouds and the light would add to the words about justice and humanity communicated in the service.

Tagore's thoughts on the prayer hall—and the service in the forest—indicate the depth of the reform Tagore was trying to achieve in his school. A primary school can help children learn to read and write. It can enhance a person's capabilities in math and science. These were foundational goals in Tagore's approach to learning. But a primary school can also create common aesthetic experiences and common ethical experiences and common social experiences in the lives of children. It can enrich the lives of children in a variety of ways. And even though Tagore does not explicitly make a political point in the letter to Gandhi the political context informing Tagore's statements in this letter is surely relevant here. In 1933, Gandhi was the head of the Indian Congress Party and a leading figure in the Indian independence movement. He could affect the behavior of many hundreds of thousands of persons through his directions and the goals he articulated in his public speeches. If the Indian independence movement led by Gandhi adopted the goal of creating a system of neighborhood schools across the country—using an approach to education that was like the one Tagore had developed at his school at Shantiniketan—the lives of all Indian children would be given a tremendous boost. Many different types of benefits would flow from this.[30]

TAGORE'S SOCIAL PROJECT

In Tagore's analysis, the British failure to educate Indian children harmed Indian society in multiple ways. It prevented Indian children from developing their mental and emotional capabilities in a context of joy and freedom. It also enhanced the power of sectarian prejudice within the country. The idea that the bodies of some persons are supposedly "impure" and sources of "pollution"—along with the more general notions of caste and social hierarchy that Tagore describes as an "incongruous anachronism" in the contemporary world—continued to be passed on from one generation to the next.[31]

The effects of unjust British educational policy in the subcontinent are extreme in Tagore's eyes. The colonial relation undermined the ability of Indian society to progress on a range of issues. The concept of the outcaste that Buddha argued against was still a feature of Indian social life. But in reflecting on this point, it is important to emphasize that the positive social program Tagore created around the concept of the person's living reality goes well beyond the theme of primary schooling. Tagore believed that the provision of food, shelter, and health care also enhance the living reality of the person. There is a societal obligation to boost the lives of persons in multiple ways.

REGAINING INDIA

Tagore's positive social program can be found in many of his writings. It is evident in essays like "My School" and the letter to Gandhi of March 1933 where Tagore lays out some of his thoughts about primary schooling. It is also evident in essays like "The Disease and the Cure" from 1908. In this ethical and social reflection, Tagore notes that what is needed in Bengal is not the Swadeshi program of boycotting British goods or a violent strategy of resisting the British Raj.[32] Instead, he frames the needs of Bengal and India as a whole through a program of public action. Tagore states:

> We must realize that when the English depart this land it will not become our motherland again. We must earn our country through our own efforts. By providing food, shelter, health, happiness and education to our countrymen, we must become their mainstay.[33]

In this passage, Tagore describes the education of all persons as a social imperative. Developing the individual's capabilities in reading and writing, math, and science *must* become the norm for all Indian children. This is the core theme of Tagore's ethical philosophy. Tagore defended the idea of a development ethic in his writings. What is distinctive about this passage, however, is the broader way Tagore characterizes this point. Tagore claims that food, shelter, and health care must also be included in this social program, along with each person's education and training. There are multiple ways a society can boost the living reality of individual persons.

The positive claims expressed in "The Disease and the Cure" are framed as social imperatives. In Tagore's view, these demands—or obligations—cannot be ignored. The growth and development of any person always and everywhere has social roots. A second point: while Tagore's claim in this passage is framed in ethical terms, it is important to consider the concrete steps that must be taken to achieve these goals. The training of teachers is, for instance, entailed by Tagore's commitment to the education of all children. Likewise, the training of doctors and nurses is required to achieve the goal of providing health care to all persons. An upbuilding of human capability at many levels is entailed by Tagore's social program. As a result, secondary schools—as well as the creation of colleges and universities—are essential to the project Tagore is affirming. It is not surprising that Tagore also founded a college at Shantiniketan—Visva-Bharati, in 1922—given the animating ideas of his social program and his ethic of development.

Tagore's social program required a lasting commitment to several levels of the institutions of learning. A system of primary, secondary, and tertiary schools should be available to all Indian children—and all of the children of the world. The *global* upbuilding of human capability is the central goal. Tagore's comments about housing and food security can also be interpreted along these lines. Building homes—and not just "rickety shelters"—for all persons requires a substantial commitment of resources and trained human talent and ingenuity.[34] There is a need for carpenters and plumbers and architects and urban planners and engineers and persons with other types of knowledge to achieve this goal. Likewise, ensuring each person's access to food required a public policy informed by agricultural science. Tagore sent his son Rathindranath to study agriculture at the University of Illinois Urbana-Champaign because Tagore knew that progress in this area was so crucial to India's future.[35]

MISERIES

When thought through in its entirety, the claim Tagore makes in "The Disease and the Cure" has dramatic implications for Indian society. A new upheaval of thought and endeavor—with an important role for public action and government policy—would be required to achieve these goals, even in part.

And here it is important to recall Tagore's comments about Buddha in *The Religion of Man*. Tagore states:

> We must be reminded that a great upheaval of spirit, a universal realization of the true dignity of man once caused by Buddha's teachings in India, started a movement for centuries which produced illuminations of literature, art, science, and numerous efforts of public beneficence.[36]

The similarities between Tagore's description of Buddha's project and Tagore's own project are striking. In Tagore's view, new endeavors in "literature, art, science and works of public beneficence" are needed to renew India and the other countries of the world. Enhancing the living reality of persons in all societies is central to Tagore's message.

Tagore's beliefs about collective action are strongly influenced by his understanding of Buddha. Like Buddha before him, Tagore clearly believed collective action could help societies progress in their realization of the dignity of the person. In making these points, however, it is important to avoid overstating the case. Tagore's first-person observations are just as relevant to his social program as the invocation of an older Indian ethical tradition. There is an important role for empiricism in Tagore's thinking here. For instance, Tagore notes in "The Disease and the Cure" that famines in Bengal were a recurring reality during British rule. Tagore was also acutely aware of the chronic malnutrition of children and adults in Bengal during his life. One does not need to take one's inspiration from the past to understand the importance of nutritious food in the lives of persons. Seeing, looking around, observation, the perceptions of the individual can resensitize the individual to food insecurity. Tagore's thoughts about health care in "The Disease and the Cure" are rooted in a similar observation. In the same passage where he discusses famine, he notes that malaria took many lives in rural Bengal. Infectious diseases such as cholera were also endemic to the region.[37]

Tagore's justifications for focusing on food and health care include a straightforward assessment of what their absence means for persons living in society. Individuals will suffer greatly and are more likely to die when their society fails to protect them from these threats. Tagore's thinking about housing is also informed by his own observations and experiences. Tagore's position as a zamindar (landlord) in rural Bengal heightened his understanding of the fragile economic conditions of his tenants. Tagore knew that large numbers of rural families were only one accident away from losing their shelter. In particular, the ability of many Bengali families to pay the rent or the mortgages on their properties depended on an unending chain of very good luck. If a person experienced unemployment or a diminution of income or an unexpected expense this person, and the family this person supported, could lose their home. Nor is this concern confined to renters. Tagore's poem "My Little Plot of Land" emphasized the economic vulnerability of small land-owners.[38] Persons who owned land but whose incomes were precarious and had mortgages on their property were also in danger of losing their homes.

From this point of view, Tagore's passage on food, health care, and shelter in "The Disease and the Cure" draws attention to Tagore's perceptions as well as Buddha's ideas. Tagore saw how the miseries of human life can quickly compound. The potential to suffer extreme forms of deprivation—the pervasive fragility of human life—clearly informed Tagore's social philosophy and his ethical views.

THE COMPARATIVE METHOD

Tagore believed the growth and development of the person was in large part dependent on the broader project of building human capability within society. Both his experience as a subject in British-controlled India and his understanding of Buddha led him to this belief. And within this context it is important to note that Tagore devoted a substantial part of his adult life to a project of "rural reconstruction" around Shantiniketan. Tagore was constantly trying to raise money for his school and university as well as a health care clinic and agricultural research in his later years.[39] But another important feature of Tagore's thinking on these issues is connected to the way Tagore was able to look outside of India to examine other possibilities. Tagore was also concerned about the dangers of isolating one's thinking from what was happening in the rest of the world.

The importance of looking abroad in Tagore's thinking is evident in some of his personal decisions. Sending his son to the United States of America to study agricultural science is an example of this attitude. It is a mistake, Tagore thought, to exclude a source of knowledge because it is supposedly alien or foreign. The individual must be willing to learn from sources of knowledge wherever they are.[40] But the look abroad is not just evident in Tagore's personal decisions; it is also evident in Tagore's formal analysis. In particular, the use of a comparative method—which examines the experience of a society in terms of what is going on in the other societies of the world—was central to Tagore's book *Nationalism* as well as *The Religion of Man* and *Sadhana: The Realization of Life*. By comparing the experiences of different societies with each other, the assumptions and existing priorities of any single society can be further explored. New upheavals of thought flow from a comparative analysis of what is happening in the lives of different peoples.

TAGORE IN JAPAN

Tagore believed the perceptions and the observations of the person can draw the person a step closer to important truths. Tagore also believed that it was important to broaden these experiences as much as possible. Comparative broadening—to use Sen's terms, can help correct against the biases that are active in any society.[41] But to better understand the importance of looking abroad in Tagore's thought it will help to consider his discussion of Japan in *Nationalism*. In this text—which was first delivered in lectures Tagore gave in the United States of America, Japan, and India during World War I— Tagore indicates that there is something persons in India and "the West" can learn about human development and society from an examination of Japanese life. In particular, Tagore focused on Japan's cultural and artistic achievements. There was a form of human consciousness—towards both persons and nature—that profoundly moved Tagore during his visit.

This point can be made more precise. At a key moment in his essay about Japan in *Nationalism*, Tagore states:

> The ideal of "maitri" is at the bottom of your culture—"maitri" of man and "maitri" of nature. And the true expression of this love is in the language of beauty, which is so abundantly universal in this land. This is the reason why a stranger, like myself, instead of feeling envy or humiliation before these manifestations of beauty, these creations of love, feels a readiness to participate in the joy and glory of such revealment of the human heart.[42]

The idea Tagore articulates here clearly draws on his own personal observations. Tagore the wayfarer, who could not speak the language and who had never stepped foot in this country prior to 1916, felt a personal connection with much of what he saw. Barriers of language and a more general lack of familiarity with Japanese life did not undermine Tagore's experience of the human and natural beauty of the country.

On one level, then, the passage on Japanese culture possesses some of the features of travel literature. It contains a kind of personal empiricism which does not abstract from the author's feelings or the shadings of mood in its descriptions.[43] Tagore's empiricism retains a sense of his whole self. A second interesting feature of this passage is its use of the Sanskrit term maitri. In the passage, Tagore translates this term as "love." This translation, however, probably does not fully capture the range of meanings Tagore is trying to express. The Sanskrit maitri is cognate with the Pali metta or loving-kindness. It is likely that Tagore is referring to the mental and emotional attitude of loving-kindness in the Metta Sutta when he is talking about the love that enhances the living reality of persons and nature in Japan. There is a cultural link—based on the historical spread of different forms of early Buddhism from India to China and then Korea and Japan—that informs this statement. But even this description of the passage understates the point; it is important to recall the details of Tagore's interpretation of the Metta Sutta in this context. Tagore believed the act of calming oneself (nibbana in Pali, nirvana in Sanskrit) and the cultivation of loving-kindness or metta are mutually constituting. Diminishing the hostile thoughts and feelings in the person is essential to the achievement of loving kindness. The love of persons and nature described in the passage from *Nationalism* is informed by the Buddhist emphasis on calming the self.

THE RAILWAY STATION

In Tagore's view, there is a link between the early Buddhist discourses, which were composed in the early centuries BCE in India, and elements of Japanese culture that are active now, in the present. The ideals of calming the self and the love of living nature are common to both. And the basis for Tagore's claim about nirvana and maitri can be traced back to texts like the discourse to Simha Sadhu. Buddha states:

> It is true, Simha, that I denounce activities, but only activities that lead to the evil in words, thoughts, or deeds. It is true, Simha, that I preach extinction, but only the extinction of pride, lust, evil thought, and ignorance, not that of forgiveness, love, charity or truth.[44]

In Tagore's view, the selective type of extinction described in this passage—the need to simultaneously diminish the hostile thoughts and feelings that arise in one's person while cultivating love, generosity, forgiveness, and truth—is affirmed by Buddha and renewed in the culture of maitri in Japan. To Tagore, there is an unbroken connection between that past and the present. Tagore also provides some concrete examples of what he means by this claim. In his lecture "The Spirit of Japan"—which Tagore delivered in Tokyo in 1916—he draws attention to a particular experience he had at a train station between Osaka and Tokyo. He states:

> While traveling in a railway train I met, at a wayside station, some Buddhist priests and devotees. They brought their basket of fruits to me and held their lighted incense before my face, wishing to pay homage to a man who had come from the land of Buddha. The dignified serenity of their bearing, the simplicity of their devotedness, seemed to fill the atmosphere of the busy railway station with a golden light of peace. Their language of silence drowned the noisy

effusion of the newspapers. I felt that I saw something which was at the root of Japan's greatness.[45]

To Tagore, the focus and training needed to achieve the dignified serenity of these monks and members of the laity—the way the goal of calming the self became an almost unconscious disposition in the lives of these individuals—is quite remarkable. The ability to give is enhanced by their ideas and their way of life. There is a connection between the dignified serenity of these persons and their generosity.

Tagore's description of the culture of maitri or metta he saw in Japan gains greater specificity when understood through this passage. "An intense consciousness of the value of reality" is communicated by the monks and the laity in their greeting of Tagore.[46] The ability to respect what is before one, now, in the present moment, is the fruit of this thinking. And while it is tempting to interpret Tagore's statements about Japanese culture or civilization as a reference to Japanese "High Art" or "High Culture" it is clear from this and other passages in "The Spirit of Japan" that this is not quite what Tagore means. In Tagore's view, the love of living nature is manifest across all sections of Japanese society and is not confined to the members of a sect. The root of Japan's greatness is evident in the greeting of the Buddhist monks and laity.

This point can be put another way. Buddhist Zen gardens in Japan are places for meditative reflection and calming the self. The Japanese term "Zen"—as well as the Korean term "Seon" and Chinese term "Chan"—is derived from the Sanskrit word *dhyana* or meditation. But the attitude of meditative reflection itself informs the way the gardens are created. These gardens blend human intention with the natural forms of trees, moss, lichen, and rocks in an extraordinary way.[47] In Tagore's language, a nonviolent, loving attitude—the attitude of maitri—is needed to create such beauty. Tagore believes, however, that the same attitude is a more general feature of this culture. Tagore states:

> This spiritual bond of love she has established with the hills of her country, with the sea and the streams, with the forests in all their flowery moods and varied physiognomy of branches; she has taken into her heart all the rustling whispers and sighing of the woodlands and sobbing of the waves; the sun and the moon she has studied in all the modulations of their lights and shades, *and she is glad to close her shops to greet the seasons in her orchards and gardens and cornfields*. This opening of the heart to the soul of the world is not confined to a section of your privileged classes, it is not the forced product of exotic culture, but it belongs to all your men and women of all conditions.[48] (italics added)

To Tagore, the way the country "will close her shops to greet the seasons in her orchards and gardens and corn fields" is akin to the attitude expressed by the persons who greeted Tagore or who created the gardens of Zen. There is a distinctive standard of value that is active throughout the country—one that cannot be traced back to commercial success. In Tagore's words, this standard of value is "*an extension of the family and the obligations of the heart* in a wide field of space and time"[49] (italics added). The themes that are active in the Brahmanadhammika Sutta and the Metta Sutta—the extension of the concept of the family to include living nature, the obligations of the heart—are still living norms in Japan.[50]

A LOVE OF HUMANITY

Tagore's statement on the culture of maitri in Japan is highly revealing. The Spirit of Japan—by which Tagore means the norms of metta and nibbana—is a living reality. It is expressed through the gardens and art and architecture and greetings produced by its people. And while Tagore does not want to homogenize all societies, remaking the entire world along the lines of one cultural expression, he does want the individuals living in different societies to be aware of what is happening in the lands of their neighbors and to reflect on this encounter. It is important, Tagore believes, to seek out and understand the experiences of other people.

Interpreted in this way, Tagore's internationalism—like his views about education—is not meant to be an abstract exercise of the intellect alone. It is also experiential and an exercise in relationship. The subconscious and the conscious mind can be nourished and broadened by travel and the engagement with other people—both in one's own neighborhood and further abroad. But one of the most important features of Tagore's reflections on the culture of maitri in Japan is connected to the way he creates a dialogue between the industrialist and the persons who affirm nirvana and metta. There is, Tagore believes, great danger in understanding society solely or strictly through the productivity of its economy or the military strength of the nation.

The passage where Tagore makes this claim is interesting. At a key moment in the narrative in "Nationalism in Japan" Tagore imagines a dialogue between himself and an industrialist who is skeptical of Indian or Asian societal achievements. The exchange is as follows:

But he says, "You do not make any progress, there is no movement in you." I ask him, "How do you know it? You have to judge progress according to its aim. A railway train makes its progress towards the terminus station,—it is movement. But a full-grown tree has no definite movement of that kind, its progress is the

inward progress of life. It lives, with its aspiration towards light tingling in its
leaves and creeping in its silent sap."[51]

The passage describes two different kinds of movement. When a train is moving from point A towards point B it is heading towards its goal. It is carrying
its cargo and its rate of forward motion can be measured. This is a valid way
of understanding the meaning of progress. But, Tagore notes, the movement
of a tree—and, more generally, the movement of any living thing—cannot be
understood in this way. A tree is growing and developing and progressing, but
it is not moving from point A to point B. Progress must also be measured by
the internal developments that are taking place within a life.

Interpreted in this way, a primary meaning of this passage is the avoid-
ance of an overly reductive understanding of the meaning of progress. The
industrialist is thinking about the progress of society through an analogy with
a machine. It is a mistake to measure a living thing solely in this way. Trains
do not grow and develop in the way people do. This epistemological point,
in turn, leads into a more substantive claim. In Tagore's view, when a love
of humanity and living nature forms in the person it brings out new potential
in all that person's existing capacities. The ability to speak and reason and
express views in public that had previously developed in the life of the individual—all the skills and abilities the person learns in the period stretching
from their infancy to their adulthood, whatever these skills and abilities may
be—blooms in a new manner. The way the person exists in the world changes.

The substantive point Tagore makes in this passage is highly significant
and represents an entryway into the most important layer of argumentation
made in this text. Tagore notes many times in *Nationalism* that a person's life
can be understood in mechanical terms.[52] How much does the person produce? Is the person an efficient worker or laborer? Does the person contribute
to the strength of the state? This point of view is well-developed in the theory
and practice of the nation. A person's life, however, can also be understood
in terms of his or her growth and development as a living reality. The aspirations of the person are also significant when thinking about their life. And this
point of view brings into consideration a very different set of concerns than
the ones articulated by the industrialist. It suggests the need for new questions
and new standards. How does the person understand their relations with their
neighbors—both local and global? Is the person gaining a new concern with
the growth and development of other people? Are norms of public reasoning
becoming more salient in the person's life? To Tagore, these considerations
should also inform a society's notion of progress; the language of efficiency
or goods produced is insufficient here. And part of the way Tagore describes
this type of movement is through the language of beauty. The development
of a nonviolent love of all people in one's mental and emotional life is like

the tingling of leaves in the sunlight and the silent movement of sap. There is something beautiful about the achievement of nonviolent norms in the life of a person and a people—a beauty that is independent of the state's ability to produce goods or wage effective war.

THE HUMAN RIGHTS TRADITION IN EUROPE

Tagore's criticism of reductive ways of thinking about the progress of the person is a culminating idea in *Nationalism*. Individuals must be understood in terms of their leading aspirations and not just their contributions to the power of the state. The inner life of the person is important to consider when measuring societal progress. Moreover, this shift in the way Tagore thinks about the person also informs his understanding of the obligations a society has towards the person. When a society boosts the lives of children and adults through its food policies and its health care policies and its housing policies and its educational policies it helps to create an atmosphere of freedom in the lives of individuals. It allows the living reality of each person to grow and develop free from violence and destitution.

In Tagore's view, individuals and societies can be assessed through the lens of maitri or metta as well as industrial output. Considering these different standards of progress improves the reasoning on both sides in Tagore's imagined exchange. This, to Tagore, is the ultimate meaning of the comparative method.[53] But the last point I would like to make in this context involves the way Tagore describes the persons living in the "western" nations in *Nationalism*. Tagore's visits to Europe and the friendships he developed with many Europeans convinced him that the love of persons and nature he found in India and Japan was also well-developed among the citizens of "the Nation." Tagore avoided a reductive point of view towards European persons and societies in this work.

Tagore's characterization of the cultural traditions in Europe is striking. One might surmise from some of Tagore's descriptions of the nation that he finds nothing good in European life. This impression, however, is a mistake. Tagore believed the living reality of all persons should be enhanced. This attitude is inclusive of Europeans as human beings. The personal basis of Tagore's conduct leads him to this conclusion. Equally important, Tagore spends some time in *Nationalism* describing Christian notions of love as well as the human rights tradition in Europe. Tagore states:

> In the heart of Europe runs the purest stream of human love, of love of justice, of spirit of self-sacrifice for higher ideals. The Christian culture of centuries has sunk deep in her life's core. In Europe we have seen noble minds who have

ever stood up for the rights of man irrespective of colour and creed; who have braved calumny and insult for their own people in fighting for humanity's cause and raising their voices against the mad orgies of militarism, against the rage for brutal retaliation that sometimes takes hold of a whole people; who are always ready to make reparation for wrongs done in the past by their own nations and vainly attempt to stem the tide of cowardly injustice that flows unchecked because the resistance is weak and innocuous on the part of the injured.[54]

This passage shares many similarities with Tagore's description of the culture of maitri in Japan. The Christian injunction, rooted in the Gospel, to "love thy neighbor as thyself"—as well as the social implications of the Christian teaching of the Good Samaritan, which radically expands the concept of one's neighbor—are similar but not identical to the attitude of loving kindness Tagore found in Japan. In Tagore's view, the theistic Christian tradition and the agnostic Buddhist tradition can each support a form of ethical universalism that is rooted in love. Even more: the persons who affirm human rights in Europe may do so from a theistic or a secular point of view. To Tagore, the person's "creed" is not the determining factor in their ethical beliefs. Instead, what is more important to Tagore is the mental and emotional developments that make possible the concern with human rights. It is a love of all persons that allows the hearts of individuals to leap up in protest at abuses of power, cruelty, and murder wherever they occur. It is the ability to reason—and feel—in terms of what another life needs to grow and develop that is the decisive factor.

From this point of view, the passage on the human rights tradition in Europe indicates that many Europeans came to think and reason in terms of what all individuals need to grow and develop. The members of this tradition defended the human rights of foreign persons even at great risk to themselves.

NOTES

1. Fakrul Alam and Radha Chakravarty, eds., *The Essential Tagore* (Cambridge, MA: The Belknap Press of Harvard University Press, 2011), 55.
2. Ibid., 3.
3. Ibid., 786.
4. Ibid, 8, 56.
5. Ibid., 57.
6. Sen notes that Tagore was especially critical of the austerity imposed on children by Mahatma Gandhi's approach to education. Sen states: "Rabindranath remained unconvinced of the merit of Gandhiji's attempt at making spinning at home (with the *charka*- the primitive spinning wheel) an important part of India's self-realization. 'The charka does not require anyone to think; one simply turns the

wheel of this antiquated invention endlessly, using the minimum of judgment and stamina.'" Krishna Dutta and Andrew Robinson, eds., with a foreword by Amartya Sen, *Selected Letters of Rabindranath Tagore* (Cambridge: Cambridge University Press, 1997), xxii.

7. Alam and Chakravarty, *The Essential Tagore*, 56.

8. Ibid., 184–85.

9. Sen—in the context of describing Tagore's criticism of Gandhi's understanding of the Bihar earthquake—notes that: "The dispute with Mahatma Gandhi on the Bihar earthquake touched on a subject that was closest to Tagore's passions and commitments: the importance of being educated in science as well as literature and the humanities." Dutta and Robinson, *Selected Letters of Rabindranath Tagore*, xxiii.

10. Rabindranath Tagore, *Gitanjali* (Song Offerings), 35. https://www.gutenberg.org/files/7164/7164-h/7164-h.htm. For Sen's discussion of this poem, see *The Argumentative Indian: Writings on Indian History, Culture and Identity* (New York: Picador, 2005), 98.

11. The pattern of referring to British rule in the context of making a broader humanistic point is also evident in the seventeenth poem of *Gitanjali*. Tagore states: "They come with their laws and their codes to bind me fast: but I evade them ever, for I am only waiting for love to give myself at last too his hands" (https://www.gutenberg.org/files/7164/7164-h/7164-h.htm). As Marc Jason Gilbert notes, Tagore is referring to laws like the "Regulating Act" (of 1784), the "Covenanted Civil Service Act" (of 1793), the "Permanent Settlement Act" (of 1793)," the "Criminal Tribes Act" (of 1871), the "Vernacular Press Act" (of 1878), and the "Arms Act" of 1878, among others—that the British foisted on Indian persons to deprive them of their freedoms. But Tagore does not explicitly elaborate on this point in the rest of the poem. For more discussion of the British legal code in the subcontinent during the colonial period see the essay "The Era of British Rule" by Marc Jason Gilbert in Roger D. Long, *A History of Pakistan* (Oxford: Oxford University Press, 2015), 283–313.

12. Yasmin Khan, "Gandhi's World," in *The Cambridge Companion to Gandhi*, eds. Judith M. Brown and Anthony Parel (Cambridge: Cambridge University Press, 1998), 14. Vincent Arthur Smith offers an especially strong indictment of British educational policy in the subcontinent. He states: "I think it likely that the percentage of literacy among the population of Ashoka's time was higher than it is now in many provinces of British India" (Smith, *Ashoka: The Buddhist Emperor of India* [Dehli: S. Chand, 1909], 139). For more on the essential importance of primary schooling for society, and especially for a society's women, see the chapter "Primary Schools" in Leavitt, *The Foreign Policy of John Rawls and Amartya Sen* (Lanham, MD: Lexington Books, 2013), 55–65.

13. Tagore, *Nationalism* (New York: Macmillan, 1917), 32.

14. For more background on Britain's exploitative educational policies in India, see Lord Macaulay's "Minute on Education" of 1835: http://www.columbia.edu/itc/mealac/pritchett/00generallinks/macaulay/txt_minute_education_1835.html.

15. At least 800,000 Indian soldiers fought for the British during World War I on the assumption that the Indian people would be granted their independence after World

War I. This promise, however, was not kept. For more discussion of this event see "The Era of British Rule" by Marc Jason Gilbert in Long, *A History of Pakistan*, 303.

16. Marc Jason Gilbert notes that Churchill "strongly believed that an enslaved India was the key to the British economy. He declared that if British troops ever marched home from there, 'they would bring famine in their wake.'" Long, *A History of Pakistan*, 309.

17. Dutta and Robinson, *Selected Letters of Rabindranath Tagore*, 421–22. Tagore's letter of March 1933 is in response to a prior letter from Gandhi.

18. As Sen and Dreze note, the concept of religious impurity in the caste system constructed an extreme form of hierarchy for the Dalits: "In large parts of India, in the old days, Dalits were not allowed to wear sandals, ride bicycles, enter temples, or sit on a chair in the presence of higher castes—to give just a few examples of the vicious system of humiliation and subjugation that had developed around the caste system." Jean Dreze and Amartya Sen, *An Uncertain Glory: India and Its Contradictions* (Princeton, NJ: Princeton University Press, 2013), 218–19.

19. Tagore makes this point a striking manner in the essay "Hindus and Muslims": "Once I began to work as a zamindar I saw that when I had to deal with my Muslim tenants as their landlord I was expected to make them sit only after the cover was removed from the couch! There is no obstacle more formidable that can separate a group of people from another as one which considers the adherents of another religion impure." Alam and Chakravarty, *The Essential Tagore*, 197.

20. For a discussion of Aggika and Buddha in the Vasala Sutta, see chapter 2.

21. Dutta and Robinson, *Selected Letters of Rabindranath Tagore*, 421–22.

22. See introduction, note 56.

23. Dutta and Robinson, *Selected Letters of Rabindranath Tagore*, 421–22.

24. Ibid., 421–22.

25. Ibid., 260.

26. As Tagore puts it in his essay "Hindus and Muslims": "Humans are unaware of a wrong if it is committed habitually." In this passage, habits primarily deaden the mind. The awareness of the person is blocked off from any sense of the harm that is done by the presence of a habit. Alam and Chakravarty, *The Essential Tagore*, 142.

27. Dutta and Robinson, *Selected Letters of Rabindranath Tagore*, 421–22.

28. Amartya Sen, *The Argumentative Indian: Writings on Indian History, Culture and Identity* (New York: Picador, 2005), 97.

29. Dutta and Robinson, *Selected Letters of Rabindranath Tagore*, 421–22.

30. Unfortunately, the push for universal education in India stalled after the nation gained independence from the United Kingdom (in 1947) and the writing of the Indian constitution (completed in 1950). For more on this point, see Dreze and Sen, *An Uncertain Glory: India and Its Contradictions*, 107–42.

31. "The thing we, in India, have to think of is this—to remove those social customs and ideals which have generated a want of self-respect and a complete dependence on those above us—a state of affairs which has been brought about entirely by the domination in India of the caste system, and the blind and lazy habit of relying upon the authority of traditions that are incongruous anachronisms in the present age." Tagore, *Nationalism* (New York: Macmillan, 1917), 135.

32. Alam and Chakravarty, *The Essential Tagore*, 141.

33. Ibid., 143.

34. This phrase is used by Sen to describe the living conditions of many persons during the colonial period. See Sen, *Identity and Violence: The Illusion of Destiny* (New York: W. W. Norton and Company, 2006), 173.

35. Tagore also lived at the University of Illinois Urbana-Champaign and wrote a letter describing his impressions. Dutta and Robinson, *Selected Letters of Rabindranath Tagore*, 98–99.

36. See introduction, note 6.

37. In "The Right Way," Tagore notes how famine and malaria have "drained the life-blood" of many Hindu regions in Bengal (Alam and Chakravarty, *The Essential Tagore*, 136). More generally, in 1951, at the end of British rule in India, the life expectancy of Indian persons was approximately thirty-two years. The average life expectancy of Indian persons in 1908 was likewise appallingly low. Tagore's observations about malaria and famine help to explain these broader trends. See Dreze and Sen, *An Uncertain Glory: India and Its Contradictions*, 6, for more discussion of these points.

38. Tagore's poem "My Own Plot of Land" describes the fragility of the individual's claim to land ownership in rural Bengal by describing the unjust eviction of the farmer Upen at the hands of a zamindar. Upen is described in the poem as floundering in debt. See Alam and Chakravarty, *The Essential Tagore*, 241.

39. Alam and Chakravarty, *The Essential Tagore*, 12–13, Tagore used the interest from the Nobel prize and the royalties from his writings to help fund his projects in and around Shantiniketan.

40. In his introduction to the book *Nationalism*, Ramachandra Guha describes the extent of Tagore's travels and quotes Humayun Kabir in this context. In Kabir's words, Tagore "was the first great Indian in recent times who went out on a cultural mission for restoring contacts and establishing friendships with peoples of other countries without any immediate or specific educational, economic, political or religious aim. It is also remarkable that his cultural journeys were not confined to the western world." Guha also notes that Tagore "visited Europe and North America, but also Japan, China, Iran, Latin America and Indo-China" and that "Tagore travelled to other lands out of curiosity, simply to speak with humans of a cultural background different from his own" (Quoted in Rabindranath Tagore, *Nationalism*, ed. Ramchandra Guha, ix–x, xi [New Delhi: Penguin, 2009]).

41. For Sen's discussion of comparative broadening, see Amartya Sen, *The Idea of Justice* (Cambridge, MA: The Belknap Press of Harvard University Press 2009), 170.

42. Tagore, *Nationalism* (New York: Macmillan, 1917), 92.

43. Tagore also describes some of the lower points of this encounter in the essay: "At first, I had my doubts. I thought that I might not be able to see Japan, as she is herself, but should have to be content to see the Japan that takes an acrobatic pride in violently appearing as something else. On my first arrival in this country, when I looked out from the balcony of a house on the hillside, the town of Kobe,—that huge mass of corrugated iron roofs,—appeared to me like a dragon, with glistening scales, basking in the sun, after having devoured a large slice of the living flesh of the earth.

This dragon did not belong to the mythology of the past, but of the present; and with its iron mask it tried to look real to the children of the age,—real as the majestic rocks on the shore, as the epic rhythm of the sea-waves. Anyhow it hid Japan from my view . . . " Tagore, "The Spirit of Japan," 3–4. https://www.gutenberg.org/files/33131 /33131-h/33131-h.htm. Accessed January 21, 2022.

44. See chapter 3, note 29.

45. Tagore, "The Spirit of Japan," 4–5.

46. Tagore, *The Religion of Man* (New York: Macmillan, 1931), 152.

47. Tagore does not name a particular place—for instance, the Ryogen-in Zen gardens in Kyoto—as a source of his descriptions. In this sense, there is an abstract quality to Tagore's impressions of the "Spirit of Japan."

48. Tagore, *Nationalism* (New York: Macmillan, 1917), 91.

49. Ibid., 92. The entirety of the section on Tagore's understanding of the Metta Sutta in chapter 3 is relevant here.

50. For more on Tagore's interpretation of these two early Buddhists discourses, see chapter 3.

51. Tagore, *Nationalism* (New York: Macmillan, 1917), 80.

52. Some of the darkest imagery in *Nationalism* is attached to this theme of the machine. In particular, Tagore thinks of the great nation states of the colonial period and the first World War as *machines of voracity*: "Before this political civilization came to its power and opened its hungry jaws wide enough to gulp down great continents of the earth, we had wars, pillages, changes of monarchy and consequent misery, *but never such wholesale feeding of nation upon nation, such huge machines for turning great portions of the earth to mincemeat*, never such terrible jealousies with all their ugly teeth and claws ready for tearing open each other's vitals" (italics added). Tagore, *Nationalism* (New York: Macmillan, 1917), 77.

53. Another example of Tagore's use of the comparative method arises during Tagore's discussion with Einstein. Einstein held the view that truth differed from beauty because truth was independent of the human mind. Tagore, however, questioned Einstein's view on this point. To Tagore, both "beauty" and "truth" are realized by human beings in the social world; it is not possible to separate truth from the living reality of the human being, in Tagore's view. Tagore's discussion with Einstein is reproduced in a slightly abbreviated form in Appendix A of Dutta and Robinson, *Selected Letters of Rabindranath Tagore*, 531.

54. Tagore, *Nationalism* (New York: Macmillan, 1917), 83–84.

Chapter 7

The International System

The arguments in Tagore's *Nationalism* and "The Disease and the Cure" are centered on the idea of enhancing human capability. By ensuring each person's access to primary schooling of high quality, health care, shelter, and nutritious food Tagore hoped to boost the growth and development of persons all over the world. In Tagore's view, every society has an obligation to enhance the living reality of every person. Equally important, in this context, is the emphasis Tagore gave to the role of public reasoning in society. Tagore did not want persons to accept ideas out of deference to the past. Instead, he believed ideas had to survive public scrutiny to gain authority. It is the "clear stream of reason"—and not the static forces of dead habit in society—that Tagore praises in the thirty-fifth poem of *Gitanjali*.

The emphasis on the growth and development of the individual in a broader context of intellectual freedom and vigorous public debate places Tagore into distinctive ethical territory. In particular, Tagore's ethical and social philosophy can be understood as an early example of what David Crocker, in his book *Ethics of Global Development: Agency, Capability and Deliberative Democracy* calls a "development ethic."[1] This form of ethical theory emphasizes the way societies have a duty to contribute to the formation of basic human capabilities in all persons, including the capability to read and write and perform investigations in math and science.[2] By defining the obligations of society in terms of the growth and development of the person, and especially the person's capacity to reason and deliberate in public, Tagore shares a core assumption with this contemporary approach to human obligation. But in making this point, it is important to avoid taking the argument too far. Tagore's ethic of development can be compared with the contemporary understanding of ethical obligation signaled by the capability approach. But it is also rooted in texts like the Metta Sutta. It is important to diminish the barriers and obstacles to a truly universal form of love, in Tagore's view.

In this chapter, I further characterize Tagore's ethic of development by examining his late essay "Crisis of Civilization." Finding a way out of what

Tagore calls "the spirit of violence" in the international system is of critical importance.[3] The human security of all persons depends on the formation of nonviolent international norms. I also examine some of Sen's thoughts on foreign policy in his book *The Argumentative Indian* as well as *Development as Freedom* in this context. Reducing violence between societies is a central theme within the ethical thought of both Tagore and Sen.

CRISIS

In Tagore's view, the idea that persons should be protected from abuses of power—along with the more general principle that society has a duty to enhance the living reality of persons through the provision of food, education, health care, and shelter—is strongly expressed in the early Indian classical period, the culture of maitri in Japan, and the human rights tradition in Europe. Tagore believed the development ethic he articulated in his writings echoed the ethical ideas he found during his travels and study. But part of what is distinctive about Tagore's thought is his willingness to analyze the foreign policy decisions of heads of state in terms of these ethical ideas. It is the duty *of the head of state* to promote the growth and development of persons, as much as is feasible.

Tagore's willingness to examine foreign policy through an ethical lens is revealing. Tagore does not separate the realm of ethics and politics. He does not wall off the competition for power from his moral thinking. But as discussed in chapter 4, this way of understanding the relation between states is also active in the early Buddhist discourses. The Cakkavatti-Sihanada Sutta—as well as the edicts of Ashoka—both indicate that it is the duty of the ruler to promote the growth and development of all people. The idea that a head of state should affirm the lives of his or her own citizens while tearing down the lives of more distant peoples is rejected in this early Buddhist tradition of political thought.

Interpreted in this way, protecting *all* persons from violence, as much as is feasible, was the bedrock principle of the Buddhist tradition of political philosophy that Tagore places himself in. Ashoka's internationalism and Tagore's internationalism share this concern. But at the time of Tagore's death in 1941 the realities of national conflict and colonial subjugation weighed heavily on his mind. In "Crisis in Civilization"—an essay from this last period of Tagore's life, whose language and imagery are closely aligned with the language and imagery of *Nationalism*—Tagore states:

> In India the misfortune of being governed by a foreign race is daily brought home to us not only in the callous neglect of such minimum necessities of life as

adequate provision for food, clothing, educational and medical facilities for the people, but in an even unhappier form in the way the people have been divided among themselves. The pity of it is that the blame is laid at the door of our own society. So frightful a culmination of the history of our people would never have been possible, but for the encouragement it has received from secret influences emanating from high places.[4]

The criticism expressed in this passage is exact and unsparing. Indian labor and Indian agricultural products propped up the British empire.[5] Churchill himself stated that the food security of England depended on the exploitation of Indian goods and Indian labor.[6] In the meantime, millions of Indian persons lacked access to primary schools, hospitals, and adequate food and shelter. Indian Hindus and Muslims were also being divided against each other by the British Raj.

Tagore's assessment of British rule at the end of his life was exceedingly grim. The future of India depended on escaping colonial subjugation. The Indian people could not develop with "the fangs" of a hostile nationalism embedded in its social life.[7] Tagore was also greatly disappointed by developments in Japan. While the Taisho period (1912–1926) saw some signs of an emerging movement towards democracy in the country this progress was swiftly reversed in the years that followed.[8] A form of militant nationalism came to dominate the thinking of Japanese heads of state. But the specific causes of this regression are especially important to keep in mind. As Karen Rasler and Jack Thompson point out in their joint book *Puzzles of the Democratic Peace*:

> The Japanese military had been impressed by the way in which Germany had been defeated and its implications for the way the next war would be fought. In the future, war would entail a total mobilization of human and material resources. If one's national stock of resources were limited, it was all the more imperative that access to the most critical resources be assured. The expectation of total war, then, increased the sense of urgency many military officers felt in the need to secure control of Manchurian coal and iron. To survive the next war some level of self-sufficiency had to be obtained.[9]

In this passage, Rasler and Thompson note that the Japanese military leadership was shaken by the possibility of losing a total war. They feared the outcome Germany experienced in World War I and this pushed Japanese military planners to consider the conquest of new territories in Asia. The lesson Japanese military planners learned from the First World War also pushed some members of the Japanese military to intervene in the domestic politics of the country. Rasler and Thompson note that heads of the armed forces "were increasingly inclined to lobby strongly at home both for more resources to

expand and more forceful action by the government." And when these interventions into domestic politics were judged to be insufficiently successful,
"military extremists begin to go beyond mere lobbying and resorted to terrorism and attempted coups to remove politicians who stood in their way."[10] Any
hope of civilian control of the military was cut off by these actions.

In Rasler and Thompson's account, it was the military incursion into
Japanese society that paved the way for the authoritarian politics that followed. A policy of violent expansionism was forced on the Japanese people
by an armed group within the state. More precisely, it was a set of observations about World War I that drove some Japanese war-planners to pursue an
authoritarian politics. By conquering the minds of these Japanese officials,
the nationalist competition for power in Europe exacted a terrible toll on the
Japanese people and the broader region.

THE POISONOUS AIR

In Tagore's view, the problems affecting India and Japan were in large
part caused by the broader forces at work in the international system. The
British were robbing India to maintain their empire within the context of an
extraordinarily hostile Europe. Likewise, the descent of Japan into a militant
authoritarianism was motivated in part by the fear of losing a total war to a
European state. In both examples, there is something about the international
system itself that was leading many heads of state to adopt an authoritarian
strategy. But what was it? Why, exactly, were so many heads of state driven
to pursue such violent goals?

In Tagore's view, the explanation for this aspect of the international system
is not hard to decipher. There is no deep mystery here. Rather, the primary
explanation is clear. If one nation has enriched itself and strengthened its army
by pursuing a colonial policy abroad it is not surprising that other nations
would follow suit. No one wanted to fall behind their existential adversaries
in military power and economic wealth. The "Scramble for Africa," Japanese
conquests in Asia, British control of India, and much else share this fear.[11] But
a second part of Tagore's understanding of this process involves the pervasive
cynicism that had taken hold of persons at the highest levels of government.
In a passage from "Crisis of Civilization," for instance, Tagore notes that
"While Japan was quietly devouring North China, her act of wanton aggression was ignored as a minor incident by the veterans of British diplomacy."[12]
This inability to condemn and resist acts of violent aggression—a kind of
moral blindness to extraordinary abuses of power—is the ultimate cause of
the crisis of civilization around the world.

Tagore's assessment of the structural causes of colonialism and the two World Wars is based on both a moral and a prudential analysis. It is the desire to keep up with the other strong states in the international system—combined with the lack of any countervailing ethical restraint—that explains why the leaders of so many nations were willing to adopt an authoritarian foreign policy from the sixteenth through the twentieth centuries. Heads of state had simply come to accept wars of conquest and territorial occupation as the norm. But perhaps the strongest statement of this point in the "Crisis of Civilization" occurs in Tagore's description of the military conflict in 1941. In one of the bleakest passages in all his writings, Tagore states:

> In the meanwhile the demon of barbarity has given up all pretence and has emerged with unconcealed fangs, ready to tear up humanity in an orgy of devastation. From one end of the world to the other the poisonous fumes of hatred darken the atmosphere. The spirit of violence which perhaps lay dormant in the psychology of the West has aroused itself and desecrates the spirit of Man.[13]

"The demon of barbarity" and the "spirit of violence" are not exaggerations in this passage. They are descriptions of the world at war. When Tagore wrote this passage, continental Europe and many North African countries were occupied by Nazi Germany and its allies, Japanese forces had gained control over a large part of Asia and the Pacific, the Battle of Britain was ongoing, the Soviet Union was under siege—and much else. What other words should one use to describe these events? All around the world, large armies were striving to annihilate each other. The reference to "the spirit of violence" in Tagore's passage reflects this fact. The image in the second sentence of the passage is also startling. Clean air is needed by persons to breathe and to live; but in Tagore's image, the violence of the conflict was so widespread that the very air itself has turned into poison. The nations of the world had become factories spewing out hatred and death.

A NEW INTERNATIONALISM

In "The Crisis of Civilization," Tagore indicates that the psychology of violence that has taken hold of the international system must be changed. Like Buddha and Ashoka before him, Tagore believed norms of nonviolence—and a program to promote the growth and development of all persons—needed to gain traction around the globe. But the specific idea Tagore defends in *Nationalism* and in "Crisis of Civilization" is especially significant. Tagore believed that if many nations simultaneously gave up their desire for new territory abroad, the terrible outcomes witnessed in the colonial period and the two World Wars could be avoided in the future. A new form of foreign policy internationalism—centered on the abandonment of territorial conquest— could lead the way forward. As Tagore puts it:

> Perhaps the dawn will come from the horizon, from the East where the sun rises. A day will come when unvanquished Man *will retrace his path of conquest* despite all barriers, to win back his lost human heritage.[14] (italics added)

The need to forgo human conquests is highlighted here. The lost human heritage that Tagore speaks, the need to calm or quiet the self and to cultivate love, which comes from "the East," from persons like Buddha and Ashoka and the culture of maitri in Japan, is especially singled out. I should also note in this context that the warning that follows this passage—where Tagore speaks about the "perils of the insolence of might" (which is among the last public statements Tagore made before his death)—points directly to the standard of the obligations of power.[15] The belief that accumulating power allows one to do whatever one wants is a deadly error, a wrong view, in Buddha's sense of the word.

The basic idea behind Tagore's foreign policy internationalism is clear. The creation of norms of nonviolence between societies in the international system was essential if persons around the world wanted to avoid the terrible outcomes of the colonial period and the two World Wars. The desire for absolute national supremacy in the international system had to be given up. In reflecting on this aspect of Tagore's thought, however, it is important to capture the nuances of his ideas. Tagore did not argue that every nation needed to completely disband its armed forces. Instead, Tagore believed that societies needed to maintain "modern weapons" to protect themselves from hostile states.[16] The need for an army and a military establishment are also endorsed in this statement.

SELF-DEFENSE

The concession Tagore makes to the need for self-defense in *Nationalism* is significant. The new international system Tagore advocated for would still possess armies and modern weaponry. The commitment to self-defense ruled out an absolute form of pacifism in Tagore's mind.[17] But in reflecting on this concession, it is important to reflect on why he makes it. Tagore wanted to reduce the amount of violence in the international system. Tagore's criticism of the spirit of violence in "Crisis in Civilization" is exceedingly clear. Why, then, is Tagore willing to endorse the need for modern weapons when he is so opposed to violent strategies of conflict resolution? What exactly is going on here?

Part of the answer to this question can be found in Tagore's experience of British colonialism. Tagore believed that one of the great harms inflicted on India at the beginning of the colonial period was the suppression of Indian agency in the area of self-defense. As Tagore puts it in *Nationalism*, England's declaration that India must "forget the use of arms for all time to come" has resulted in a situation where "India is being turned into so many predigested morsels of food ready to be swallowed at any moment by any nation which has even the most rudimentary set of teeth in its head."[18] The entire experience of Tagore's adult life had shown him what happens to a society that lacks the means to ensure its own self-defense.

In Tagore's view, an international system with excessively large asymmetries of power is an invitation to injustice. A society without an army can easily become prey to the societies that do. Tagore makes a similar but more precise comment in the context of his discussion of Japan in *Nationalism*. He states:

> I should not for a moment suggest that Japan should be unmindful of acquiring modern weapons of self-protection. But this should never be allowed to go beyond her instinct for self-preservation. She must know that real power is not in the weapons themselves, but in the man who wields the weapons; and when he in his eagerness for power, multiplies his weapons at the cost of his own soul, then it is he who is in even greater danger than his enemies.[19]

In this passage, Tagore again emphasizes the need for the weaker countries in the international system to protect themselves from military aggression. Tagore understood why Japanese heads of state were anxious about the First World War. In this conflict, European heads of state proved they were willing to sacrifice hundreds of thousands of persons to win a war of attrition. This reality could not be neglected by Japanese war-planners and leaders. But in validating the Japanese focus on its own self-defense Tagore makes an important qualification. He did not believe that massive, expansionist, military buildups were needed to defend Japanese society from the European states. The Japanese people could successfully ward off an invasion without conquering new territory abroad. But doing so would require allying with other states in the region. A joint commitment to self-defense could unite the like-minded societies in Asia. This is part of the reason Tagore draws attention to a more peaceful period in Asian history towards the beginning of his essay about Japan in *Nationalism*. Tagore's comment—"I cannot help but bring to your mind those days when the whole of eastern Asia from Burma to Japan was united with India in closest friendship, the only natural tie which can exist between nations"—is meant to remind Japanese leaders and heads of state that a more peaceful relation with one's neighbors also has the effect of increasing one's security.[20]

Interpreted in this way, the military strategy Tagore is arguing for in *Nationalism* is not based on the idea of overwhelming the enemy in an existential battle. At no point does Tagore make claims like "the best defense is a good offense" or "it is better to be the hammer than the anvil" or some other similar idea. Instead, Tagore's notion of self-defense is based on the idea of inflicting enough damage on an invasion force—through violent means—to prevent that invasion from succeeding. By substantially raising the costs of an invasion in the eyes of the invader a society is best able to preserve its freedom.

BALANCE OF POWER

Tagore's thoughts about self-defense—like his ethic of development—place him into distinctive territory. Tagore's thinking contains an element of "balance of power." It is important to avoid extreme asymmetries of power in the international system. The possession of modern weapons is therefore acceptable to Tagore. But Tagore also believed that an effective balance of power could be achieved without imitating the massive military buildups of the European nation states or engaging in expansionist wars. Japan and India did not need to blindly fall into the "psychology of violence" when considering their own strategies of self-defense.

As can be seen from this discussion, Tagore made a historically informed judgment about what a society needs to do to defend itself in *Nationalism*. There are alternative ways of approaching self-defense that do not involve embracing the nationalist theory of "Total War." But it is not just that Tagore believed in the efficacy of a certain type of military strategy in this passage; he is also making an ethical argument. In Tagore's view, the head of state who "multiplies his weapons" out of an "eagerness for power" has adopted the intention of killing hundreds of thousands of innocent persons to increase the territory of his nation. By adopting this intention, Tagore believes the head of state who builds up his power to unleash an expansionist war has "lost his soul." This person's ability to reason and feel in terms another life's needs has been completely dissolved by their fear of other states and the desire to dominate other peoples.

THE UNITED NATIONS

Tagore's comment on the proper uses of modern weaponry reveals a great deal about the international system he was hoping to construct. The intention of using violent force to protect life from predatory power and nothing else is endorsed by Tagore. If many societies adopted this approach to the use of power in their foreign policies, Tagore believed the amount of violence in the international system would diminish. In this sense, Tagore's foreign policy shares many commonalities with the foreign policy articulated by Ashoka. The thirteenth "Major Rock Edict" of Ashoka—with its moral critique of war, its commitment to self-defense and its focus on the human capability to love—is a source for Tagore's views.[21] And while Tagore did not live to see the defeat of the Axis powers, it is important to note that something like his point of view gained a foothold in the awareness of heads of state around the globe at the end of World War II. The United Nations was formed in 1945 and the "Universal Declaration of Human Rights" was ratified in 1948. The Geneva Conventions were also revised and expanded. A substantial change occurred in the international system at this time.

The reforms of the international system in the immediate period after World War II reflected many of Tagore's leading ideals. A forum for peacefully resolving international conflicts was created and the human right to food, shelter, health care and education—as well as freedom from poverty, among other important economic and social rights—was formally affirmed.[22] However, when viewed through the perspective of Tagore's thoughts about the self-defeating nature of violent competition, the kind of compromise involved in the formation of the United Nations is also clear to see. In particular, the "Security Council" of the United Nations gave special status to the victors of the Second World War. The ability to veto measures put forward at the Security Council was granted to five nations only. As a result, these states could advance their interests without fear of a global rebuke. The military decisions of these five nations—including the decision to invade another country or incite a civil war or orchestrate a coup d'etat—could not be condemned by the United Nations.

Understood in this way, the creation of the United Nations did not do away with the competition for power that culminated in the World Wars. Instead, it created a system where this competition was limited to a handful of nations who were shielded from global censure. No amount of reasoning, argument, and evidence, no amount of personal testimony or the weight of human experience could override the veto powers of these states.

The structure of the United Nations' Security Council discounts the opinions and experiences of the non-veto member states. Russia (the successor to the Soviet Union), China, Britain, France, and the United States of America have special status within this system. But the flaws in the structure of the Security Council are not limited to the two-tiered international system it established; the Security Council also created a distorted system of incentives for the remaining states in the international system. In particular, the states that lacked veto power had an incentive to align with a state that did possess veto power. In this way, a non-veto state could continue to abuse its powers without fear of sanctions or a global rebuke.

The structure of the United Nations Security Council falls well short of the international system Tagore hoped to construct. It allowed the competition for power to take a different form, shielded the most powerful nations from international collective action, and incentivized division. The states of the world aligned themselves in an entirely new way during this period. At the most basic level, however, the reforms of the international system after 1945 did not address the issue of political economy that Tagore raises so forcefully in his English language writings. The United States of America and the Soviet Union devoted a large amount of their social product to the construction of the most powerful militaries on the earth to win the Second World War. And although these militaries were scaled back in the immediate aftermath of the war this proved to be a momentary pause. The economies of these countries were very large—and each state was able to extract enough wealth from these economies to develop and produce many new types of weapons, including thirty thousand nuclear weapons.[23] From this point of view, the problem Tagore identified in *Nationalism* and "Crisis in Civilization" only became worse.

ESCALATIONS

The formation of the United Nations and the outbreak of the Cold War illustrates the paradox at the heart of the international system that was created at the end of World War II. By the time of the Cuban Missile Crisis in 1962, the nuclear arsenals developed by the United States of America and the Soviet Union were powerful enough to destroy civilization. As Sen has pointed out, President Kennedy believed the chances of a nuclear war that would end humanity were one in three or perhaps fifty-fifty.[24] Heads of state, in their "eagerness for power," had multiplied their weapons in a staggering way. And yet the international system that could produce such deadly arsenals and such extreme situations was also characterized by the affirmation of human rights by societies all over the world. The growth and development of all persons and the destruction of all persons became potential realities from this point forward.

When Tagore died in 1941 nuclear weapons did not yet exist. Thus, there is no specific statement calling for nuclear disarmament in Tagore's writings. However, it is important to note that Sen, drawing on the passages on self-defense and modern weaponry in *Nationalism* which were just discussed, argues that Tagore would oppose the construction and eventual use of nuclear weapons. More precisely, Tagore would hold the belief that the construction of a single nuclear weapon is immoral—and therefore also simultaneously imprudent.

The basis for Sen's argument is as follows. Human action, Tagore notes in many contexts, does not occur in a vacuum; the decision of a head of state to increase their military spending does not disappear into the ether. Instead, heads of state are continuously responding to the actions of their neighbors. These persons are constantly adjusting and reacting to each other. And since a large increase in military spending is act of tremendous hostility, the decision of a single head of state to substantially increase their military spending will reverberate in the minds of other leaders. These persons will notice this decision and act to counter it.

To Tagore, the nature of human action in the international system is such that the decision of one head of state to dramatically increase the size and the power of the army will lead other nations to consider new action. It is a mistake to assume that heads of state will not respond to an increased level of military threat. But in Sen's view, the construction of nuclear weapons can be analyzed in the same way. The construction of a single nuclear weapon—like the creation of immense "conventional" arsenals—is an act of tremendous hostility. Its creation gives the head of state the power to kill hundreds of thousands of persons in an instant. As a consequence, the construction of a single nuclear weapon will set in motion a series of responses. No head of state will stand idly by when their adversary constructs a nuclear weapon. Indeed—as the history of Britain and France's decision to develop nuclear weapons indicates—even allies can become uneasy at the large asymmetry of power that is established by these devices.[25]

Understood in this way, the construction of a single nuclear weapon is akin to the other cases of military escalation that Tagore discusses in *Nationalism*. Developing nuclear weapons sets in motion a series of counter-responses that makes everyone worse off. And it is important to emphasize in this context that Tagore and Sen really do believe that every person is made worse off by these choices. If the decision to construct nuclear weapons results in a situation where one's adversary also constructs nuclear weapons has any real advantage been gained? Both countries are spending more on their armed forces and their power to take human life has also massively increased. But the people living in these countries are not made safer. The dangers of a nuclear exchange have been added to preexisting threats.

The conclusion Sen draws from this discussion is striking. Tagore, Sen notes, identified "the conundrum . . . about the weakening effects of military power."[26] An early version of what is now identified as the "security dilemma" by scholars of international relations was articulated by Tagore.[27]

RESOLVING THE SECURITY DILEMMA

Sen's invocation of Tagore in *The Argumentative Indian* is highly interesting. In Sen's interpretation, "Tagore was not merely making a moral point" in *Nationalism*. Tagore was not just speaking about the immorality of rapidly expanding the size of a country's arsenal in order to conquer another people. He was also making a point "of pragmatic importance, taking into account the responses from others that would be generated by one's pursuit of military strength."[28] It is the way Tagore combined an ethical perspective with a model of international relations that is akin to the "security dilemma" model that makes his work so prescient and relevant. Sen's reading of Tagore's statements about an ethically acceptable form of self-defense can also be read in this light. As previously discussed, the construction of a modern arsenal that is sufficiently large enough to fend off invasion is supported by Tagore. Joint commitments to self-defense are also central to the way Tagore considers this issue. But Tagore also believed his approach to self-defense would not arouse fear in the remaining members of the international system. A just principle of self-defense will not set in motion a set of escalating counter-responses in Tagore's view.

On this reading, Tagore believed the idea of the obligations of power could satisfy the need for self-defense without initiating a form of militarism that would endanger the other peoples of the world. Tagore's approach to self-defense shows a viable way of responding to the security dilemma—*if* the heads of state that currently possess nuclear weapons and vast conventional arsenals can see the danger.

NOTES

1. David Crocker, *Ethics of Global Development: Agency, Capability and Deliberative Democracy* (Cambridge: Cambridge University Press, 2008). For Sen's discussion of the idea of a development ethic, see *The Idea of Justice* (Cambridge, MA: The Belknap Press of Harvard University Press, 2009), 381.

2. For more on this point see chapter 5—"The Centrality of Education"—in Jean Dreze and Amartya Sen, *An Uncertain Glory: India and its Contradictions* (Princeton, NJ: Princeton University Press, 2013), 107–43.

3. Rabindranath Tagore, *Crisis in Civilization: A Message on Completing His Eighty Years* (Birbhum: Santiniketan Press, 1941), 12. Accessed from https://indianculture.gov.in/reports-proceedings/crisis-civilization-message-completing-his-eighty-years.

4. Tagore, *Crisis in Civilization*, 10.

5. For more on the role of Indian soldiers in World War I see Roger D. Long, ed., *A History of Pakistan* (Oxford: Oxford University Press, 2015), 302–3. For a discussion on the role of Indian soldiers in World War II, see Sarah Ansari's discussion in *A History of Pakistan*, 389–340. Ansari notes that: "at least 50%" of the British India army "was made up of Muslim soldiers" and that "much of the war effort was likely to rest on Muslim-majority provinces such as the Punjab and Bengal."

6. "However, [Churchill] strongly believed that an enslaved India was the key to the British economy. He declared that if British troops ever marched home from there, 'they would bring famine in their wake" Long, *A History of Pakistan*, 309.

7. "I ask you what disaster has there ever been in the history of man, in its darkest period, like this terrible disaster of the Nation fixing its fangs deep into the naked flesh of the world, taking permanent precautions against its natural relaxation?" Tagore, *Nationalism* (New York: Macmillan, 1917), 41.

8. "The Taisho adjective refers to the decade or two (roughly 1910s–1920s) in Japan's political history that is considered an era of movement towards democratization and liberalization." K. Rasler and W. Thompson, *Puzzles of the Democratic Peace: Theory, Geopolitics and the Transformation of World Politics* (New York: Palgrave Macmillan, 2005), 80. The entire discussion from 80–85 is relevant here.

9. Rasler and Thompson, *Puzzles of the Democratic Peace*, 84.

10. Ibid., 84–85.

11. The Berlin Conference of 1884 partitioned much of the African continent among the European powers.

12. Tagore, *Crisis in Civilization*, 9.

13. Ibid., 12.

14. Ibid., 13.

15. Ibid., 13.

16. See note 20.

17. For more on this point, see chapter 5, pages 91–92 and 99–100.

18. Tagore, *Nationalism* (New York: Macmillan, 1917), 149.

19. Tagore, *Nationalism* (New York: Macmillan, 1917), 95.

20. See introduction, note 7.

21. For a discussion of the thirteenth Major Rock Edict of Ashoka, see chapters 4 and 5.

22. These rights are identified in Articles 25 and 26 of the Universal Declaration of Human Rights. https://www.un.org/en/about-us/universal-declaration-of-human-rights.

23. Melvyn P. Leffler and Odd Arne Westad, eds., *Cambridge History of the Cold War*, vol. 1 (Cambridge: Cambridge University Press, 2010), 387.

24. See Amartya Sen, *The Argumentative Indian: Writings on Indian History, Culture and Identity* (New York: Picador, 2005), 262. The claims about President

Kennedy's understanding of the Cuban Missile Crisis come from Theodore Sorenson, who was Special Counsel to the president: "John Kennedy never lost sight of what either war or surrender would do to the whole human race. His UN Mission was preparing for a negotiated peace and his Joint Chiefs of Staff were preparing for war, and he intended to keep them both in rein. . . . He could not afford to be hasty or hesitant, reckless or afraid. The odds that the Soviets would go all to the way to war, he later said, seemed to him then 'somewhere between one out of three and even.'" Theodore C. Sorenson, *Kennedy* (London: Hodder and Stoughton, 1965), 705. Sen also notes in this context that the "Kennedy Tapes" likewise "bring out how close the world came to a nuclear annihilation."

25. I should also point out that Mao wanted China to develop nuclear weapons in part because of his distrust of the Soviet Union. See Leffler and Westad, *Cambridge History of the Cold War*, vol. 1, 358–59.

26. Sen, *The Argumentative Indian*, 252.

27. For more discussion of the security dilemma, see Levy and Thompson, *Causes of War* (Chichester, UK: Wiley, 2009), 30. As Levy and Thompson note, "the core of the security dilemma" involves the idea that the "actions that states take to increase their security often induce a response by adversaries, and actually result in a decrease in security."

28. Sen, *The Argumentative Indian*, 252.

Chapter 8

Human Security

In the analysis of Tagore and Sen, the decision to rapidly expand the armed forces of a society—as well as the decision to construct a nuclear weapon—leads to an escalating pattern of response and counter-response that leaves everyone worse off. Finding a way out of this irrational pattern of escalation is an urgently important endeavor in the view of both thinkers. And within this context it is important to note that Tagore and Sen's analysis of the international system points to the need for several concrete reforms. As Sen puts it in *The Argumentative Indian*:

> the world order on weapons needs a change and in particular requires an effective and rapid disarmament, particularly in nuclear arsenals.[1]

By abolishing nuclear weapons, reducing conventional arsenals, curtailing the arms trade, and devoting scientific talent to non-militaristic objectives, a new international system can be created.[2]

The basic idea in Tagore and Sen's approach to foreign policy is clear. A strategy in which all states simultaneously reduce their capacity for violence—*regardless of regime type*—is defended. Sen does not rely on the idea of a "democratic peace" in his approach to human security.[3] But Tagore and Sen's analysis of violence is not just limited to foreign policy. The same type of arguments can be found in their reflections on sectarian violence. In particular, Tagore and Sen believe that sectarian forms of violent conduct also exhibit an escalating pattern of response and counter-response in the absence of the rule of law. The destabilizing quality of the violent act is at work in both the foreign policy and the domestic policy spheres.

In this chapter, then, I discuss Tagore and Sen's analysis of the sectarian violence that plagued British controlled India in the years leading up to the partition of the subcontinent in 1947. I also develop Sen's argument in "Peace and Democratic Society" in this context. Calcutta, unlike other cities in India, has avoided sectarian conflict in the post-Independence period.

A politics focused on the idea of the obligations of power has proven to be empirically effective at diminishing all forms of violent conduct in Calcutta in the recent past.

THE BRITISH ROOTS OF HINDU-MUSLIM CONFLICT

As discussed in chapter 7, Tagore believed a strategy of violent aggression in foreign policy had a wide range of negative effects. Persons around the globe were made worse off by the politics of hostile nationalism during the great wars period. However, a distinctive feature of Tagore's writings is his belief that violent strategies of conduct also have a similar effect *within societies*. The inherently escalating quality of violent conduct is evident in domestic contexts as well.

The basis for this claim can be found in some of Tagore's earliest social and political essays. In "The Disease and the Cure" (from 1908) Tagore draws attention to a reality Indians had to consider in their relationship with the British. He states:

> Right at the beginning, we must remember a truth. For whatever reason or through whatever means, if we try to retaliate against the English, then they certainly will do something about it. The consequence of their action will not be beneficial to us.[4]

The form of analysis evident in this passage is clear. It may seem like a strategy of taking up arms and violently resisting British occupation—or, for that matter, pursuing a strategy of boycotting English goods sold in Indian stores—would strengthen the standing of Indian persons in their relations with the British.[5] By harming or retaliating against the British rulers of India some measure of agency would be achieved by Indian persons. But in making this point Tagore also draws attention to the inevitable response. The British authorities in India would not ignore the strategy of boycott or armed insurrection. They would do something about it. In Tagore's view, the British would retaliate in a proportionate way—or even possibly in a disproportionate way—if the Indian resistance movement adopted these goals. And if the British did respond to Indian retaliation with further aggression, is it accurate to argue that Indian persons had gained from their initial strategy? Would Indian persons truly benefit from a boycott or armed rebellion?

The problem Tagore draws attention to in this passage is highly significant. There are few good options available to persons when the government they live under is well organized and willing to abuse its power. In this context, any hostile strategy is bound to backfire. However, in reflecting on the conundrum that faced all Indian persons under British rule it is important to note that Tagore did offer a way forward. Tagore believed a better strategy for Indian persons to pursue during the colonial period involved healing the social divisions that existed within Indian society while continuously and stridently advocating for their freedoms with their British rulers. By forming a common identity centered on the idea that "food, shelter, health, happiness and education" should be provided to all persons—including Indian Hindus, Indian Muslims and the members of all other faiths as well as persons of no faith at all—Indian persons would be better positioned to achieve their freedoms in the long run.[6]

Tagore's answer to the conundrum posed in "The Disease and the Cure" is resolved by avoiding hostilities all together. There are steps Indian persons can take to improve their own society that do not involve a direct military or economic confrontation with the British. Tagore argues for a form of nonviolent protest against British rule in this essay. I should also point out that Tagore's letter to Lord Chelmsford is informed by a similar logic. Tagore did not advocate that Indian persons take up arms against the British Raj after the Amritsar massacre of 1919. Instead, he criticized the decisions of the British military commander who ordered the killings. Tagore states:

> The enormity of the measures taken by the government of the Punjab for quelling some local disturbances has, with a rude shock, revealed to our minds the helplessness of our position as British subjects in India. The disproportionate severity of the punishments inflicted upon the unfortunate people and the methods of carrying them out, we are convinced, are without parallel in the history of civilized governments, barring some conspicuous exceptions, both recent and remote. Considering that such treatment has been meted out to a population, disarmed and resourceless, by a power which has the most terribly efficient organization for destruction of human lives, we must strongly assert that it can claim no political expediency, far less moral justification.[7]

Tagore's description of the British commander's action in this passage is exact and unsparing. The British commander's action involved intentionally targeting a large group of unarmed and nonviolent protestors. Perhaps 379 innocent Indian persons were killed and over a thousand were wounded by rifle fire in the space of fifteen minutes.[8] This violent and unjust action, however, also set in motion a wave of shock and anger through the Indian populace. Hundreds of thousands of Indian persons condemned this act. And this response, as Tagore notes, undermined British rule. The British commander's decision to kill many unarmed civilians had the effect of weakening—not strengthening—the British standing in India.

Tagore's comments in the letter to Lord Chelmsford reveals the way a violent strategy *of governance* diminishes *the ruler*. The commander harmed his own cause through his orders. The subcontinent became less governable through this decision. But a third instance of this type of social analysis can be found in "Crisis of Civilization." In a key passage for understanding Tagore's views on sectarianism—as well as Tagore's views on the proper goals of government—Tagore states:

> It is the mission of civilization to bring unity among people and establish peace and harmony. But in unfortunate India the social fabric is being rent into shreds by unseemly outbursts of hooliganism daily growing in intensity, right under the very aegis of "law and order." In India, so long as no personal injury is inflicted upon any member of the ruling race, this barbarism seems to be assured of perpetuity, making us ashamed to live under such an administration.[9]

The point made in this passage is critical in the extreme. Tagore notes that the institutions of "law and order" did exist in India in 1940 and 1941. There was a very large police force—and a very large prison system—run by British officials in India.[10] However, this entire system of "law and order" was centered on the purpose of protecting British administers and British rule. The goal of shielding Indian persons from violence was not a priority. As a consequence, acts of violence perpetrated by Indian Hindus against Indian Muslims—as well as acts of violence perpetrated by Indian Muslims against Indian Hindus—were not investigated or prosecuted by British authorities. The persons who committed these acts were not brought to justice.

In Tagore's analysis, the unwillingness of the British Raj to maintain the rule of law in regions with large numbers of both Hindus and Muslims contributed to the outbreaks of hooliganism and sectarian violence that were beginning to occur in India at the beginning of World War II. By failing to act the British Raj insured the escalation of tensions between members of these two groups. But even this point understates the case. Not only were British officials unconcerned with stopping the outbreaks of violence between Indian Hindus and Indian Muslims that was rending Indian society. In Tagore's view, these officials were actively contributing to this conflict. A strategy of pitting Indian Hindus and Indian Muslims against each other was a long-standing feature of British rule in Tagore's eyes. This is evident in Tagore discussion of the partition of Bengal into a predominantly Hindu and a predominantly Muslim administrative unit in 1907. In "The Right Way," Tagore characterized the strategy of Lord Curzon as one of "divide, weaken and rule."[11] This strategy of governance is also evident in the public statements of leaders like Churchill, who claimed that British rule in India was needed to protect Muslim persons from "Hindu domination."[12] But the culmination of this policy of dividing Indian persons against each other was the intentional indifference of British authorities to the outbreaks of violence between Hindu and Muslim persons that were beginning to take place with more frequency in the subcontinent in 1940. The British administrators of India knew these outbreaks of violence were occurring. And yet they did not fulfill their duty to protect the Indian people. A violation of the obligations of power is evident here.

KADER MIA

Tagore believed the outbreak of Hindu-Muslim violence that took place at the beginning of the Second World War was the byproduct of an intentional, long-term project of sowing division. As Tagore puts it: "So frightful a culmination of the history of our people would never have been possible, but for the encouragement it has received from secret influences emanating from high places." It is "the way the people have been divided against themselves" that offers the most damning indictment of British rule in the subcontinent in Tagore's eyes.[13]

The way the British rulers of India targeted preexisting religious tensions to strengthen their control over the country was unforgivable to Tagore. The British rulers in India did not pursue the mission of civilization in the subcontinent. But while Tagore experienced the outbreak of sectarian violence with the eyes of an elderly adult, who had seen his faith in British civilization entirely eroded, Sen witnessed the events of the 1940s with the eyes of a child. Sen was born in 1933. Moreover, Sen's reflections on this tumultuous period of Indian history attempt to retain this perspective. In his book *Identity and Violence: The Illusion of Destiny*, Sen narrates several events from this period in a way that retains the point of view of his younger self.

Sen's descriptions of sectarian violence in India are calm but unflinching in their detail. At the beginning of the chapter entitled "Freedom to Think" Sen states:

> My first exposure to murder occurred when I was eleven. This was in 1944, in the communal riots that characterized the last years of the British Raj, which ended in 1947. I saw a profusely bleeding unknown person suddenly stumbling through the gate of our garden, asking for help and a little water. I shouted for my parents, while fetching some water for him. My father rushed him to the hospital, but he died there of his injuries. His name was Kader Mia.[14]

The reality of sectarian violence is brought out in a stark way in this passage. The potential asymmetries of power that always exist in society—the ability of persons to band together into armed groups to harm individuals—suddenly came out into the open. An innocent man was viciously attacked and ultimately died from his wounds.

The passage on Kader Mia illustrates the great importance of norms of nonviolence in society. Ultimately, it is the shared understanding that killing an innocent person is harmful and wrong that protects persons from violence. When the norms against murder break down in a society, individuals are exposed to the human capacity for violence with no countervailing restraint. Nor is Kader Mia the only victim of this act. As Sen's father drove Kader Mia to the hospital, they were able to learn more about his story. Kader Mia was a Muslim day laborer with a family to support. But the nature of his poverty was so extreme that he felt obligated to go out in search of work even in the midst of a very terrible communal riot. Kader Mia's wife had urged him to stay home that day.[15] It is clear from these details that Kader Mia was part of a family who loved him and depended on him for their survival. Kader Mia's wife and children were also greatly harmed by his death.

From this point of view, the murder of Kader Mia had multiple effects. The attack was painful to Kader Mia and ultimately ended his life. Kader Mia's capacity to act was taken from him. The murder also exposed Kader Mia's wife and child to extreme destitution. How, exactly, would Kader Mia's family purchase food or pay the rent after his passing? In British administered India, there was no national programs in place to help these persons. But a third layer of Sen's analysis is centered on the wider social effects of Kader Mia's murder. Sen notes that some Muslim persons were threatened and simultaneously enraged by this act. The killing of Kader Mia had the effect of leading some Muslim persons to retaliate against Hindus. And these retaliatory acts by some Muslim persons in turn lead some Hindus to respond in kind. A cycle of violent response and counter-response was furthered by the murder of Kader Mia. As Sen notes, a "fragmentary logic"—in which it became all important "to kill the enemies who kill us"—took hold in the minds of many persons on both sides.[16]

IMPOVERISHED INDIVIDUALS

Sen's analysis of the murder of Kader Mia shows several levels of harm. The victim, the family of the victim, and the wider society are wounded by the murder. Moreover, Sen's analysis in this text contains within it many of the same critiques of sectarian violence found in the Attadanda Sutta discussed in chapter 1. The idea that "Fear results from resorting to violence"—or the idea that "Fear is born from arming oneself," which is Olendzki's translation of the first verse of the Attadanda Sutta—is active in these passages from

Sen.[17] Individuals will feel fear and terror and may take actions to protect themselves when confronted with the perceptions of an angry mob. The second verse of the Attadanda Sutta—"Seeing people struggling, like fish, writhing in shallow water with enmity against one another, I became afraid"—is also at work in Sen's description.[18] When persons or families or societies are caught up in feelings of fear, punctuated by recurring episodes of violence and killing, the result is a massive constriction of human freedom. Existence itself becomes an intense struggle for these persons. Everyone feels fear.

Sen's description brings out the escalating nature of Hindu-Muslim violence within the context of a breakdown of the rule of law. When political authorities allow the social world to descend into sectarian violence, persons become trapped within highly destructive patterns of behavior. A tremendous loss of freedom and life is evident here. But an additional feature that stands out in Sen's account of this period is his focus on the poverty of the Hindu and Muslim victims of sectarian violence. Why does Sen bring the theme of poverty into his retelling of the murder of Kader Mia?

Part of the reason Sen focuses on poverty in this context is personal in nature. Sen notes that the oppressive sense of poverty in Kader Mia's story—the necessity that drove Kader Mia to risk his life to feed and shelter his family—changed Sen's own thinking as a child. The connection between poverty and loss of freedom, Sen says, "was a shocking realization that hit my young mind with overpowering force."[19] Kader Mia and his family were highly food insecure. His actions were sharply constrained by this fact. As Sen puts it, Kader Mia "had to go out in search of work, for a little income, because his family had nothing to eat."[20] Indeed it is likely that a one- or two-week period without work would make it impossible for Kader Mia to gain any income at all. Kader Mia would become too weak to work if he missed too many meals.

The depth of Kader Mia's poverty placed him and his family on the brink of starvation. Kader Mia was not free to wait things out. Moreover, what was true for Kader Mia was true for the large number of extremely impoverished Bengali persons at this time. Many of these persons were on the brink of starvation. Indeed, Sen points out in another context that a large famine broke out in Bengal in 1942 and especially 1943. Two to three million persons died of starvation during this calamity. But the cause of this famine was not a scarcity of food. The supply of food in Bengal was roughly stable in 1942 and 1943—and higher than in 1941. There was more rice and wheat available in the famine years. Instead, the cause of this famine was the inability of impoverished Bengalis to buy the food that was available. The price of rice had gone up by 900 percent from the previous year in some retail markets in Bengal in 1943 due to the war economy in Bengal.[21] It was the extreme destitution of so many Bengalis that made them vulnerable to this economic shock.

From this point of view, the situation Kader Mia faced in 1944 was not an isolated incident. Many hundreds of thousands of other Muslims and Hindus in Bengal where in the same circumstances. These persons had to go out in search of work in the face of a communal riot because the alternative was worse. It was this group of highly impoverished persons on both sides who were the principal targets of the attackers. And even if a highly impoverished family did decide to wait things out that did not ensure their safety. Sen notes that many of these families lived in "rickety shelters" and were therefore easy targets for the large, armed, mobs that were roaming Dhaka in 1944, or Calcutta in 1946.[22] The failure to provide adequate housing to impoverished Bengalis also made these persons easy targets of sectarian rage.

The comments Sen makes about extreme poverty—as well as the food insecurity and inadequate shelter extreme poverty is synonymous with—sharpens the initial account of Kader Mia's death. The British failure to maintain the rule of law during this period was not symmetrically experienced by all Bengalis. Instead, this failure was most acutely felt by the poorest members of Bengali society. These individuals were at risk both in their homes and on their way to work. The sense of a world without shelter—the description in verse 3 of the Attadanda Sutta—stands out in Sen's account of these persons.[23]

The connection between extreme poverty and loss of freedom is starkly expressed in the murder of Kader Mia as well as the "thousands upon thousands" of the poorest Hindus and the poorest Muslims who were killed in events of this kind.[24] This is a staggering loss of life. Many relationships of love and loyalty were torn apart by these events.[25]

THE POST-INDEPENDENCE ERA

Sen's discussion of the period that led up to the partition of British India into India, West Pakistan and East Pakistan is extraordinarily grim. Indian persons suffered greatly during the second World War and its immediate aftermath. When the head of state fails in the tasks of protecting individuals from violence and extreme destitution the result is a calamity for many people. The echo of the Sutta Nipatta and the Cakavatti Sihanada Sutta is evident here.[26] However, even as he discusses these terrible realities, Sen does point to a way forward. As Sen's discussion of Kader Mia indicates, there is a connection between the social and economic human rights—such as the human right to food and shelter and an adequate income—and *human security*. A person is better able to protect their own life if they are free from the condition of extreme poverty.

In Sen's view, diminishing poverty increases the agency of persons. Individuals are better able to take actions to protect themselves when they can feed themselves and shelter in place. Likewise, individuals with higher incomes can move away from dangers and are more likely to survive. Extreme poverty constrains what a person can do and be. But the last set of themes I would like to address in this context concerns the changes that took place in India after India's independence from Britain. What happened in India on the question of human security after independence?

The point Sen makes in this context is clear. There have been no outbreaks of sectarian violence on the scale of the Hindu-Muslim riots of the 1940s in India's recent past. India freed itself from the worst forms of sectarian conflict after independence. In fact, this change has been so dramatic that it has injected a sense of unreality into Sen's childhood memories. Sen notes that "over sixty years after Kader Mia's death, as I try to recollect the deadly Hindu-Muslim riots in the 1940s, it is hard to convince myself that these terrible things really did happen." In another passage, Sen notes that the breakdown of norms of nonviolence in the communal riots of the 1940s was an "ephemeral and transitory" moment in the history of Hindu-Muslim relations in the subcontinent.[27] A massive change occurred in the country on this question.

The first point, then, to note in Sen's analysis of human security in India after independence is an acknowledgment of dramatic improvement. There has been nothing like the death of thousands upon thousands of persons through sectarian violence in the subcontinent that occurred in the 1940s. And part of this transformation must be attributed to the transition to democracy in India as opposed to the authoritarian system of British rule. Indian persons—when given the chance to vote within a democratic, constitutional system—did not initially elect leaders who used the power of the state to sow sectarian fears. When persons in positions of power do not pursue the strategy of "divide, weaken and rule" new norms of nonviolence can quickly form.

CALCUTTA IN 2005

In Sen's analysis, the lifting of a malevolent governing intention from Indian society had a dramatic effect on the country. Indian society was able to evolve in a new direction. The human security of Indian persons significantly increased in the post-Independence years. But as Sen also points out, the depth of this transformation is easy to understate. It is not just that India has mostly avoided the terrible events of the 1940s after the turn to democracy. It is that some Indian cities are currently among the most peaceful cities on the planet. Many Indian cities have very low rates of violent crime relative to their international peers.

The passage where Sen makes this observation is highly interesting. In the introduction to the book *Peace and Democratic Society*—which also contains the "Report on the Commonwealth Commission on Peace and Understanding"—Sen notes that:

> Calcutta (also called Kolkata) . . . is not only one of the poorest cities in India—and indeed the world—it so happens that it has a very low crime rate. Indeed, in serious crimes, the poor city of Calcutta has the lowest incidence among all the Indian cities. The average incidence of murder in the 35 cities of India is 2.7 per 100,000 people—2.9 for Delhi. The rate is 0.3 in Kolkata. The same lowness of violent crime can be seen in looking at the total number of all violations of the Indian Penal Code put together. It also applies to crime against women, the incidence of which is very substantially lower in Calcutta than in all other major cities in India.
>
> It also emerges that Indian cities in general are strikingly low in the incidence of violent crime by world standards, and Calcutta seems to have the lowest homicide rate not only in India, but also in the world. In 2005, Paris had a homicide rate of 2.3, London of 2.4, New York of 5.0, Buenos Aires of 6.4, Los Angeles 8.8, Mexico City 17.0, Johannesburg 21.5, Sao Paulo 24.0, and Rio de Janeiro an astonishing 34.9. Even the famously low-crime Japanese cities have more than three times the homicide rate of Calcutta, with 1.0 per 100,000 for Tokyo and 1.8 for Osaka, and only Hong Kong and Singapore come close to Calcutta (though still more than 60 per cent higher), at 0.5 per 100,000 each, compared with Calcutta's 0.3.[28]

This data from 2005 reveals a striking pattern. Indian cities in general had a much lower homicide rate than many of their international peers during this year. But within this context, Calcutta really stands out. Calcutta had the lowest homicide rate of any large urban area in the world in 2005.[29] Violence against women was also lower than the other Indian cities during this period.[30]

The passage on Calcutta from *Peace and Democratic Society* illustrates a remarkable achievement on several levels. It is an achievement when viewed through Calcutta's past. For instance, the four-day period of Hindu-Muslim violence in Calcutta between August 16 and August 19 of 1946 resulted in 5,000 to 10,000 deaths and 15,000 wounded.[31] Meanwhile Calcutta—whose population has grown substantially since 1946—recorded forty-one homicides in all of 2005. From this point of view, the transition to democracy has brought extraordinary benefits to the city. When viewed through the mostly peaceful post-independence years, one can understand why Sen's childhood memories might appear so unreal. But Calcutta's achievements also stand out when viewed through an international comparison with other democratic urban areas. More precisely, Calcutta, Paris, London, New York, Buenos Aires, Los Angeles, Mexico City, Johannesburg, San Paulo, Rio de Janeiro, Tokyo and Osaka are all governed by a democratic political process. The holding of elections and other institutional features of democracy are common to each. However, the homicide rates in these cities vary greatly. There is a large difference between Calcutta's homicide rate (0.3 per 100,000 persons) and the homicide rate of Rio De Janeiro (34.9 per 100,000 persons).

From this point of view, there is something distinctive about Calcutta that goes beyond the institutional features of the democratic process. The institutional features of democracy are not enough, by themselves, to explain why the homicide rate is so low in this city. But what is it? Why, exactly, has Calcutta achieved so much in the area of human security in the post-independence years?

ETHICAL NORMS AND POLITICAL HISTORIES

In responding to this question Sen makes a general comment and a more specific point. The general comment concerns methodology. In Sen's analysis: "Cultural and social factors as well as features of political economy are all important in understanding violence in the world today."[32] A new form of social investigation is needed to better understand the homicide rates of different regions. The more specific point involves a cultural, social and political economy analysis of Calcutta. Sen states:

> the prevailing politics of Calcutta and of West Bengal, which is very substantially left of center, has tended to concentrate on deprivation related to class and, more recently, to uses and abuses of political power. That political focus, which is very distinct from the religion and religion-based community, has made it much harder to exploit religious differences for instigating riots against minorities, as has happened, with much brutality, in some Indian cities, for example Bombay (or Mumbai) and Ahmedabad.[33]

The core of this passage is centered on the government of Calcutta and West Bengal. Diminishing extreme deprivation and removing abuses of power has taken root in the politics of this region. More precisely: persons in Calcutta made voting decisions based on alleviating deprivation and diminishing abuses of power. Concurrently, political parties in Calcutta have responded to this voting behavior. It is the responsiveness of parties to the demands of the voting public that has sustained this norm. And while it might be the case that the realities of the Great Bengal Famine and the sectarian violence of the 1940s helped to initially set these priorities in motion that does not necessarily explain their longevity or their continued hold. There are other factors at work here. In particular, Sen indicates that the disaggregation of ethical and political identities from religious identities in Bengal has played a crucial role in the longevity of these norms. By justifying ethical and political identities in terms of experiences that all persons can observe—with special emphasis on observations related to economic class—Calcutta has been inoculated against a resurgence of sectarian violence in the recent past.

Interpreted in this way, Sen's explanation of the low homicide rate in Calcutta is rooted in several factors. The institutional features of democracy contribute to this achievement. The holding of competitive elections is a key part of the story. The movement away from the malevolent governing intentions of the British Raj was very important. But to truly understand Calcutta's homicide rate it is necessary to examine the history of Calcutta as well as its leading norms and its public reasoning. It is the stability of a certain kind of norm and a certain type of public reasoning in the city over time that best explains why the homicide rate of Calcutta is so much lower than its democratic and nondemocratic urban peers. The comparison within India Sen sets in motion in this passage is also highly revealing. As Sen notes, the approach taken in Calcutta and West Bengal has proven to be more empirically effective at reducing homicides and other forms of violent crime than the approach taken in Bombay and Ahmedabad. Calcutta's homicide rate of 0.3 per 100,000 persons in 2005 compares favorably with the homicide rates of these two cities. Equally important, there have been no sectarian riots in Calcutta in the recent past. In Mumbai and Ahmedabad, however, the situation is different. There have been communal riots that targeted a Muslim minority population in these two cities. These riots may have been much smaller than the ones that took place during the British Raj. They were still very brutal.

CALCUTTA AND THE OBLIGATIONS OF POWER

In this chapter, I have discussed Tagore and Sen's analysis of sectarian conflict in India in more detail. Both Tagore and Sen identify the British strategy of inciting sectarian conflict within India as a determining factor in the sectarian riots of the 1940s. As Sen notes, when the long-term strategy of dividing Indian persons against themselves was lifted sectarian violence immediately declined. Sen also draws attention to the importance of justifying ethical and political obligations in nonreligious terms in this context. By disaggregating ethical and political ideas from ideas of divinity—by drawing on experiences that all persons can perceive when reasoning in public about state policy— Calcutta has avoided sectarian conflict altogether. This aspect of Calcutta's ethical, social, and political life plays an important part in any explanation of its extremely low homicide rate.

Sen's discussion of the homicide rate in Calcutta and other urban areas around the world brings his discussion of peace and democratic society into sharper relief. Some democratic societies are better than other democratic societies in providing human security because of their social histories and political norms. From this point of view, the study of Calcutta has much to offer to the urban areas of the world. But the last comment I would like to make in this context concerns the way the argument in *Peace and Democratic Society* fits together with the broader themes under consideration in this book. In particular, the idea of the obligations of power—which requires individuals in positions of power to (1) protect persons from abuses of power, and (2) protect persons from extreme deprivation (including homelessness and starvation), while (3) disaggregating religious identity from ethical and political life—is a theme in Sen's interpretation of the Sutta Nipata as well as Sen's argument in *Peace and Democratic Society*. There is a clear overlap here. And this, in my view, is revealing. In Sen's analysis, something like the idea of the obligations of power was a norm in the city of Calcutta in 2005. The urban area with the lowest homicide rate in the world shares many of the same priorities as Buddha's ethic. Grounding ethical and political norms in religious identity, however, has not yielded the same outcomes. Religious communitarianism, as well as the idea of "civil religion" espoused by thinkers like Locke and Rousseau, does not have the same record of protecting persons from violence as the obligations of power. A difference in norms leads to a difference in outcomes in this case.[34]

NOTES

1. Amartya Sen, *The Argumentative Indian: Writings on Indian History, Culture and Identity* (New York: Picador, 2005), 267.

2. See Leavitt, *The Foreign Policy of John Rawls and Amartya Sen* (Lanham, MD: Lexington Books, 2013), chapter 9 for more on these points.

3. The idea of a "democratic peace" is described in Rawls, *The Law of Peoples with "The Idea of Public Reason Revisited"* (Cambridge, MA: Harvard University Press, 1999), chapter 5, as well as K. Rasler and W. Thompson, *Puzzles of the Democratic Peace: Theory, Geopolitics and the Transformation of World Politics* (New York: Palgrave Macmillan, 2005).

4. Fakrul Alam and Radha Chakravarty, eds., *The Essential Tagore* (Cambridge, MA: The Belknap Press of Harvard University Press, 2011), 141.

5. Tagore is referring to the Swadeshi program of boycotting foreign goods and schools in this passage in the "Disease and the Cure."

6. See chapter 6, note 31.

7. See introduction, note 22.

8. See introduction, note 23.

9. Rabindranath Tagore, *Crisis in Civilization: A Message on Completing His Eighty Years* (Birbhum: Santiniketan Press, 1941), 11. Accessed from https://indianculture.gov.in/reports-proceedings/crisis-civilization-message-completing-his-eighty-years.

10. See chapter 6, note 11.

11. Fakrul Alam and Radha Chakravarty, *The Essential Tagore*, 134.

12. See introduction, note 21.

13. Tagore, *Crisis in Civilization*, 10.

14. Amartya Sen, *Identity and Violence: The Illusion of Destiny* (New York: W. W. Norton and Company, 2006), 170.

15. Ibid., 173.

16. Ibid., 172.

17. See chapter 1, note 6.

18. See chapter 1, note 6.

19. Sen, *Identity and Violence*, 173.

20. Ibid., 173.

21. Ibid., 106. See also Sen, *Poverty and Famines: An Essay on Entitlement and Deprivatio* (Oxford: Oxford University Press, 1982), 52–86.

22. Sen, *Identity and Violence*, 172.

23. See chapter 1, note 6.

24. Sen, *Identity and Violence*, 172.

25. August and September 1947 were very bloody and continue to live on in the historical memory of persons living in the subcontinent. See, for instance, this retrospective in the *Washington Post*: Vidhi Doshi and Nisar Mehdi, "70 Years Later, Survivors Recall the Horrors of India-Pakistan Partition," *The Washington Post*, August 14, 2017. https://www.washingtonpost.com/world/asia-pacific/70-years-later-survivors-recall-the-horrors-of-india-pakistan-partition/2017/08/14/3b8c58e4-7de9-11e7-9026-4a0a64977c92_story.html.

26. For Buddha's discussion of violent sectarianism in the Sutta Nipata, see chapter 1. The Cakkavatti-Sihanada Sutta is discussed at the beginning of chapter 4.

27. Sen, *Identity and Violence*, 172.

28. Sen, *Peace and Democratic Society* (Cambridge: OpenBook Publishers, 2011), 17–18.

29. Ibid.

30. Ibid.

31. Ibid.

32. Ibid., 17.

33. Ibid.

34. For more on the idea of civil religion see Locke, *A Letter Concerning Toleration*, ed. James Tully (Indianapolis, IN: Hackett, 1983), and Rousseau, *The Social Contract*, trans. Donald A. Cress, introduction by David Wootton (Indianapolis, IN: Hackett, 2019). Sen's criticism of communitarianism is especially pronounced in *Identity and Violence, The Illusion of Destiny*.

Chapter 9

Open Impartiality

I have now covered the main passages from the writings of Tagore and Sen that refer or seem to refer to Buddha and the early Indian classical period. For both thinkers, Buddha (1) presented an account of human ethical obligation that (2) emphasized diminishing violence and sectarian conflict in society while (3) consciously avoiding appeals to religious concepts and ideas. Both thinkers also emphasize (4) the way Buddha grounded his ethical arguments in observations and experiences that all persons can have. A form of social empiricism is central to the way Buddha justified his ideas when speaking in public. Moreover, in the process of developing these general ideas, I have emphasized the specific ethical principles Tagore and Sen find in Buddha's statements as well as the Ashokan inscriptions. In particular, (5) the idea of the obligations of power and (6) the notion of a development ethic is central to the way Tagore and Sen interpret Buddha and Ashoka. The foreign policy internationalism of Tagore and Sen is firmly rooted in the early Indian classical period.

The link between Buddha's ethical philosophy and the ideas of Tagore and Sen should now be clearer. But what I would like to do in this final chapter is to compare Sen's foreign policy internationalism with the social contract tradition. The idea of the obligations of power—as well as the closely related idea of the development ethic—differentiates Sen's foreign policy internationalism from the foreign policy ideas of Thomas Hobbes and John Rawls. Tagore and Sen do not ground their approach to foreign policy in the concept of a "democratic peace" as Rawls attempts to do.

SEN AND THE SOCIAL CONTRACT

As discussed throughout this study Sen believes that "The perspective of obligations of power was presented powerfully by Gautama Buddha in the Sutta Nipata."[1] Part of Sen's argument in *The Idea of Justice*—as well as *The*

Argumentative Indian and the "Contemporary Relevance of Buddha"—is devoted to defending this interpretation of Buddha's ethical teaching. But in the process of describing the idea of the obligations of power in the Sutta Nipata, Sen develops a contrast with a different ethical tradition. Sen states:

> The mother's reason for helping the child, in this line of thinking, is not guided by the rewards of cooperation, but precisely from her recognition that she can, asymmetrically, do things for the child that would make a huge difference to the child's life and which the child itself cannot do.[2]

In this passage, the adult is vastly more capable—and therefore vastly more powerful—than the infant child. There is a very large asymmetry of power between adult human beings and the newly born. And yet the adult can use their superiority in power to promote the growth and development of the child. It is the way persons choose to use their skills and abilities that defines the ethical basis of their conduct in Sen's reading. But what, exactly, is Sen getting at with the reference to rewards or cooperation in this sentence? And why does the theme of rewards or cooperation fail to capture what is going on in the Metta Sutta?

The basic idea informing Sen's argument is as follows. A person may choose to take on the responsibility of caring for a child. An adult can focus on creating a world of loving-kindness in a child's life. But the obligation to do so does not flow from a mutually beneficial agreement. An infant is not yet able to enter into contracts, make promises or engage in cooperation. Nor can an infant reciprocate the goods deeds of their caregiver. Newborn children simply cannot do these things. And while it is possible to reframe this relationship in terms of the idea of tacit consent—in this line of reasoning, the infant would, retroactively, consent to the way they are looked after as a child when they reach adulthood—Sen notes that this type of explanation is very "round about" and obscures the question of the adult's mental and emotional life.[3] It is the way the caregiver is responding to the presence of the child that is distinctive and most in need of clarification.

Reframing the relationship between an infant and an adult in terms of cooperation or an agreement is, in Sen's view, a mistake. The idea of a contract between an adult and an infant is cumbersome and is not something any person can ever see or experience. There is an unempirical quality to this kind of explanation. Buddha's point in Sutta Nipata, however, is more thoroughly grounded in experience. An infant needs a great deal of care and attention to grow and develop. Many concrete interventions are required to successfully sustain the life of a child into maturity. In particular, an adult must feed and shelter and clothe and clean and teach and protect a child on a daily basis for a long period of time to further that child's growth and development. Doesn't the sense of the adult intervening in the life of the child—because the adult understands they can "do things for the child that would make a huge difference to the child's life and which the child itself cannot do"—better characterize what is happening here? More generally, there are over seven billion persons now living on the earth and each one of these persons required—and requires—a large number of interventions from many different people during infancy and childhood to grow and develop. It is the widespread perception of adults intervening in the life of children that makes Buddha's analogy so easy to understand and so powerfully communicative.

THE ORIGINAL POSITION

In Sen's view, the notion of cooperation between equal agents is an important ethical idea. There are many aspects of human life where the idea of cooperation is illuminating and reveals important truths. However, the belief that cooperation can explain all aspects of a person's ethical obligations is clearly an overreach. It is a distortion to redescribe all of a person's responsibilities in terms of one type of interaction that can play out between equally situated adults.

Sen does not believe the idea of cooperation is the best point of departure in explaining the obligations an adult might have towards an infant. This point, however, can be extended to other types of cases. In the social contract tradition of ethical and political philosophy, the idea of cooperation or an agreement between free and equal persons is given very great prominence. It is used to work out the basic principles of justice at work in an ideal society. Only what all persons (or their representatives) can consent to in a hypothetical "original position" is given priority in this way of thinking.[4] But here, too, Sen finds a distortion. Is the idea of a social contract—that is, a hypothetical agreement between equally situated persons that specifies the basis for social cooperation—really the best approach for thinking about the most important political obligations at work in a society? Is, for instance, the relation between the newly born and the heads of state in a society best understood through the idea of a hypothetical agreement? The same point can be made when considering the human relation with nonhuman species. Persons cannot enter into contracts with other animals and other plants and other forms of life. A tree or a bird or a deer or a fish simply cannot do these things. As a consequence, using a contract to frame the obligations persons have towards the nonhuman environment involves the adoption of several additional steps that gets in the way of the primary issue. And since the idea of tacit consent—which was appealed to in the case of adults and children—cannot be invoked in the relation between persons and animals the discussion must delve into even more complexities. The framework of the social contract tradition is not a very promising one for addressing these concerns.

Sen does not believe the social contract adequately captures the head of state's obligations towards infant children or other species. But a second area of divergence between Sen and the social contract tradition centers on the area of foreign policy. As noted in chapters 5 and 8, Tagore and Sen never justify the idea of intentionally targeting civilians with weapons of war. There is nothing like the idea of the supreme emergency exemption in the writings of Tagore and Sen. But these notions are defended by Thomas Hobbes in *Leviathan* and John Rawls in *The Law of Peoples*. Hobbes and Rawls have a more permissive attitude towards the use of violence by the state.

The difference in substance between the two ethical traditions on this question is important and has many roots. It is possible that these diverging attitudes can be traced back to Thucydides on the one hand and Buddha on the other.[5] But however this may be, the passage where Hobbes articulates the main assumptions of his approach to foreign policy in *Leviathan* is well known. In the thirteenth chapter of part I of *Leviathan*, Hobbes states:

> But though there have never been any time, wherein particular men were in a condition of warre one against another; yet in all times, Kings, and Persons of Soveraigne authority, because of their Independency, are in continuall jealousies, and in the state of posture of Gladiators; having their weapons pointing, and their eyes fixed on one another; that is, their Forts, Garrisons and Guns upon the Frontiers of their Kingdomes, and continuall spyes upon their neighbors, which is a posture of War.[6]

The ideas expressed in this passage are exceedingly grim. To Hobbes, every state is an existential threat to every other state and every state is always preparing for the next war. The international system is in a state of perpetual conflict in Hobbes's analysis.

Hobbes likens the relationships between states in the international system to that of gladiators who are fighting to the death or preparing to do so. What matters in this contest is the strength of the antagonists and little else. And it is within this context that Hobbes makes a claim about justice or right. Hobbes notes that: "The notions of Right and Wrong, Justice and Injustice have there no place."[7] Justice is not real—it is not present—in the international system.

INNOCENT PERSONS

Hobbes's description of the international system is slightly modified at other points in *Leviathan*. He notes that an agreement or "covenant" or treaty between societies is possible and establishes a common but limited sense of transnational justice. But outside of the case of states that have formally agreed to cooperate with each other, there are no limits on what can be done. Hobbes states:

> But the Infliction of what evil soever, on an Innocent man, that is not a Subject, if it be for the benefit of the Commonwealth, *and without violation of any former Covenant*, is no breach of the Law of Nature.[8] (italics added)

The point Hobbes makes here draws attention to a key assumption in his understanding of human obligation. For Hobbes, justice is an emergent property in the international system. It is created by treaties and is always minimal in nature. In the absence of these treaties all kinds of violent conduct are permissible. More precisely, the "infliction" of "evil" on an "innocent man" is acceptable conduct to Hobbes if: (1) the action benefits the Hobbesian state and (2) the innocent persons who are targeted are members of a state that has not made a contract or a "covenant" with the Hobbesian sovereign. In this way of thinking, the idea of an abuse of power in foreign policy can only be invoked *after* two states make a treaty—not before.

The picture of the international system that emerges from these passages is clear. States are like gladiators fighting to the death and this conflict can be limited to a certain extent by formal agreements. But outside of the context created by these treaties there are no ethical constraints on the decisions of the head of state in foreign policy. In Hobbes's view, the state of war is the reality in international relations. However, when viewed through the kinds of arguments that have been under examination in this study the problem with Hobbes's ideas are also readily apparent. At no point in Hobbes's discussion of foreign policy does he reflect on the way his arguments would impact the decisions of other heads of state in the international system. Hobbes never stopped to consider how other heads of state would respond to these claims. And this is a big oversight. Hobbes believed the domain of foreign policy is an existential struggle that is akin to a gladiatorial conquest. He also believed the innocent civilians living in other nations can be targeted in the absence of treaties. If you were a neighboring head of state in the region reflecting on Hobbes's comments, what would you think? How would you respond to Hobbes's claims?

One problem with Hobbes's account of the international system is its shortsightedness. There is no acknowledgment of anything like the security dilemma in Hobbes's approach to foreign policy. Hobbes does not consider the ways in which his ideas can lead to conflict spirals that leave everyone worse-off. A second problem with Hobbes's theory, however, is connected to Hobbes's belief that treaties create a minimal sense of transnational justice.

Hobbes may have thought this. But this is in fact a highly dubious idea. Persons do not need a contract or agreement with other persons to understand why abuses of power are wrong. The existence of a contract or a "covenant" between two different peoples is not the primary or the only source of the ethical obligation to avoid abusing one's power. On the contrary: abuses of power are often understood to be wrong independent of the presence or absence of contracts and agreements. The idea of a contract has no bearing on the ethical idea of an abuse of power in most cases.

When analyzed in terms of Sen's ethical theory, Hobbes's error is also connected to the way he justifies his ethical ideas. The predatory use of power is not wrong because it violates a contract. It is wrong because it harms innocent human beings. It causes pain, severs relationships of love and loyalty, and robs large numbers of persons of the capacity to act. One can invoke the ideas in Ashoka's thirteenth "Major Rock Edict" in this context. Or again: the predatory use of power is not wrong because heads of state have decided that it is wrong. Abuses of power are wrong because they create feelings of fear and the desire for retaliation in the society that has been attacked. The "historical memories" of societies are most definitely shaped by acts of violent aggression.[9] And these thoughts—which are decisive in their own right—just touch the surface of the kinds of arguments that are possible here. There are many reasons that can be invoked to explain why abuses of power are immoral and should be avoided that have nothing to do with a contract or treaty. There is—to use Sen's term—plural grounding on this point.[10] And among the arguments that condemn abuses of power one should include the perspective of the development ethic and the obligations of power. According to these notions, there is an imperfect duty to promote the growth and development of all persons around the world. Whenever a head of state attacks the innocent civilians of another nation to gain power or territory they are violating this principle.

THE SUPREME EMERGENCY EXEMPTION

Hobbes's understanding of foreign policy can be criticized from many points of view. Hobbes did not think about the way his ideas would affect the heads of state living in other societies. But Hobbes also mischaracterizes the origins of justice in his theory. A contract or an agreement is not required to understand why abuses of power are wrong. Abuses of power do not require the existence of contracts or agreements to become viable ethical ideas.

Interpreted in this way, there is a kind of comprehensive error or misunderstanding evident in Hobbes's approach to foreign policy. It is not just that Hobbes endorses the idea that the head of state can invade their neighbors, or initiate coup d'etats, or order assassinations. It is that Hobbes's notion of morality is itself distorted by his belief in contracts. The idea that heads of state must enter into agreements with each other to create a minimal, trans-national sense of justice basically ensures that the entire analysis will be extraordinarily permissive in regard to state violence.

Hobbes's foreign policy ideas can be sharply criticized from the perspective of the obligations of power and the idea of the development ethic as well as other ethical points of view. But what about the foreign policy ideas of the social contract thinker John Rawls (1911–2002)? Why did Rawls believe it was permissible to target the civilian populations of "outlaw regimes" in times of "Supreme Emergency"?[11]

Rawls's passage on the supreme emergency exemption in *The Law of Peoples* lays out the conditions of its use. Rawls states:

> (The supreme emergency exemption) allows us to set aside—in certain special circumstances—the strict status of civilians that normally prevents their being attacked in war. We must proceed with caution here. Were there times during World War II when Britain could properly have held that civilians' strict status was suspended, and thus could have bombed Hamburg or Berlin? Possibly, but only if it was sure that the bombing would have done some substantial good; such action cannot be justified by a doubtful marginal gain. When Britain was alone and had no other means to break Germany's superior power, the bombing of German cities was arguably justifiable.[12]

In reflecting on this passage, it is clear that Rawls believes the supreme emergency exception should only be invoked in very dire cases. Rawls did not, for instance, believe the conditions of the supreme emergency exemption were met in the United States of America's war with Japan at the end of World War II. Rawls opposed Truman's decision to drop atomic bombs on Hiroshima and Nagasaki.[13] However, in Britain's war with Germany between 1939 and 1942 the situation was different. Britain was in danger of losing the war to Germany at this time. In Rawls's view, Britain was justified in targeting German civilians during this most desperate phase of the war.

Rawls's defense of the supreme emergency exemption is presented as a last resort. Rawls constrains the use of violence in the international system in a way that Hobbes never does. But why does Rawls claim that the targeting of civilians "cannot be justified by a doubtful marginal gain"? What is at stake in this idea? And here it seems that Rawls is drawing on the idea of total war. If the civilian population is subjected to terror bombings, then Rawls may believe that the civilian population's morale and resolve to support the war will decrease. This might be what Rawls is referring to when he speaks of Britain breaking "Germany's superior power." It is also possible that Rawls believes the ability of the outlaw regime to produce weapons of war might be diminished through these bombings. By targeting the labor force in the manufacturing centers of the outlaw regime, the war effort of the outlaw regime may be slowed down. On this interpretation, the outlaw regime's ability to construct new weapons could be diminished by these bombings. Perhaps this is what Rawls means by a "substantial good" in this context.

RAWLS AND HOBBES

Rawls's interpretation of the supreme emergency exemption is framed in terms of the events of World War II. The realities of this conflict convinced Rawls that the supreme emergency exemption was a necessary principle in any discussion of self-defense. But it is also the case that there is a parallel between Rawls's ideas here and the claims made by Hobbes in *Leviathan*. When Hobbes argues that "the Infliction of what evil soever, on an Innocent man, that is not a Subject, if it be for the benefit of the Commonwealth, and without violation of any former Covenant, is no breach of the Law of Nature" he is making the same type of claim that Rawls is making with the supreme emergency exemption. In both cases, the targeting of persons who are acknowledged to be innocent is permitted if it benefits the state. It is just that Rawls has a stricter sense of when this type of thinking can be invoked.

Rawls shares an assumption about the use of violent force with Hobbes. But there is also an important procedural and methodological similarity between Hobbes and Rawls. Rawls—like Hobbes—believes justice in the international system must be understood through the idea of a contract.[14] Justice in the international system is an emergent property in the thought of Rawls and Hobbes. And this assumption is highly significant. In Rawls's discussion, outlaw regimes deny human rights and wage war against their neighbors. They have not entered into an international social contract with surrounding societies. As a consequence, they are outside of the hypothetical system of law that Rawls has created in *The Law of Peoples* and their civilians can be intentionally targeted in situations of extreme emergency. The fact that outlaw regimes are not "members in good standing" in the law of peoples is all important here.[15]

CONTRACTS AND NUCLEAR BOMBARDMENT

Rawls believes less is owed the civilians of an outlaw regime than the civilians of societies that adhere to the international social contract. If the outlaw regime is on the verge of winning a war, its civilian population is no longer protected by nonviolent norms. I should also point out in this context that Rawls believes the possession of nuclear weapons is justifiable within the law of peoples. In Rawls's view, there must be some societies with nuclear weapons to counteract the threat of outlaw regimes. This means, among other things, that the civilian population of an outlaw regime can be targeted with nuclear weapons in a situation of supreme emergency. The terrors of a nuclear bombardment can rain down on these persons.

For Rawls—like Hobbes—the assumption that international justice is based off the idea of a contract exposes large groups of innocent people to the horrors of war. There is an extraordinarily grim reality embedded within both Hobbes's and Rawls's theory of justice. But this parallelism between Hobbes and Rawls on state violence also means that Rawls is open to the same types of criticism that arose in the discussion of Hobbes. First, there is the question of how heads of state would respond to Rawls's reasoning. Rawls endorses the supreme emergency exemption and argues that the "some nuclear weapons must be retained."[16] How would neighboring heads of state view this decision? What actions might neighboring heads of state take in response to this situation?[17] And while it is difficult to answer this question within Rawls's framework because he is talking about the defense of an ideal society in *The Law of Peoples*—one that does not yet exist—the real-world history of nuclear weapons has been one of proliferation.[18] The construction of nuclear weapons and their use at the end of World War II has led other states to adopt the same military strategy. There are now nine states in the world who possess nuclear weapons. There are also several other states that are considering this path. Is the world really a safer place for humanity as a result of these actions?

Rawls's thoughts on the supreme emergency exemption and nuclear weapons can be criticized in terms of their empirical effects. The strategy of producing—and possibly using—nuclear weapons has led to a series of responses that have left everyone worse-off. In the real world the decision to construct a nuclear weapon has led to a sharp escalation in the dangers confronting all human beings. But the problem here is not just the imprudence of this strategy. There is also a problem with the underlying ethical framework of the social contract in this context. Is the idea of a contract needed to decide if the nuclear bombardment of an innocent civilian population is unjust? Does the presence or absence of a treaty determine the morality of this idea?

A DEMOCRATIC PEACE?

The supreme emergency exemption can be criticized from a moral point of view. Targeting innocent men, women, and children is an abuse of power. The supreme emergency exemption can also be criticized from a prudential point of view. Authoritarian adversaries will adopt the rationale of the supreme emergency exemption and develop nuclear weapons in response to the decisions of the leading democracies. Everyone is made worse-off by these events. But even limited means/ends reasoning calls the supreme emergency exemption into question. As Stephen Nathanson notes in his book *Ethics and the Terrorism of War*, analyses of the bombing of German cities during World War II concluded that they "did not significantly help to defeat the Germans."[19] The effectiveness of the supreme emergency exemption has not been corroborated by historians of war. And if one asks the question "Why not?" Nathanson's reply is as follows:

> [Then] there is the fact that people in the military play a direct role in fighting a war and therefore that killing or disabling combatants is generally more likely to weaken an enemy's war-fighting capacity than killing or disabling people who are not involved in war-fighting. Effective war-fighting generally requires attacking the enemy militarily.[20]

Here Nathanson notes that a successful war of self-defense requires diminishing the military capabilities of the attacker. Winning battles between combatants is the most important thing. Moreover, Nathanson gathers a large amount of evidence to support this claim. In particular, Nathanson notes that civilians made up 5 percent of the total deaths in World War I, 48 percent of the total deaths in World War II, 84 percent of the total deaths in the Korean War, and 90 percent of the total deaths in the Vietnam War.[21] And yet the targeting of civilians by either side did not confer any military advantage in these cases. These attacks did not play a meaningful role in the resolution of these conflicts. As Nathanson notes: "As long as combatants could fight on, the civilian deaths did not directly weaken the enemy forces and therefore did little to achieve military success."[22]

Nathanson questions the supreme emergency exemption on means/ends grounds. The supreme emergency exemption or something like it does not help one achieve the goal of waging a just war of self-defense or any other type of war. In fact, one could make the opposite argument. When a head of state decides to bomb a civilian center in a situation of supreme emergency the head of state is siphoning off military capacity from the fight against the attacking forces. The efforts of war planners, the training of soldiers, the military equipment involved in the operation, and much else, including the use of natural resources, are diverted away from the principal objective of engaging combatants.

The fact that the supreme emergency exemption can be criticized from so many different perspectives is a sign that it is not well founded. The

supreme emergency exemption and the doctrine of mutually assured destruction—which is also grounded in the supreme emergency exemption—should
be abandoned. Article VI of the Nuclear Non-proliferation Treaty must be
pursued anew.[23] At the very least, the nuclear arsenals of the United States of
America and Russia should be further reduced. As of January 2021, the United
States of America has 1,800 nuclear warheads actively deployed while Russia
has 1,685 nuclear warheads actively deployed. Moreover, each country has
several thousand nuclear warheads in reserve. China, the United Kingdom,
France, Pakistan, India, Israel, and North Korea also possess nuclear warheads. Getting the numbers down in the United States and Russia constitute a
critical first step towards the larger project of nuclear disarmament.[24]

The need for a reduction in nuclear arsenals is urgent. In the absence of
this project several very terrible outcomes are just around the corner. Another
problematic idea in international relations is the notion of a "democratic
peace." According to this hypothesis, functioning democracies do not—for
the most part—attack functioning democracies. As Rawls notes, the "great
wars of history" were not fought by established democracies. And this
empirical finding is a cause for optimism in Rawls's view. If established
democracies do not, for the most part, attack each other, a world in which
every society becomes a functioning democracy constitutes a genuine path
toward perpetual peace.[25] However, the problem with this notion is that it
abstracts away from the reality of the existing conflict between democratic
and authoritarian regimes. If the leading democratic and authoritarian states
in the international system continue to expand their conventional arsenals, sell
weapons to countries around the world, pursue new cyber weapons, develop
unmanned systems for waging war, pursue the militarization of space, and
maintain existing stockpiles of long-range nuclear weapons while increasing
medium range nuclear weapons—all of which are currently happening—the
idea of a democratic peace becomes too remote to be of much use. Finding a
way to de-escalate the conflict between democratic and authoritarian states in
the short term should be the priority. Slowing down the mutually reinforcing
rush to increase military capacity is critically important.

Interpreted in this way, the idea of democratic peace is an important idea.
And I do not in any way wish to diminish the attractive possibility of a
world of well-established and functioning democracies. But the notion that
"democratic peace" will enhance human security in the international system
by itself is an overreach. Human security is not enhanced by the strategy
of arming the democratic and the nondemocratic regimes to the hilt. Even
more: by adopting the view that it is permissible to use nuclear weapons to
defend democracy, the supreme emergency exemption basically ensures that
the conflict between democratic and authoritarian states will continue indefi-
nitely. No authoritarian and no democratic state will unilaterally disarm when

its adversaries are committed to the construction and possible use of nuclear weapons. International collective action—to slow down the rush to militarize in several different areas—is needed as a first step. The obligations of power require heads of state to consider this course.

CONCLUDING REMARKS

The approach to foreign policy described in this book—as well as the approach to violent conduct within a society—is centered on the inherently escalating nature of the violent act. Persons will not stand idly by if their lives are threatened. Persons will take actions to defend themselves. Finding ways to protect persons and advance human security without initiating irrational escalations is a more promising path. But the last point I would like to make in this study is taken from a passage in the *The Idea of Justice*. Sen states:

> There are powerful traditions of reasoned argument, rather than reliance on faith and unreasoned convictions, in India's intellectual past, as there are in the thoughts flourishing in a number of other non-Western societies. In confining attention almost exclusively to Western literature, the contemporary— and largely Western—pursuit of political philosophy in general and of the demands of justice in particular has been, I would argue, limited and to some extent parochial.[26]

The reference to Buddha in the first sentence of this passage is clear. In Sen's view, it was Buddha who adopted the unique strategy of disaggregating ethical and religious argumentation in the early Indian classical period. The ethical ideas put forward by Buddha is one of the many "powerful traditions of reasoned argument" Sen is referring to here. But the point Sen makes in the second part of this passage is also significant. There is great danger, Sen indicates, when the examination of justice is confined to a single tradition. Important assumptions may go uncontested. Other possibilities of thinking and reasoning are overlooked. The demands of open impartiality are not met when attention is limited to only one tradition of impartial thought.[27]

The danger of systematically excluding alternative conceptions of impartiality is a problem in any investigation. It is necessary to pay attention to impartial and reasoned argument wherever it arises. Seeking out different concepts of impartiality is built into Sen's idea of justice. But these concerns are also amplified by the connection between morality and prudence in Sen's writings. If the moral ideas informing a perspective are distorted, then it is going to be very difficult for a person or a group of people or a head of state to act in a prudent manner. Mistakes in ethical reasoning will echo in the concrete decisions people make. And nowhere is this more evident than in reflections on violence and human development. By reflecting on the practical reasoning evident in the Sutta Nipata and other early Buddhist discourses, as well as the Ashokan inscriptions and Tagore's writings, Sen develops an ethical understanding that is less permissive of violence and more focused on the growth and development of persons than the social contract thinkers. The study of justice—and especially the study of ethics and international relations—can be improved by the engagement with non-European traditions.

NOTES

1. Amartya Sen, *The Idea of Justice* (Cambridge: The Belknap Press of Harvard University Press, 2009), 205.

2. Ibid.

3. Ibid., 206.

4. Ibid., 56.

5. In the Athenian way of thinking about the relations between states described by Thucydides, justice is not real in and of itself. Instead, justice is an emergent property that depends on the underlying power relations between different states. Justice can only arise *if* two states are equal in military strength, in the Athenian view. It should also be noted in this context that Hobbes translated Thucydides's *History of the Peloponnesian War* into English. More generally, there is a connection between Thucydides's writings and what is now called "political realism." As Stephen Nathanson has noted "Realists trace their key ideas to Thucydides, Machiavelli and Hobbes" (Nathanson, *Terrorism and the Ethics of War* [Cambridge: Cambridge University Press, 2010], 80). In this context, Rawls's praise of Hobbes's *Leviathan*—"surely the greatest book of political philosophy in English"—gains greater significance. Rawls, *Justice as Fairness: A Restatement*, ed. Erin Kelly (Cambridge, Ma: Harvard University Press, 2001) 1. See also Rawls, *A Theory of Justice* (Cambridge, MA: Belknap Press of Harvard University, 1971), 10 note 4.

6. Thomas Hobbes, *Leviathan*, ed. C. B. Macpherson (Harmondsworth, UK: Penguin, 1985), 187–88.

7. Ibid., 188.

8. Ibid., 360.

9. Rawls notes this reality in his discussion of the conduct of war: "The way a war is fought and the deeds done in ending it live on in the historical memories of societies and may or may not set the stage for future war" (Rawls, *The Law of Peoples with "The Idea of Public Reason Revisited"* [Cambridge, MA: Harvard University Press, 1999], 96). However, Rawls does not argue for the principle of noncombatant immunity in all cases in this text.

10. Sen, *The Idea of Justice*, 2.

11. Rawls, *The Law of Peoples*, 98–99.

12. Ibid., 98.

13. Ibid., 95.

14. "This idea of justice is based on the familiar idea of the social contract, and the procedure followed before the principles of right and justice are selected and agreed upon is in some ways the same in both the domestic and the international case." Ibid., 4.

15. "Gradually over time, then, well-ordered peoples may pressure the outlaw regimes to change their ways; but by itself this pressure is unlikely to be effective. It may need to be backed up by the firm denial of economic and other assistance, or the refusal to admit outlaw regimes as members of good standing *in mutually beneficial cooperative practices*" (italics added). Ibid., 93. Rawls also makes a similar point in the context of his discussion of Hitler's Germany: "The peculiar evil of Nazism needs to be understood. *It was characteristic of Hitler that he recognized no possibility at all of a political relationship with his enemies*" (italics added). The inability to seek out or adhere to treaties or contracts or agreements—the unwillingness to cooperate with other societies—is the defining feature of Hitler's conduct, in Rawls's description. Ibid., 99.

16. Ibid., 9.

17. Indira Gandhi was the head of state who ultimately sanctioned India's development of nuclear weapons.

18. For more on this point, see Leavitt, *The Foreign Policy of John Rawls and Amartya Sen* (Lanham, MD: Lexington Books, 2013), chapter 9.

19. Stephen Nathanson, *Ethics and the Terrorism of War* (Cambridge: Cambridge University Press, 2010), 187. See also A. C. Grayling, *Among the Dead Cities: The History and Moral Legacy of the WWII Bombings of Civilians in Germany and Japan*, 91–116. Note that Grayling's analysis of the bombing of Japanese civilian centers—including the nuclear bombings of Hiroshima and Nagasaki—reaches the same conclusion as his discussion of the bombings of German city centers.

20. Nathanson, *Ethics and the Terrorism of War*, 202.

21. Ibid., 203.

22. Ibid., 202.

23. Article VI of the "Nuclear Non-proliferation Treaty" reads as follows: "Each of the Parties to the Treaty undertakes to pursue negotiations in good faith on effective measures relating to cessation of the nuclear arms race at an early date and to nuclear disarmament, and on a treaty on general and complete disarmament under strict and effective international control" ("Treaty on the Non-Proliferation of Nuclear Weapons [NPT]," United Nations, n.d. https://www.un.org/disarmament/wmd/nuclear/npt/text/).

24. According to the Stockholm International Peace Research Institute (SIPRI), the United of America has 1,800 actively deployed nuclear war heads while Russia has 1,625. The United Kingdom has 120 actively deployed nuclear weapons while France has 280. Meanwhile, The United States of America (3,700), Russia (4,630), the United Kingdom (105), France (10), China (350), India (156), Pakistan (165), Israel (90), and North Korea (40–50) each have nuclear warheads which are not actively deployed but which are stored or held in reserve or retired warheads that may be dismantled. This data is from January 1, 2021. "Global Nuclear Arsenals Grow as States

Continue to Modernize—New SIPRI Yearbook Out Now," Stockholm International Peace Research Institute, June 14, 2021. https://www.sipri.org/media/press-release /2021/global-nuclear-arsenals-grow-states-continue-modernize-new-sipri-yearbook -out-now.

25. Rawls, *The Law of Peoples*, 52–53.

26. Sen, *The Idea of Justice*, xiii–xiv. The point Sen makes about parochialism in the study of justice in this passage is akin to the point George Gheverghese Joseph makes about the study of mathematics at the end of his book *The Crest of the Peacock*: "And yet if there is a single universal object, one that transcends linguistic, national, and cultural barriers and is acceptable to all and denied by none, it is our present set of numerals. From its remote beginnings in India, its gradual spread in all directions remains the great romantic episode in the history of mathematics. It is hoped that this episode, together with other non-European mathematical achievements highlighted in this book, will help extend our horizons and dent the parochialism that lies behind the Eurocentric perception of the development of mathematical knowledge." Joseph, *The Crest of the Peacock: Non-European Roots of Mathematics* (Princeton, NJ, and Oxford: Princeton University Press, 2011), 512.

27. For more on Sen's concept of open impartiality and "the need to invoke a wide variety of viewpoints and outlooks based on diverse experiences far and near," see Sen, *The Idea of Justice*, 44–46.

Bibliography

Alam, Fakrul, and Radha Chakravarty, eds. 2011. *The Essential Tagore: Rabindranath Tagore*. Cambridge, MA: The Belknap Press of Harvard University Press.

Amaravati Sangha. 2013. "Karaniya Metta Sutta: The Buddha's Words on Loving-Kindness." November 2. Accessed January 21, 2022. https://www.accesstoinsight.org/tipitaka/kn/snp/snp.1.08.amar.html.

Bhikku, Thanissaro. "The Shorter Exhortation to Malunkya," Dhammatalks.org. Accessed January 21, 2022. https://www.dhammatalks.org/suttas/MN/MN63.html.

Brechert, H., and Richard Gombritch. 1991. *The World of Buddhism: Buddhist Monks and Nuns in Society and Culture*. London: Thames and Hudson.

Bronkhorst, Johannes. 2007. *Greater Magadha: Studies in the Culture of Early India*. Leiden: Brill.

Brown, Judith M., and Anthony Parel. 2011. *The Cambridge Companion to Gandhi*. Cambridge: Cambridge University Press.

Collins, Steven. 1998. *Nirvana and other Buddhist Felicities: Utopias of the Pali Imaginaire*. Cambridge: Cambridge University Press.

———. 2010. *Nirvana: Concept, Imagery, Narrative*. Cambridge: Cambridge University Press.

Crocker, David A. 2008. *Ethics of Global Development*. Cambridge: Cambridge University Press.

Doniger, Wendy. 2009. *The Hindus: An Alternative History*. New York: Penguin Books.

Doshi, Vidhi, and Nisar Mehdi. 2017. "70 Years Later, Survivors Recall the India-Pakistan Partition." *The Washington Post*, August 14. Accessed January 21, 2022. https://www.washingtonpost.com/world/asia-pacific/70-years-later-survivors-recall-the-horrors-of-india-pakistan-partition/2017/08/14/3b8c58e4–7de9–11e7–9026–4a0a64977c92_story.html.

Dreze, Jean, and Amartya Sen. 2013. *An Uncertain Glory: India and its Contradictions*. Princeton, NJ: Princeton University Press.

Dutta, Krishna, and Andrew Robinson, eds., with a foreword by Amartya Sen. 1997. *Selected Letters of Rabindranath Tagore*. Cambridge: Cambridge University Press.

Goodin, Robert. 1985. *Protecting the Vulnerable: A Reanalysis of Our Social Responsibilities*. Chicago: University of Chicago Press.

Grayling, A. C. 2007. *Among the Dead Cities: The History and Moral Legacy of the WWII Bombings of Civilians in Germany and Japan*. New York: Walker and Co.

Harvey, Peter. 2013. *An Introduction to Buddhism: Teachings, History and Practices*, Second Edition. Cambridge: Cambridge University Press.

Hobbes, Thomas. 1985. *The Leviathan*. Edited by C. B. Macpherson. Harmondsworth, UK: Penguin.

Holder, John J., ed. and trans. 2006. *Early Buddhist Discourses*. Indianapolis, IN: Hackett.

Huxley, Andrew. 1996. "Buddha and the Social Contract." *Journal of Indian Philosophy* 24, no. 4: 407–20. Accessed January 21, 2022. http://www.jstor.org/stable/23448397.

Joseph, George Gheverghese. 2011. *The Crest of the Peacock: Non-European Roots of Mathematics*. Princeton, NJ, and Oxford: Princeton University Press.

Kangle, R. P. 1965. *The Kautilya Arthashastra Part III: A Study*. Delhi: Motilal Banarsidass.

Kenoyer, Jonathan Mark. 1998. *Ancient Cities of the Indus Valley Civilization*. Karachi; New York: Oxford University Press.

Kristensen, Hans M., and Matt Korda. 2021. "Global Nuclear Arsenals Grow as States Continue to Modernize." Stockholm Institute of Peace Research Initiatives Yearbook, June 14. Accessed January 21, 2022. https://www.sipri.org/media/press -release/2021/global-nuclear-arsenals-grow-states-continue-modernize-new-sipri -yearbook-out-now.

Leavitt, Neal. 2013. *The Foreign Policy of John Rawls and Amartya Sen*. Lanham, MD: Lexington Books.

Leffler, Melvyn P., and Odd Arne Westad, eds. 2010. *Cambridge History of the Cold War*, vol. 1. Cambridge: Cambridge University Press.

Levy, Jack S., and William R. Thompson. 2009. *Causes of War*. Chichester, UK: Wiley.

Locke, John. 1983. *A Letter Concerning Toleration*. Edited by James H. Tully. Indianapolis, IN: Hackett.

Long, Roger D., ed. 2015. *A History of Pakistan*. Oxford: Oxford University Press.

Macaulay, T. B. 1835. "Minute by the Hon'ble T.B. Macaulay." Accessed January 21, 2022. http://www.columbia.edu/itc/mealac/pritchett/00generallinks/macaulay/txt_minute_education_1835.html.

Mascaró, Juan, ed. 1973. *The Dhammapada*. London: Penguin Books.

———. 1965. *Upanishads*. London: Penguin Books.

Matilal, Bimal Krishna. 1986. *Perception: An Essay on Classical Indian Theories of Knowledge*. Oxford: Oxford University Press.

McClish, Mark, and Patrick Olivelle, edited and translated with an introduction. 2012. *The Arthashastra: Selections from the Classic Indian Work on Statecraft*. Indianapolis. IN: Hackett.

Nathanson, Stephen. 2010. *Ethics and the Terrorism of War*. Cambridge: Cambridge University Press.

Norman, K. R., ed. 1996. *The Rhinoceros Horn and other Early Buddhist Poems: The Group of Discourses (Sutta Nipata)*. London: The Pali Text Society Oxford.

Nussbaum, Martha C. 2000. *Women and Human Development: The Capabilities Approach*. Cambridge: Cambridge University Press.

Olendzki, Andrew. "Attadanda Sutta: Arming Oneself." November 2. Accessed January 21, 2022. https://www.accesstoinsight.org/tipitaka/kn/snp/snp.4.15.olen .html.

Olivelle, Patrick, trans. 1996. *Upanishads*. Oxford: Oxford University Press.

Olivelle, Patrick, Janice Leoshko, and Himanshu Prabha Ray, eds. 2012. *Reimagining Ashoka: Memory and History*. New Delhi: Oxford University Press.

Pletcher, Kenneth. 2021. "Jallianwala Bagh Massacre." Britannica, April 6. Accessed January 21, 2022. https://www.britannica.com/event/Jallianwala-Bagh-Massacre.

Rangarajan, L. N., ed. 1987. *The Arthashastra*. Gurgaon: Penguin Books.

Rasler, K., and W. Thompson. 2005. *Puzzles of the Democratic Peace: Theory, Geopolitics and the Transformation of World Politics*. New York: Palgrave Macmillan.

Rawls, John. 2001. *Justice as Fairness: A Restatement*, edited by Erin Kelly. Cambridge, MA: Harvard University Press.

———. 1999. *The Law of Peoples with "The Idea of Public Reason Revisited."* Cambridge, MA, Harvard University Press.

———. 1971. *A Theory of Justice*. Cambridge: Belknap Press of Harvard University.

Reich, David. 2019. *Who We Are and How We Got Here: Ancient DNA and the New Science of the Human Past*. New York: Vintage Books.

Reidy, David and Martin, Rex, eds. 2006. *Rawls' Law of Peoples: A Realistic Utopia?* Malden: Blackwell.

Rhys, Davids. Ambatha Sutta. Accessed August 20, 2022. https://www.sacred-texts.com/bud/dob/dob-03tx.htm.

Rousseau, Jean-Jacques. *On the Social Contract*, second edition. Translated by Donald A. Cress, introduction by David Wootton. Indianapolis, IN: Hackett.

Saddhatissa, H., ed. and trans. 1994. *Sutta Nipata*. Abingdon: Curzon Press.

Satyamurti, Carole. 2015. *Mahabharata: A Modern Retelling*. New York: W. W. Norton and Company.

Sen, Amartya. 2005. *The Argumentative Indian: Writings on Indian History, Culture and Identity*. New York: Picador.

———. 2014. "The Contemporary Relevance of Buddha." *Ethics and International Affairs* 28, no. 1: 15–27.

———. 1999. *Development as Freedom*. New York: Anchor Books.

———. 2009. *The Idea of Justice*. Cambridge, MA: The Belknap Press of Harvard University Press.

———. 2006. *Identity and Violence: The Illusion of Destiny*. New York: W. W. Norton and Company.

———. 2011. *Peace and Democratic Society*. Edited by Amartya Sen. Cambridge: OpenBook Publishers.

———. 1982. *Poverty and Famines: An Essay on Entitlement and Deprivation*, reprint with corrections. Oxford: University of Oxford Press.

Sen, Kishiti Mohan. 2005. *Hinduism*. London: Penguin Books.

Singh, Upinder. 2017. *A History of Ancient and Early Medieval India: From the Stone Age to the 12th Century*. Noida: Pearson.

———. 2017. *Political Violence in Ancient India*. Cambridge, MA: Harvard University Press.

Smith, Vincent Arthur. 1909. *Ashoka: The Buddhist Emperor of India*. Delhi: S. Chand.

Sorenson, Theodore C. 1965. *Kennedy*. London: Hodder and Stoughton.

Tagore, Rabindranath. 1941. *Crisis in Civilization: A Message on Completing His Eighty Years*. Birbhum: Santiniketan Press. Accessed January 21, 2022. https://indianculture.gov.in/reports-proceedings/crisis-civilization-message-completing-his-eighty-years.

———. 2021. *Gitanjali*. September 27. Accessed January 21, 2022. https://www.gutenberg.org/files/7164/7164-h/7164-h.htm.

———. 1917. *Nationalism*. New York: Macmillan.

———. 2009. *Nationalism*. Edited by Ramachandra Guha. New Delhi: Penguin Books.

———. 1931. *The Religion of Man*. New York: Macmillan.

———. 1913. *Sadhana: The Realization of Life*. New York: Macmillan.

———. 2010. *The Spirit of Japan*. July 10. Accessed January 21, 2022. https://www.gutenberg.org/files/33131/33131-h/33131-h.htm.

Thapar, Romila. 1997. *Ashoka and the Decline of the Mauryas*. Oxford: Oxford University Press.

Thucydides. 1996. *The Landmark Thucydides: A Comprehensive Guide to the Peloponnesian War*. Edited by Robert B. Strassler. New York: Free Press.

United Nations. 1995. "Treaty on the Non-proliferation of Nuclear Weapons." May 11. Accessed January 21, 2022. https://www.un.org/disarmament/wmd/nuclear/npt/text/.

———. 1948. "Universal Declaration of Human Rights." December 10. Accessed January 21, 2022. https://www.un.org/en/about-us/universal-declaration-of-human-rights.

Index

abuse of power, vii–viii, 2, 8, 10, 49, 61, 85, 87n26, 113, 159, 165–66, 169–70
Africa, 94, 136
agnosticism, 6, 40n4, 128
Ahmedabad, 157–58
Alexander the Great, 93–94, 99
Amitraghata, Bindusara, 76
Amritsar massacre, 8, 19, 149
Andrews, Charles Freer, 116
Ansari, Sarah, 145
army, 11, 12, 13, 26, 73, 78–79, 94–96, 99, 136, 138–39, 143, 145n5
artha, 82–83
Arthashastra, 77, 78, 81–87, 90–91, 100n4
  centrality of conquest in, 78–84
  domestic social capitol in, 83
  duty in, 83
  empiricism of, 79–81
  envoys in, 90–91
  famine prevention in, 82–83
  food as source state power in, 80, 82–83
  foreign policy uses of census in, 78–79
  on institutional sources of power, 78–79
  internal life of conqueror in, 80–81

lack of compassion in approach to war, 78–81
as a science, 82
spies in, 80, 93, 98
on split between domestic and foreign policy, 82–84
on when to wage war, 78–80
Ashoka
  Ahraura Minor Rock Edict of, 40n5
  army of, 94, 99
  conversion to Buddhism, 75–76, 81
  critique of sectarianism, 97–99
  envoys of, 13, 90–92
  first "Major Rock Edict" of, 96–97
  first "Minor Rock Edict" of, 52, 75–77
  internal change of, 13, 75–77, 89
  international approach to foreign policy, 13, 89–95
  public reasoning and, 97–99
  science of warfare and, 91, 99
  and spread of Buddhism, 52
  on suffering caused by war, 13, 76
  as teacher, 13, 74–76, 89–91, 93–94

Index

About the Author

Neal Leavitt is a senior lecturer in the humanities at Boston University and the author of *The Foreign Policy of John Rawls and Amartya Sen*. He received his doctorate in philosophy from Boston College and his bachelor of arts in philosophy from Harvard College. He lives with his wife, Irene, and son, Kyle, in Cambridge, Massachusetts.